MINOR KEYS

Gender, Inequality and Work in
Electronic Music

Samantha Parsley

BRISTOL
UNIVERSITY
PRESS

First published in Great Britain in 2025 by

Bristol University Press
University of Bristol
1–9 Old Park Hill
Bristol
BS2 8BB
UK
t: +44 (0)117 374 6645
e: bup-info@bristol.ac.uk

Details of international sales and distribution partners are available at bristoluniversitypress.co.uk

© Bristol University Press 2025

DOI https://doi.org/10.51952/9781529240443

British Library Cataloguing in Publication Data
A catalogue record for this book is available from the British Library

ISBN 978-1-5292-4041-2 hardcover
ISBN 978-1-5292-4042-9 paperback
ISBN 978-1-5292-4043-6 ePub
ISBN 978-1-5292-4044-3 ePdf

The right of Samantha Parsley to be identified as author of this work has been asserted by her in accordance with the Copyright, Designs and Patents Act 1988.

All rights reserved: no part of this publication may be reproduced, stored in a retrieval system, or transmitted in any form or by any means, electronic, mechanical, photocopying, recording, or otherwise without the prior permission of Bristol University Press.

Every reasonable effort has been made to obtain permission to reproduce copyrighted material. If, however, anyone knows of an oversight, please contact the publisher.

The statements and opinions contained within this publication are solely those of the author and not of the University of Bristol or Bristol University Press. The University of Bristol and Bristol University Press disclaim responsibility for any injury to persons or property resulting from any material published in this publication.

Bristol University Press works to counter discrimination on grounds of gender, race, disability, age and sexuality.

Cover design: Hannah Gaskamp
Front cover image: iStock/master1305

Contents

List of Figures and Tables		iv
About the Author		v
Acknowledgements		vi
Prelude (Or, Middle-Aged Lady Plays with GarageBand in Her Shed)		viii
1	The Warm-Up: Being a Gender Minority in Electronic Music	1
2	There Aren't Any Women Producers	16
3	Good Music is All That Matters	37
4	But … Nobody Discriminates!?	59
5	Positive Action Is Just Not *Fair*	76
6	Women Don't Make Their Own Music	91
7	Girls Just Aren't into Tech	108
8	Women Just Need to Be More Confident	131
9	Conclusion: Manifestos for an Inclusive Industry	152
Appendix: Knowing the Industry Inside Out		161
Notes		169
References		184
Index		198

List of Figures and Tables

Figures

1	Artwork for 'Lift 51' by Dovetail	15
2	Artwork for 'Keep Your Disdance' EP by Dovetail	35
3	Artwork for 'Almost Like' by Dovetail	57
4	Artwork for '1984' EP by Shawnonymous and Dovetail	74
5	Artwork for 'Sea Organ' EP by Dovetail	89
6	Artwork for 'Fall Away (22 Mix)' by Dovetail	106
7	Artwork for *Acid Vol 3* compilation featuring 'Therapist Drift' by Dovetail	129
8	Artwork for 'Just Dance (Dovetail's Funky Breaks Remix)' by Dovetail and Bungalow	150

Tables

A1	Data generation activities	162
A2	Sample characteristics	166

About the Author

Samantha Parsley is a writer, coach, DJ and founder of In the Key, a directory and platform championing the careers of women, trans and non-binary electronic music producers (www.inthekey.org). She is Professor of Organization Studies at the University of Portsmouth and coaches research-led writers as Curious View (www.curiousview.co.uk). Samantha DJs and produces music as Dovetail and lives with her husband on the south coast of England.

Acknowledgements

This book has been a lifetime in the making. I'd like to thank my brother for being the audience for my first Fisher Price DJ sets, my mum and dad for buying me my first record player and Tom Arnfeld, Donna Stewart and Steve Stewart for their Christmas gift of my first DJ controller. Thank you to Joe, Laura and Elijah for christening me 'Disco Nanny' and to Andy Beckett and Gary Wood for showing me the ropes of how to DJ when I didn't have a clue where to start. I'm grateful for all the encouragement to take the plunge in the first place from the DJs I interviewed in my pilot project and I'm forever grateful to the wonderful DJs and producers whose voices brought this book to life, for giving me their time and heartfelt insights into a world they love so much and find frustrating in equal measure – you are all awesome and I feel proud to know you.

Thank you too to everyone who has cheered me on from the sidelines on social media as I've written this book. To Marjana, my tardigrade chum, I extend huge gratitude for being such a source of support and sanity when I 'went native' and wanted to jack it all in and quit academia, and for working with me so tirelessly to refine the concept of ameliorative work. I hope you think it's been worth the wait! I'm grateful to The Leverhulme Trust for the grant that enabled me to immerse myself in the project and to the record labels who have liked my music enough to release it for sale. Thank you especially to the Association for Electronic Music for enabling me to participate in so many industry events and see things from a different angle, and to Sisu, MPW, Deevstock, Threads Radio, and Unmade Radio for the opportunities to DJ, learn, organize events, and host radio shows. Thank you, Deev, for believing in me.

I am indebted to my publishers, Paul Stevens and Isobel Green of Bristol University Press, for loving this project so much and for their patience while I battled my ADHD tendencies and took months and months to produce a proposal – I hope the end result has been what you hoped for back at the start.

But there quite simply wouldn't have been an end at all if it wasn't for the incredible Susanne Schotanus, who has coached me through my first book-length project and taught this old dog so many new tricks that she feels she's only just learned how to write at all. Thank you to my anonymous peer reviewers and my critical readers Claire, Beatriz and Tim for their time and valuable feedback on the manuscript too. Almost finally, to Claire Spooner-Loveday, my music BFF, sounding board and all-round Z-list celebrity – I love you in a slightly gay way, but don't tell Aimie in case she punches me in the face.

And last of all, Drew, my biggest fan, rock to my firework and sexiest man in Portchester – thank you for always believing in me and for announcing with such conviction that I would write a book as we lounged by the pool in Ibiza after no sleep. Thank you for not thinking I am a complete cock for wanting to be a DJ when other wives are reading *Heat*, painting their toenails and watching 'Strictly'. I love you.

Funding acknowledgement

This project was funded by The Leverhulme Trust, Grant Number 2019-598-7.

Prelude (Or, Middle-Aged Lady Plays with GarageBand in Her Shed)

In 2017 I took a long hard look through my record collection and realized I owned almost no electronic music made by women. I also realized that until that moment I had never noticed that fact. If your response to this is, 'So what?', then this book is for you. If you're thinking, 'Wow, I wonder why?', then this book is also for you. And if, like me, your reaction is more along the lines of, '*Never even noticed?* What the hell kind of trickery means that an engaged academic feminist, Professor of Work and Organization and long-time clubber could overlook the fact that pretty much all of the dance music she loved was made and played by *men?*', then this book is most certainly for you.

In that moment I'd woken up to the fact that I could probably name less than a handful of women DJs. It was rare that I had I even *seen* one perform during my 30 years dancing in clubs and festivals, let alone be able to name any women artists who *produced* music. My mind was racing. Why were there so few women DJs and even fewer making their own electronic music? Or if they were out there, why didn't I know about them? And why had I never thought about this before? And then I realized. This was the first time I had ever really paid attention to the artists' names on the music I was buying – because I'd recently learned to DJ and produce music myself. It had become personal.

But why does a middle-aged professor learn to DJ and produce music in the first place? The reason is simple. Because she'd always wanted to, but never even considered she could. I don't mean that some careers teacher at school said, 'No, Sam, you can't be a DJ.' It was more that during my childhood in the 1970s and 1980s nothing about music, or DJ culture, gave me any indication whatsoever that this was something an ordinary girl from an ordinary working-class background could ever do. It was only through interviewing underground DJs for an academic research project in my mid-40s, that I discovered how accessible digital DJing (and indeed electronic music production) now is, and it was those conversations that inspired me to become Dovetail. At 44 years old, I was done worrying about whether I was being an idiot for wanting to learn to DJ after all these years, and cared way less than younger me would have done about what anyone else thought. In the end it was simple. These nice guys I was interviewing told me what equipment I needed to get started, and so that's what I did. The fact that they were all guys is important. But you probably realize that since you're reading a book about why women are so marginalized as electronic music artists.

You will find out more about why this book is about electronic music *artists* who produce their own music, and not 'just DJs' in Chapter 1. Throughout the book I'll be explaining how being a DJ/producer is vital for career success nowadays, and that everyone is at it. Including me, in my shed at the end of my garden. The reason for this is that in the digital music age, it is no longer enough to just play other people's music if you want to make it as a DJ – no matter how good you are at that. You have to be a *producer* as well, which means writing, composing, recording, producing and engineering your own tracks. Unless you are woman, it appears.

But it was not gender that I first set out to explore. As an academic scholar of work and organization, even on my nights off, I'd always found it fascinating that at 2 am, while I was partying and dancing my socks off, the DJ on the stage was at work. Or were they? As I bounced up and down to 150 bpm hard house and traced psychedelic patterns with my glowsticks, I pondered whether DJs even feel like they are at work at 2 am, playing music to a dancefloor packed with sweaty bodies losing their minds to the music. Are DJs still 'at work' when they join the crowd to dance after their set? Were the DJs I saw after-partying with the event's promoters, racking up lines of cocaine and knocking back Jack Daniels purely having fun, or was that also just work? An element of the networking necessary to be successful in the electronic dance music industry, perhaps?

So, I set out to investigate these things by interviewing some DJs I'd met through friends, and to be honest I was surprised by how professional DJing actually is and how seriously DJs take their work. A lot of the time they would much rather not be partying, and be at home with their families, curled up with a boxset instead, no matter how much they also loved their job, and felt lucky to be living the dream. I developed an idea that DJs are creative labourers, showing how, yes, DJing is most certainly work, but not work as we know it. My focus at that time was most firmly on the job and on DJing as work, and I was actively ignoring anything to do with gender. For example, I gave a conference paper about this in 2014, dismissively presenting my 90 per cent male interview sample as perfectly acceptable because it was the 'industry norm'. I pushed back against questions from the audience that perhaps gender would be an interesting avenue to explore – a familiar, fiercely fearful knot tying itself in my stomach at the mere thought. How could I accuse my DJ mates, and all those cool people in clubland I was frankly a bit in love with, of being sexists? I did not want to be 'that woman'. Nope. Not going there. And it would still be almost three years before I did.

This reticence to become a gender researcher probably needs some contextualization. I'm from a 'non-traditional' academic background and was raised in an inner city – the first of my immediate family to go to university, which I did after having two children and separating from my first husband, aged 26. The men and women in my family fulfilled traditional gender roles as I was growing up, in a culture where I learned that men were basically to be pleased at the expense of my own needs, which usually meant not upsetting them – and certainly not rocking the boat with the 'F word'. Until my late 30s I struggled to call myself a feminist with pride. Alongside all this, music has always been a huge part of my life. My brother and I had a request show when we were little – we used his Action Man walkie-talkies and our wind-up Fisher Price record player to 'broadcast' between our bedrooms. He'd pretend to be different callers, and I'd be the DJ. The show did not include a banging set-list, to be fair, as we only had six records of children's nursery rhymes to play, but as I grew up the tunes got better, and I started making mixtapes recorded illegally from the UK Top 40 show on Radio 1 on a Sunday night. This turned into curating collections from legitimately bought vinyl records, then CDs, and a brief dalliance with minidiscs. It was always me who controlled the music at parties, in the car, *anywhere.*

But let's return to 2014. Six months after that conference presentation, my son and friends gave me my first (digital) DJ equipment for Christmas. By New Year's Eve I'd worked out the basics and was hooked. As an avid user of creative tech for photo and video editing, design and podcasting – this just felt like learning some new software. Why had I been so afraid of doing this my whole life? Why had I been so *scared*, feeling so out of place if I went into a record store? So terrified of the equipment? And then it hit me that I *had* been out of place. DJing was never for me because I never saw anyone like me on the stage at gigs, in the magazines I loved, or hanging around the record stores. Even in the high street chains like HMV or Virgin, I never went into the 'listening booths' to sample the music I was about to buy – they were far too intimidating – and so I literally bought new dance music on the strength of what the cover looked like.

When digital MP3 files burst onto the scene in late 1990s things did begin to change. To buy dance music I no longer had to go into record stores staffed by blokes who either ignored me or gave me withering looks that made me feel intensely uncomfortable and out of place. But it took until I was 47, had learned to DJ myself, and begun to produce my own electronic music that I felt ready to unpick and examine all this. Over the years since I had been challenged at that conference and then became a DJ, the political had become personal, culminating in the epiphany that opens this Prelude. *I didn't own, play or dance to music made by women.* I didn't know any women producers in electronic music genres, and I wanted to know why. And like Neo taking the red pill in the movie *The Matrix*, after that, I knew there was no going back.

This book is the culmination of the research project that followed, and which I carried out predominantly between 2018 and 2022, with the generous support of a Research Fellowship from The Leverhulme Trust. Back then, it was called 'In the Key of She: Women, Technology and Cultural Production', but in 2022 after a frank conversation with a non-binary transgender producer, I quietly dropped the pronoun 'she' in order to be more publicly inclusive, which is why you'll now find the project online as just 'In the Key'. Using a gendered pronoun when the 'In the Key' directory on the project website included lots of transgender, non-binary and gender-expansive artists, as well as cis-gendered women, was the right thing to do, no matter how nice the assonance between 'key' and 'she' is, as Paul my publishing editor laments!

At the time of writing this book, that directory includes the details of over 300 women, and gender-expansive artists across electronic music genres. On the project website (www.inthekey.org) you'll also find recordings of 35 episodes of a radio show I produced in collaboration with UK-based DJ collective Sisu where I interview women producers about their careers and showcase their music. Since the start of In the Key, I've spent six years immersed in the music industry, making countless presentations to industry folks; I've written several articles for high-profile music press outlets, started performing as a DJ and begun releasing music. I've upgraded from GarageBand to Ableton but I still make music in my shed, and now I've written this book. It's by far my proudest academic achievement, and the most exciting, and enriching thing I've ever done in my career. I hope you enjoy it too.

Samantha Parsley,
31 March 2025

1

The Warm-Up: Being a Gender Minority in Electronic Music

Psy-sisters: The work is worth it

> We started Psy-sisters collective because of a lack of female DJs in the psytrance scene at the time and I really missed that female energy when I was playing at gigs. So, we put on our first event at the Union Club in Vauxhall in 2013, and it was a big success. There were eight female DJs on the line-up, which was pretty much all there were in the UK at that time. It was the first time there had ever been a party like that with all female psytrance DJs on the line-up, and I think a lot of people came to that party because it was just something new, it was like, wow, it's all the girls on the decks! It was really great energy, and the success of that just kept going and the collective was formed.

Meet Psibindi, a psytrance DJ, producer and vocalist. Although she says 'we' in her story related here, when Psy-sisters was founded it was really just *her* taking the initiative to make a space for women to come together in a heavily male-dominated genre of electronic music. Psy-sisters is one of the longest-standing collectives for women and gender-expansive artists in the UK and, although its main focus is still psytrance, it has expanded to welcome people from all electronic genres who identify with a marginalized gender. At the time of writing, Psy-sisters includes a record label, events brand and several staff, all managed by Psibindi alongside her own music career *and* a day job. It's a huge amount of work – a full-time job in itself – and requires a lot of financial resources: 'costs such as website, IT systems, paying interns and contractors … marketing is a huge chunk, graphic design, release campaigns, PR, event production, it goes on and on …'. She told me: 'So yeah, the investment is high, the hours are high, but the reward is worth it.'

What makes it 'worth it' is the good that the collective does in the music industry, giving emerging DJs a chance to play at their events, championing producers who are women of Asian and Middle-Eastern heritage, and focusing on disadvantaged women: 'There are a lot of women out there that don't have access to studios, and don't have the money to get into production or DJing and we want to help,' Psibindi explained. But beyond the events and special projects, the collective provides everyday support for its members too. For some reason, misogynistic online comments seem especially prevalent in the psytrance community and at the time I was writing this, a member from the collective was subject to a barrage of sexualized, hateful comments on her Facebook feed in response to simply posting a video of her DJing with a comment about the importance of representation. The Psy-sisters community came out in force to support her – although women, trans or non-binary people often feel too unsafe to challenge this kind of trolling directly, the power of weaving a safety net from solidarity to lift fellow artists back up and help them heal after they've been attacked is not to be underestimated.

Introduction

This book shines a light on the hidden lives of women and gender-expansive people who produce and perform electronic music. People like Psibindi and the members of the Psy-sisters collective, who have to expend considerable effort to get in, get by and get on in electronic music as DJs and producers in an industry that is over 90 per cent men.[1] The central premise is that gender inequality in the electronic music industry can be explained through a concept I'm calling 'ameliorative work' – the hidden and not-so-hidden efforts women and gender-expansive people undertake as part of their career, purely on account of their gender. It is *work* because, as we shall see, it demands considerable emotional, practical and financial resources from those who undertake it, and it has real, material effects on these artists' careers. This theory is the end-point of a qualitative investigation, where common themes have been extrapolated from the lived experiences of all the people whose thoughts and feelings have contributed to the project.[2] Two (or more) *individual* working lives will never be exactly the same, because our circumstances, personalities and privileges are not identical.

However, when you put all those lives together and trace patterns between them, you start to generate a theory about the issues they face. In my case this started out as 'Why are there so few women producing electronic music?', which led to many more sub-enquiries which you will explore in the pages to come. At the end of the book are three manifestos for change, which turn the stories, experiences and ideas you are about to read into blueprints for action.

This book is a story of hope, resilience and passion – of people fighting to follow their dreams, and that includes me – a middle-aged university academic who learned to be a DJ, and to produce and release her own music. My artist name is 'Dovetail', which symbolizes the bringing together of my passion for electronic music with my professional skills as an academic researcher, and it's this unique combination that's made this book possible.[3] I have yet to meet another DJing business school professor, let alone one who's a woman. But it is not just my story. I present data from six years of immersive research in the electronic music industry – including 63 in-depth interviews with women producers and industry gatekeepers, reflections on DJ and music production courses I've attended, and my participation in electronic music conferences, parties and events. It also draws on insights gleaned from my work as a co-chair of the diversity working group of a professional body, and as a coach, advisor and often friend to women and non-binary artists working in the industry.[4,5] I have changed the names of people who have taken part in private conversations with me to protect them from any possible harm, but where information about organizations, initiatives or individuals is in the public domain, I refer to them by their real names.

Listening to the voices of DJ/producers

To my knowledge, this is the first book that specifically looks at the career experiences of women electronic music DJ/ producers – a unique combination of stage performance using DJ decks in the club (or at the festival) and music composition behind the scenes in home studios. The DJ's job is to blend, mix and/or cut two or more pre-recorded pieces together in creative combinations live in front of dancers with the aim of producing a new and different whole – DJs sonically shape energy and 'vibe' in order to make people dance, usually in a club, or via the radio. In contrast, the job of the electronic music producer is to make the music tracks that the DJ plays. This involves composition, sound engineering and audio production, and making electronic music is very 'tech-heavy'. Unlike traditional music made and performed with analogue instruments, like guitars, violins, trumpets or pianos, electronic music is made with machinery. It is an inherently 'techie' process, and always has been since its earliest roots. The first electronic synthesizers were huge room-sized contraptions made of valves, cables and reel-to-reel tape, but now it's possible to make beats with a computer you can carry anywhere, as I explain later. But music production and audio engineering remain more akin to mathematics, physics and computer programming than they do to playing an instrument, for example, and I have always had a strong hunch that this is a fundamental reason why men are so over-represented in this occupation. That's why I started this project in the first place – to investigate the relationships between gender, technology and cultural production.

Both DJing and music production are roles in which, increasingly, DJ/producers must demonstrate competence in order to be accepted as legitimate members of the occupation. What makes this context unique is the sheer breadth and complexity of skills that are required, On the one hand, as DJs they are crowd entertainers, flamboyant extroverts leading the party,[6] selecting, playing and manipulating music on the fly to create energetic 'journeys' for crowds to dance to. On the other, they are producers who are solitary sound engineers, writing music by themselves, hidden away at home, staring at their computers for hours at a time.[7] On top of all that, artists also need to continually create content for social media to attract and retain fans, demonstrating the likes, shares, and follows that count as evidence of popularity to open doors to getting their music signed by record labels, and bookings for gigs.

While some DJs have always been producers, in the days of analogue recording technologies and pressing vinyl records, being an artist writing and recording music and being a DJ were two distinct roles, if not totally separate careers. But once the digital revolution in music took hold, the numbers of 'DJ/producers' proliferated – so much so that it is rare to see a cis-male DJ who now does not refer to themselves as a producer too. The reason for this is, at least in part, technological. It is now possible to buy (or download a pirated copy of) software that allows you to make music with your computer in ways that were previously incredibly expensive, and time-consuming. Known as 'self-producers'[8] these artists don't work in professional studios, recording and producing music written and performed by other people. Instead, they compose, arrange and engineer music of their own with software 'digital audio workstations' (DAWs) running on their computers. Although some do play a musical instrument, sing and/or have formal musical training, many don't and are often self-taught. The outcome of this opening up of music production to the masses is that producing your own tracks has become the new calling card of the modern-day DJ in a digital age as we will see further in Chapter 6.

The electronic music industry also works a little differently to other music sectors. Broadly, because of its roots in 'DIY' music-making and counter-culture (as we will be exploring in various ways in the book), the motif of 'the underground' is very strong – even when figures show that the industry is worth billions of dollars worldwide. This 'independent' ethos in electronic music (for example record labels and gatekeepers outside the handful of huge commercial companies such as SONY, Universal, and Warner) means that smaller clubs and record labels proliferate, and routes to market are highly decentralized, fragmented and pretty much entirely dependent on contacts and networks, as we shall see in Chapter 3. It also means that the industry operates with more liberal contractual arrangements – artists are rarely contracted to a record label in the ways they are in pop music, for example. Instead, it is individual pieces of music that are 'signed', and I'll say more about this and its effects in Chapter 2.

All of this means that being a DJ/producer in electronic music is not something that is straightforward for women, trans and non-binary people, despite there being no reason whatsoever why they cannot admirably fill the role requirements for the job. That said, it's important to note that many of the themes covered in this book are similar to those in others' accounts of what it is like to be a woman in the music industry more generally,[9] and there are almost certainly parallels that can be traced out to gendered experiences in the wider creative and cultural industries too. Film, TV, games design, software engineering, and so on, all report similar dynamics at play. However, there are unique challenges – and opportunities – that the distinctive traits of the DJ/producer job and the electronic music industry throw up in particular, and that's where this book comes in as the first of its kind.

Chapter 2 shows just how dramatically men dominate all areas of the electronic music industry – and especially production. The playing field in this industry is far from level, as we see in Chapters 3 and 4, and efforts to address this are met with hostility and derision, as we'll discover in Chapter 5. Electronic music production and performance is exceptionally technology-dependent which, as we shall see, is still regarded as a (cis-)male domain – the focus of Chapters 6 and 7. Likewise, DJ gigs often take place at raves, as opposed to traditional performance spaces. Raves are all-night parties, characterized by a high degree of hedonism, and recreational drug-taking, sometimes taking place in disused buildings in rundown areas. Women and gender-expansive people face threats to their safety, challenging environments and the need to be on their guard against unwelcome advances from intoxicated crowds, and unfortunately fellow artists and venue staff too, as I will discuss in Chapter 8. Dealing with all this is work. Work that women and gender-expansive people have to do *just because* they are women, trans and/or non-binary. And while I don't want to overclaim the generalizability of the situations and experiences I describe in this book, in some respects what you are about to read mirrors gender relations in wider society, and you might recognize resonances in other sectors too.

Dancing between toil and hope: introducing the idea of ameliorative work

In the chapters that follow I'll be showing how ameliorative work[10] is done by women, and gender-expansive artists, day in, day out, in addition to all the usual creative angst, hustle and grind that goes with being a musician. I'm using this introduction to explain the theory, but the rest of the book will bring it to life, structured around seven common myths about inequality in electronic music, and in many places told through the voices and experiences of the ameliorative workers themselves.

The term 'ameliorative work' encompasses all the efforts women and gender-expansive people go to in the course of their occupation simply because of their gender, over and above the activities and tasks required by the job. It's sustained and ongoing work and, importantly, it is not optional. It *matters* to artists' careers. As our opening vignette shows, ameliorative work is an overlapping constellation of private, hidden, public and visible efforts that costs energy, time, money and emotional resources – all aimed at bringing about change. So, it's *ameliorative* work because it's done to make the working lives of minoritized gender artists better, or at least bearable, which includes fighting the system and advocating for industry and policy change as well as managing quieter feelings of imposter-ism, self-doubt and general unease.

Naming things is important because it fixes our attention onto them. By gathering a collection of things and giving them a name, we bring them into existence, which means we also give them meaning. In this case, I'm bringing together a disparate collection of effortful feelings, behaviours, outcomes and actions into the concept of 'ameliorative work' in order to recognize them as more than the sum of their parts. Usually, to begin with, there are eyerolls and moans of '*Why do we need yet more words?*'. But as the take-up of recent terms such as 'inclusion', 'microaggressions' and 'non-binary' suggests, when a concept accurately describes something that previously we didn't have language to describe, people are quick to start using it and, importantly, *doing* things with, and about, the thing they now have a name for. If we don't develop concepts, we can't study them, let alone develop solutions for them – because to all intents and purposes they don't exist.[11] And that's what is important here. For far too long only cis men's achievements and experiences have defined the world of electronic music, keeping everything experienced by other genders hidden. Even when those experiences *are* recognized, they are minimized, because taken one by one they might indeed seem trivial (for example, feelings of exclusion in the music classroom or recording studio, or patronizing comments after a gig). And where experiences are more visible and harder to ignore, such as misogynistic trolling, or sexual harassment, dealing with them is not seen as *work*, and definitely not work that takes time and resources away from the real job of being an electronic music producer and performer. Furthermore, all the positive and progressive effects that result from being an 'ameliorative worker' also get ignored if we don't have the language to identify them. Bringing them all together, therefore, gives them power – we can see just how significant they are when taken together as ameliorative work: and it could well be that gender inequality in electronic music is so entrenched because women, trans, and non-binary people are doing way more work than cis-gendered men. They are working a second shift but no-one can see it. And this is the value of theory – a much-maligned concept that many regard as too abstract and too intellectual to have much value in the 'real world'. But this is far from true.[12]

Ameliorative work includes the intensely personal feelings of not belonging, feeling excluded, lacking confidence, not being skilled enough, or undeserving of the success that comes your way. These feelings are often kept well hidden, experienced as shameful and rarely voiced, so the 'work' remains invisible. Performing ameliorative work requires an astute understanding of the dynamics of each situation, responding creatively and reflexively in ways that make the best (or limit the worst) of a situation.[13] One is always on alert, watching one's back or second-guessing – 'Did he *really* mean that?' – which is tiring and depleting. Yet it these same feelings that fuel determination and the resolve to dust oneself down, put on a brave face and keep going. Ameliorative work costs time as well as energy, as we can see in the vignette that opens this introductory chapter. Time spent responding to misguided or downright misogynist comments online about gender inequality is time taken away from making music or working on one's career, for example, not to mention the emotional toll it takes to constantly be defending one's own existence and proving one's own disadvantage to the very people who cause it.[14] But posting content to educate often pays off, and people *do* wake up to realize things they had never considered before. Helping people 'get woke' is an important step towards change. If people don't believe there are problems, there will never be solutions. The ameliorative work might be more visible here, but is still not recognized *as* work. Finally, ameliorative work can be high-profile, public and highly resource-intensive, as we see in the case of Psy-sisters, and many other organizations like them too.[15] Forming collectives, and setting up initiatives that actively platform and support diverse artists requires a whole additional shift in your schedule alongside your creative work – and it's work that falls almost exclusively to women, trans and non-binary folks themselves, and particularly those who are black and/or queer, as we will see further in Chapter 8. But challenging 'bro culture' in this way, is *such powerful work*, driven by incredible passion – learning the craft of DJing and music production in a safe space among others like you transforms the confidence of so many newbies to the scene – and confidence is something they'll need in order to face the darker side of this work – sexual harassment, misogyny, traumatizing online comments, being groped as you're trying to work in the DJ booth, assumptions you've slept your way onto the line-up or being refused entry to the stage you've been booked to play because you look like a groupie. I can personally vouch for the strength and power of those support networks when you're faced with some of this crap, and without them it will take way longer to boot these behaviours out of the industry.

Moving beyond awful

Seeing this more complex, 'double-edged' version of the 'gender inequality in electronic music' story has driven me throughout this research, and I have used the twin tools of 'appreciative inquiry' and 'reparative reading' to guide me. Appreciative inquiry is a 'positive psychology' technique that focuses on the things that people and organizations do well already to counterbalance our obsession with what is going badly.[16] Often counsellors and consultants focus on what's *wrong* with their clients – emphasizing what they lack – in order to help them to improve. In the present context, this looks something like this: Sure, if you want to get your music signed to a record label you're likely to have your skills questioned, and your music doubted, just because you are not a man. Yes, it's true that often if you want to get booked for DJ gigs you'll need to look more 'marketable' (read: pretty and sexy) than your male counterparts. But you are also bravely showing up with your feminine identity so you are leading an assault on people's implicit bias just by 'you doing you'. With every person you blow away with your talent, you're chipping away at the stereotypes that women can't do tech, and disrupting the idea that pretty, sexy people can't also be DJs and producers just by existing. Although you'll face challenges, with every new fan you gain, or public appearance you make, you have the potential to change minds and ignite passions. Just by being up there and looking different from how people expect, you sow the seeds of possibility in the eyes that are upon you. Which is something worth doing.[17]

The beauty of appreciative inquiry is that it helps us avoid all-encompassing doom and gloom – the swamping and sensationalist 'oh, isn't it all *awful*' perspective that plagues most discussions of gender issues and occupational inequality. This is what Eve Sedgwick – a wonderful writer from the 1980s – calls 'paranoid reading'– an inevitable focus that everything is dreadful, people are terribly oppressed and the facts of the matter must be regarded critically and with suspicion even when people say that things aren't really so bad.[18] It's become a hallmark of 'good' academic research to be a paranoid reader, especially in the 'critical management studies' tradition I've been schooled in.[19] We spend several years as postgraduate student researchers learning not to take things at face value and to look for deeper, hidden (and often more negative) meanings that define people's reality. Make no mistake, all of these are super important. Sedgwick's work doesn't mean that we slip into the cult of toxic positivity and annihilate the very real consequences of the negative stuff from people's experiences.[20] Paranoid readings and associated activism have got us a long way, and are undoubtedly accurate portrayals of how things are for minorities at work: harassment, discrimination, microaggressions and exclusion are all *very* real, and account for inequality and a persistently bad deal for those who experience life as a minority in their chosen occupation. But they are not the *only* story and they downplay the creative and resilient ways in which people resist their marginalization and oppression. They gloss over the good things that emerge from those acts, as my previous examples show.

So, appreciative inquiry starts by recognizing what is already strong and working well as a way to inquire how things could be better. It's a subtle shift, because, after all, we're still trying to understand how to improve things so there is some element of deficit being addressed,[21] but it's also an approach that empowers the people who have most likely come to counselling or consultancy in need and doubt. In an appreciative inquiry, they start from a position where they can appreciate what they are doing already is pretty damn good. This is what Eve Sedgwick calls 'reparative reading' – where the intention is to repair the damage caused by negativity. Eve was a queer woman writing at a time when being 'out and proud' was something that often caused you serious harm. Her ideas were a powerful challenge to the narratives circulating at the time and I'm inspired and humbled to draw on them here. This was broadly how I approached the formal interviews with women producers and DJs, and other gatekeepers that were undertaken for this book – 63 formal conversations that lasted around 90 minutes[22] focusing on career success strategies, artists' achievements and the pride they felt in their work and professional development. Inquiring appreciatively is also a philosophy that I carried with me during my more informal interactions with the music industry too – at conferences, events, during my role as industry body co-chair, when observing artists' lives online, and in my own learning to be a DJ and producer over the past few years. What are they doing well, and how and why do they do that?

A note on pronouns

Most of the research this book is built on is about cis women. I am a cis-gendered woman myself and, to my knowledge, the people I formally interviewed for the project were cis-gendered. Six were men, two were non-binary and the remaining 55 identified as women. So, at its heart, this is a story about women and about me. However, my wider interactions with the music industry – particularly as the project progressed, confirmed that gender inequality is wider than a 'woman problem'. The 'bro culture' and masculine character of electronic music impacts anyone who doesn't identify as a cis-gendered man, albeit with some important idiosyncrasies. With this in mind, throughout the book I refer to 'women and gender-expansive people' whenever it makes sense to. This is unless I am specifically referring to gender-expansive people who identify as, for example, trans and/or non-binary, or indeed discussing issues that more specifically face women, where I do use the pronouns 'she/her'.

This is an important conversation to have – and I urge you to consider it in your own life too. Using gender-sensitive language is something that is hugely important to me. It makes my blood boil when I read 'he/him' in a text where the author is not specifically referring to a man. The words 'man', 'men', 'he' and 'him' do not stand for all of humanity, nor are they gender-neutral terms. I feel alienated and unimportant when I am asked by an author to think of myself as 'he/him' when the text is about experiences that apply to all genders. Using a person or community's preferred pronouns is to say 'I see you and I respect you'. It is both a matter of common courtesy and a political act of recognition – a public acceptance that others have the right to identify themselves in whatever ways feel right for them.[23] Using appropriately gendered language is not – as tabloid-newspaper-reading boomers lament – 'political correctness gone mad'. I believe language is one of the most significant ways bias is reproduced in society – and by the same token I believe language is an incredibly powerful weapon to dismantle it too.[24]

The more difficult question that slips out of all this, though, is why I didn't involve more trans and non-binary folks in the first place. I made a special effort to include black and brown women's voices in my study, so why not gender non-conforming people too? These are powerful questions that are hard to answer without sounding like whining excuses borne of my own privilege, but here goes anyway. When I started this research in 2017, we were still very much in a space where gender was seen as a binary construct and gender fluidity had yet to be talked about as seriously as it is now – conversations about *women* in electronic music were really only just starting at an industry level. After the #metoo movement erupted in the screen industries, music was forced to take a long hard look at itself too. On top of this, because of my own identity (read: privilege) as a cis-gendered woman, that's where my (self)interests lay. I knew hardly any trans and/or non-binary people back then, so I never really questioned that this project would be about the struggles that *women* face as they forge their careers as female producers, DJs and artists in an industry that's overwhelmingly made up of men.

I'm pleased to say that's changed over the years – and has particularly come about through my encounters in the electronic music industry and with a range of 'non-straight-white-male' collectives that have been formed over the past couple of years. Sex-positive, gender non-conforming and queer parties like He.She.They, Pornceptual, Boudica, BBZ, Unorthodox, to name just a fraction, are currently blazing a trail through rave to radically disrupt mainstream clubbing. In 2024, as I was writing this book, He.She.They completed their first residency in Ibizan superclub Amnesia, and you can't get more high profile than that. So, lately, gender-expansive voices have definitely been part of the research on which this book is based, through informal conversations and my generally more heightened attention to gender-identity issues.

The line-up

Each chapter of the book tackles one of seven 'myths' about gender and electronic music that I have heard on repeat during my research, and which drive much of the ameliorative work I am going to present. Although there is a logical flow to the chapters, each deals with a standalone topic so you can pick and choose where you jump in if reading them one after the other doesn't work for you.[25]

Why myths?

Myths are a particularly useful way to think about entrenched inequality in social settings because they symbolize beliefs and assumptions that are rarely questioned.[26] They are not entirely fiction but definitely not the whole truth either – often because their origins have long been forgotten and are rarely questioned. Myths legitimate unequal power dynamics in ways that appear 'normal' and/or 'right' and which usually cause disadvantage to others. For example, the myth of rationality in business, institutions and especially change processes obscures the fact that much decision-making is based on the personal interests of the leaders involved.[27] Historically it has also provided a convenient reason to exclude women from senior leadership positions because they are regarded as unsuitably 'irrational'. Likewise, the myth of the 'heroic' leader masks the fact that there are usually entire teams behind the achievements of the hero' – a figure who is, of course, almost always a cis man.[28] In this book, we deal with a bunch of myths about gender inequality in electronic music production and my aim in each chapter is to interrogate each one through appreciative inquiry and reparative reading – to kill them with kindness, if you will.

'There aren't any women producers' comes first in Chapter 2. The title encompasses the assumption that women (and gender-expansive people), quite simply, don't make electronic music, and the fact that very few people can name producers from minoritized genders if asked. The key point for this chapter is that there are, in fact, lots of women producing music and DJing out there but structural inequality has kept them hidden. The myth that there aren't any stops majority players in the industry needing to do anything about it. I'll present all the current facts and figures that show how heavily gendered the industry is, and explain how it is only in recent years that this has even been noticed. The ameliorative work here is that women, trans and non-binary people have to fight against a system that has already decided that they don't exist.

Chapter 3 tackles the emphatic statement that 'Good music is all that matters'. This phrase encapsulates the 'common-sense' and oh-so-pervasive myth that the music industry is a meritocracy. It addresses the myth that 'good music will always shine through' and that musical quality is the only criteria on which artists should be booked, promoted, developed, and considered as 'talent'. It is a myth, because why else would it just so happen that the vast majority of talent is white, cis-gendered, male, often heterosexual and usually wearing a black T-shirt? Coincidence? Refusing to accept that these are pre-requisites for good music-making I explore the production of 'talent' as a gendered process. I explain the freelance and heavily networked character of the industry in which 'who you know' is of paramount importance. I will show how this dependency on others for success perpetuates 'bro culture', as gatekeepers justify their selection decisions on 'talent.' The ameliorative work described in this chapter centres around the difficulty that gender-expansive and women artists face breaking into 'bro culture' and raises the issue that it may be dangerous for them to even try.

Chapter 4, 'But … Nobody Discriminates?', continues this theme and deals with the concrete ways in which minoritized genders – and especially women – are judged and treated on different terms to cis men. I show that the statement 'nobody discriminates against women, trans and non-binary folks' is a myth by discussing different shades of discrimination which are unrelated to conscious intention. In an industry obsessed with women's image, attractiveness and sexualization, even though it likes to pretend it's not, you either don't look the part (read: not cool and/or sexy enough), so your value is diminished, or you're *too* sexy, and slated for using your sexiness to get fake success. Women deal with this in various ways that intersect particularly with age, but also colour. The ameliorative work explained in this chapter therefore arises from the effort that goes into navigating the politics of fitting in versus standing out, particularly in the misogynistic glare of social media, online abuse and the expectation that women will just grow a thicker (attractive, but not too attractive) skin.

Chapter 5 returns to the sloping playing field described in Chapter 3 and discusses the widespread myth that 'Positive action is just not fair', discussing how initiatives to platform and develop minoritized gender artists are seen as special treatment which is 'reverse discrimination' against white, straight, cis men, instead of a corrective to a biased system. The impacts of positive action are controversial, with artists feeling they've only been chosen to 'tick a box' on a gatekeeper's 'diversity action' scorecard, leading to a general undertone of 'not belonging' in the industry corrosive to self-belief and resilience, and requiring quiet, hidden ameliorative work to stop the rot. At the same time, gatekeepers often reap reputational benefits of virtue signalling or performing diversity with no real substance, offloading the actual work of positive action initiatives onto their women and gender-expansive employees as an 'identity tax' that is not levied on cis men. Nonetheless, there is strong evidence, from this study and elsewhere, that positive action works and, as we see in Chapters 6 and 7, is particularly needed on account of electronic music's technology-dependent character.

'Women don't make their own music' is the myth that is tackled in Chapter 6, looking at the readiness of gatekeepers to doubt the technical skills of women, accusing them of using ghost producers or needing to work with audio engineers in order to obtain the proficiency required to be a good producer. This also applies to gender-expansive people but the more you can 'pass' as a cis man, the less you'll find yourself doubted, because technological prowess is transgressive of the feminine identity in particular. This chapter begins to examine these associations and explores the idea that men and women have particular traits and dispositions around music. It also explains how the myth that women don't make their own music legitimates gatekeepers' tendency to pair women with engineers, or offer them ghost production options. The ameliorative work that women artists have to perform around this is the constant need to justify one's abilities to a high standard, leading to a paralysing perfectionism.

Chapter 7, 'Girls Just Aren't Into Tech' explores why women are consistently under-represented in tech-heavy creative industries at all levels, and in tech-related education. Where they do appear in music courses, for example, they tend to be in the songwriting or performance cohorts and not the audio engineering or music tech courses. This chapter explains how gendered socialization affects preferences for and ambitions to use technology. It establishes that taking the statement 'girls aren't into tech' at face value is a convenient excuse not to change learning environments to be more welcoming of diverse genders. This is also a major reason for why it's so hard to move the needle on gender equality in tech-heavy industries and I pick this up through a discussion of expressive technology. The ameliorative work that this chapter deals with centres on the effort it takes to deal with always feeling out of place, but also celebrates the powerful representational work that women, trans and non-binary artists do to refute stereotypes.

'Toughening up' is the subject of Chapter 8, where we unpick the seemingly positive idea that 'women just need to be more confident'.

Why is this a myth? Because it urgently needs reframing to recognize that women are being blamed for not being able to 'cope' with unwelcoming and/or unsafe environments, and expected to thrive in spaces that were never designed for them, and where they constantly have to battle the damaging effects of not-belonging. Dealing with the fallout from these is perhaps the toughest form of ameliorative work I'll discuss in this book, and I'll tell some bleak stories here from my interviewees and the wider industry with reports about assault, harassment, exclusion, online abuse, ridicule, mansplaining, and other miseries that women face on a regular basis – in fact so regularly that they rarely report them. Women needing more confidence is a particularly pervasive discourse that is bought into by almost everyone in the industry – including the women and gender-expansive communities themselves. But what has emerged as a result of this perception that women need to support each other to succeed is a mighty source of solidarity for women, trans and non-binary artists. There are now hundreds of collectives for women, queer women, trans women, women of colour, and despite my use of the word 'women' here, they're spaces for including and supporting anyone marginalized on account of their gender identity. They're brave spaces, where marginalized folks can be bold and *just be themselves.* But on the flip side, although they can be powerful agents for change, they still represent yet more ameliorative work for the women who run them. As we saw from Psibindi and her work with Psy-sisters, we are asking those who are most disadvantaged to fix the system that broke them.

Chapter 9, 'Conclusion: Manifestos for an Inclusive Industry', summarizes the ameliorative work uncovered in each chapter and sets out what we can all do about it. Throughout the book, it will have become clear just how much extra women and gender-expansive people do in comparison to their cis-male counterparts, just to make their working lives better, or at least bearable. In line with the appreciative inquiry approach, this chapter reiterates just how strong and brave women and gender-diverse artists in this industry are, and how they show enormous creative resilience, acting as inspirational role models for the next generation. To conclude, I offer three manifestos to ignite thinking about your own practice as artist, ally, educator, music lover, or just a decent human interested in ways to empower women, trans and non-binary electronic music artists to tackle inequality.

Chapter track: 'Lift 51'

'Lift 51' is named after one of the lifts at my workplace and it was the very first piece of electronic music I made, hence why I've included it in the opening chapter to the book. I called it 'Lift 51' because the vocal in the track is a recording of the 'voice' of the

Figure 1: Artwork for 'Lift 51' by Dovetail, reproduced with kind permission of Rave Support Machine

Source: Available as a free download from https://soundcloud.com/ravesupportmachine/advent-day-13-dovetail-lift-51

lift – a woman speaking in the 'Queen's English' accent of the English upper classes. To 'come up' in the electronic dance music world means to feel the first rush of effect from psychoactive drugs, so the words 'Going Up' spoken in that 'deadpan' plummy voice always amuse me as I ride the six floors up to my office.

I made the basics of 'Lift 51' in a couple of hours because it's a 'loop-based' project with a few samples thrown in. It's quick because you just sequence and layer pre-made sounds together in an arrangement that pleases you (in the case of electronic music usually in a form that will work on a dancefloor). Rather like cut and paste. Many would definitely not consider this proper electronic music production, but why not? It's a simple track, for sure, but even if the components were pre-made, no one has arranged them in this combination and order before, and by the time I've added effects and filters on top, this track is as original as any other.

2

There Aren't Any Women Producers

It's Time to Draw the Line

Jacki-E is a UK-based DJ and producer based in Northampton, UK. Every single week from April 2018 to October 2024 she has researched, compiled, recorded and broadcast an episode of *Draw the Line* – a two-hour show aired on internet radio stations in the UK and Canada with the express aim of raising the profile and increasing awareness of women, trans and non-binary electronic music artists. As the name of the show suggests, it's a call to arms – 'It's Time to Draw the Line' under the cis-male domination of electronic music and do something concrete to bring about change.

Each episode of *Draw the Line* starts with a one-hour mix from Jacki-E herself playing only music made by non-cis-male producers. In the second hour she airs a mix prepared by a guest DJ from the worldwide, female and gender-expansive community. During the series' run, Jacki-E produced over 300 shows, which is astonishing stamina and shows quite remarkable dedication. In my experience, once you know what you're doing, it takes at least a full day to research, plan and record a radio show, plus hours spent trawling online record stores and social media to find music to play. There is also the financial outlay to buy that music and then you pay the radio station for your airtime. Quite simply, *Draw the Line* has been a huge labour of love gifted by Jacki-E to the electronic music community. You only need to listen to an episode to hear new music by new artists, all from under-represented genres curated and collated into one place. It's time to draw a line under the myth that opens this chapter – that there are 'no women producers'.

Introduction

My primary aim in this chapter is to challenge the myth that *Draw the Line*[1] so effectively blows apart: that women, or gender-expansive artists, don't produce electronic music. As Jacki-E's tremendous commitment shows, there are *lots* of non-cis-male artists across all sorts of electronic genres if you know where to look, and are curious enough to do so. So why this enduring assumption? Are men the only people creative and technically minded enough to write, compose, produce and arrange their own tracks? Of course not. In essence that's the question behind the whole book, but in this chapter I'll be starting to look at the top-level reasons, reasons that set the scene for what's to follow in future chapters.

It's clear that the myth that there aren't any women producers is very well fed and fattened up by the fact that we can't see them, so people can rarely name any besides the few big superstars that dominate the top slots in charts, music sales and headline performances at events, as we shall see in this chapter. And that doesn't just apply to men, it's everyone. When I questioned my interviewees about their journeys into the industry, few other women came up in conversation. Angelica, an artist based in North America, explained to me that not only was she the 'only woman DJ on the circuit back in the 1990s and 2000s' when she began her career, but back then there were even less women she'd heard of in the production world. 'Nope, there were no women in production that I knew personally,' she told me, after spending a little while staring off into the mists of time trying to recall some. That's a career of some 25 years, including time spent operating in Berlin – one of the biggest dance music cities in the world. Likewise, Tess, a UK-based artist, had trouble bringing to mind *any* female role-models she'd had at the beginning of her career in the 2000s – 'I'm definitely coming across more females bit by bit,' she told me. 'But when I first started out? Literally, hardly ever.' This sentiment echoed across many of the interviews I carried out with the mid- to experienced-stage artists, and felt like something they'd only just started being aware of themselves – either through me approaching them as a researcher interested in gender in their industry, or because they'd been seeing gender issues becoming more prominent in recent years and reflected on their own experiences. Speaking of her previous career in nightclub security, itself a heavily gendered profession, Dee summed this up neatly during a revelation she shared during our conversation: 'D'you know, in the 18 years that I worked in clubs as security I don't think I've *ever* worked where there's been a woman [DJ] on the decks. Wow. I've just realized that.' Zara too told me that initially she'd never noticed her gender but then 'obviously you get to a point that you realize that being one of one is not good, and that's not progressive'.

In this chapter I'll be unpacking these experiences through lots of statistics and data that reveal the numbers of women in the industry working as producers and DJs, as well as explaining why it's so hard to generate accurate numbers. In discussing why it's tough to find the numbers, I'll be describing a bit more about what the occupation of being an electronic music DJ/producer actually involves, and in fact why some would contest that it's an occupation at all. I'll show how these idiosyncrasies of the job feed back into the reasons why it's so hard to find artists producing and performing electronic music who are not cis men. By the end of the chapter you might even find yourself convinced that there actually *aren't* any women producers out there, so compelling is the evidence that most of the music we buy, stream, see performed, dance to, and hear on the radio is made by men. I found this chapter difficult to write for this very reason – statistics and 'hard data' are difficult to argue with and numbers are seductive. After all, if there *were* women producers out there, then we'd see them in the places we see men, right? Perhaps. But I'm going to ask you to think about that differently – not as evidence of a lack of women, but as evidence that shows just how hard-baked into the foundations of the music industry structural inequality is – which paves the way for the ideas in the rest of this book.

Beginning to draw the line

The first reason why the assumption that women don't make electronic music is incorrect is that there is clear evidence to the contrary, as Jacki-E's dedication to finding and platforming women (described at the start of the chapter) illustrates. Her considerable ameliorative work in preparing and broadcasting *Draw the Line* shows that there *are* women – and gender-expansive folks – out there just waiting to be discovered. Jacqueline Palmer (aka Jacki-E) was one of the first people I connected with when I began my research in 2018. At the time I was still labouring under the misapprehension that finding women who produced electronic music rather than just playing it as DJs was going to be like finding needles in a haystack as there were so few of them. That's what the whole premise of my research rested on – why do so few women produce electronic music?

Seeing Jacki-E's social media advert for her new radio show, then, came as a quite a surprise. My immediate reaction was to think 'OH NO! I've got this all wrong!' because here was this brilliant person with a radio show leading the way by sharing all this great music that wasn't made by men, and here *I* was, going around saying 'Hey! Why don't women make electronic music?' Jacki-E was going to put together a mix of music made by women *every single week* – so there must be loads of artists that I had yet to discover. As she later told me in an interview for my own radio show,[2] 'rather than wittering online about the lack of gender diversity in dance music ... do something positive, and what more positive thing can you do than find music by women and play it!'

But where was she finding all these people? Why couldn't I see them? It was clear that I needed to change emphasis. Instead of asking why there weren't any women music producers, the real questions were 'Why are they so hard to find?' and 'What makes and keeps them less visible than the cis men?' It was through conversations with Jacki-E about how she found her music, that I started to work out a strategy for finding those needles in the haystack. Plundering the tracklists Jacki-E published for each of her shows, I discovered new artists left, right and centre. From there I would look at the artists' profile on the industry's leading online record store for DJs – Beatport[3] – and see if they had any charts compiled.[4] 'Women tend to play music by other women,' Jacki-E told me when we chatted over a drink at a music conference. 'DJs charts are an excellent source of finding them because we lift each other up by including each other's music there.' To find black artists (of all genders and genres) you can search the Black Artists Database (BAD).[5] Scouring the DJ charts landing pages is also a handy at-a-glance way of finding non-cis-male producers, and black and brown artists, since DJs often use a photo of themselves as the banner for the chart, although take care not to mis-gender, or indeed mis-race – do your homework.[6]

I also quickly learned that producers from marginalized genders tend to collaborate with one another as well as share each other's music on their charts, so scanning down the credits of the releases listed on the artist's page usually revealed more names to follow up. Women also often release music on 'profile-raising' compilations put out by record labels, or collectives intended to address gender imbalance, for example to mark International Women's Day/Women's History Month in March. Clicking on the release title would then take me to all the other tracks on that album, and the names of more women to investigate. Once I've identified an artist, I simply click 'follow' on my platform(s) of choice to be notified when they release more music. You can also do this across all their social media profiles, where artists often share work in progress and upcoming collaborations and preview unreleased material. Hunting down music made by women and gender-expansive people in this way was probably my first introduction to the time and effort involved in ameliorative work, and it ultimately led to the In the Key Producer Directory[7] listing 350 women and gender-expansive electronic music artists – one of the resources from the research that I am most proud of. To my knowledge, it was the first – and is still the only – exclusively electronic music, multi-genre resource in the world for finding non-cis-male producers.[8]

This process was important not only to amass the In the Key Directory, but also to diversify my own record collection. As soon as I went public with In the Key there was no way I could ever DJ a set that wasn't diverse, even accidentally. I was committed to walking my talk, and up until I began the project, cis men were the producers of almost all the tracks in my electronic music library. But I had to confess to finding diverse genders hard in some genres where there just seemed to be an endless sea of cis-male producers, often white, and often young. And if *I* was finding it hard, then it was certainly not something that anyone *without* my determination to do things differently would ever think of doing, even if they thought it was necessary.

There is no getting away from the fact that this process *does* take time, perseverance and effort. That it is ameliorative work. The more usual way that DJs find music to play is by receiving 'promos' (promotional copies) from record labels. These come for free in the hope that the DJ will give the tracks exposure by playing them in their sets, raving about them on social media, and ultimately influencing others to buy or stream the music. But the promos are curated and forwarded via promo distribution services by the record labels, who are largely run by white cis men and whose rosters are almost exclusively other white cis men. Relying on promos will certainly not diversify your record collection or introduce you to new gender-diverse artists – as I've heard from so many women during this project 'I only get sent promos made by male artists'. I'm only on a couple of promo lists myself, but I can probably count on one hand the number of tracks I've been sent that are made by marginalized-gender producers.

The ameliorative work of finding gender minorities' music

Hunting out music made by gender-diverse artists, then, is a rewarding and exciting work of discovery. But it is also the first instance of ameliorative work that I'm highlighting in this chapter because, as I alluded to previously, it's often women and gender-expansive folks who lift up and champion each other – collaborating on productions, playing each other's music and otherwise celebrating and sharing each other's work. We often have good contact books with details of lots of producers who don't identify as cis male and it took us a long time to assemble those. Why is this work undertaken by the very people who are in the minority? Where are all the cis guys spending hours trawling through DJ charts to make their record collections more diverse? Why are *they* not reaching out to collaborate with people from different genders? Where are the allies who are actually doing some of this work too?

It's a tricky issue. On the one hand, it's utterly delightful when a dude from a record label, promoter or fellow DJ asks us if we can recommend any women they can approach for promos or book for their gigs. It's just *brilliant* that they care enough to even ask. But on the other, they are asking us to hand over a list we have spent time and effort searching for ourselves so they can just take their pick. After a panel at an industry conference recently I had a respectful but frank conversation with a well-known male DJ about how non-diverse his record label is. He was pretty dismissive – citing the usual clichés about talent shining through, and telling me 'It's not my job to go out there and find women if they are too shy to get in touch with me.' I gave him my card, we agreed to disagree and went our separate ways. So, I was bowled over when a week later I received an email from him asking me to send any 'decent producers' his way.

YES! SUCCESS! Our conversation had clearly made an impression after all. Delighted, I listened to some recent tracks from his label, and sent emails to the producers I could think of that fitted the sound. I was passing on the personal email address from the boss of a prestigious label, so most were pleased to hear from me. Yet, no matter how much delight I felt at potentially being able to make one more record label just slightly less cis-male-dominated, I nonetheless spent a good couple of hours doing this work on the label owner's behalf. Labour that he didn't pay for. Scouting out and finding talent with the right sound is the cornerstone of the artists and repertoire function (hereafter A&R). A&Rs are literally *paid* for doing what I'd just done. And it's almost always men who hold these roles.[9] Now, of course, I have the luxury of an academic salary, and engaging with industry is part of my job – but the principle is the same. A member of the dominant majority (a cis man) did not have to expend any resources to do his job – he outsourced it to me, with no recompense.

I've heard many similar stories of how minoritized artists are asked to find female or gender-expansive remixers for their tracks themselves. Heather, an early-stage producer who was starting to get some traction on bigger labels, explained to me how this worked: 'I was asked to find other girls to remix [the track] … the label only puts out two-track EPs, see. I don't know many other girls, so was weird just emailing cold, but I found someone in the end.' Heather's qualifier 'in the end' here suggests that she put a fair bit of time and effort into finding her remixer. At no point in our conversation did she seem to think she'd asked to do anything unreasonable; in fact, like me when the big-name DJ asked for my help, she sounded pleased that the label was wanting to include more women on their releases. We are eager to help in the battle for better gender representation and take it for granted that it's our job to do so. However, this artist involvement in their own creative product is rarely so forthcoming when the remixers are men. 'Oh yeah, they just took my track and got a bunch of white dudes to remix it,' Naomi told me. 'That's quite normal – not to have a say in what kind of remixes get done.'

This idea that it's the minoritized individuals who take on the load of fixing their own disadvantage is known in psychology as 'identity taxation'[10] – a concept I will refer to quite a lot in the chapters that follow. It's a big part of ameliorative work – your time is taxed because of your identity, when the majority individuals get away lightly and, indeed, often pick up the accolades for being forward-thinking, diversity-friendly players.

So … if there are so many women producers out there, why do people keep saying there aren't?

The answer to this question is precisely because they are so hard to find, and doing so requires a fair deal of effort that dominant groups do not consider it necessary to expend. Women – let alone gender-expansive folks – are not visible anywhere where people come into contact with music. They are a tiny minority across all measures, which is what you are about to discover in this section of the chapter. This is partly because, undoubtedly, there *are* more men who make electronic music for reasons I discuss in later chapters, but this easy, go-to, answer is not the whole story. The measures themselves, and the ways they are put together are part of a cloaking mechanism that hides women in plain sight. So, as well as showing there is a lack of non-cis-male artists across measures like employment metrics, production credits, gig appearances, label rosters, radio plays, streaming numbers, rankings and awards lists, in this section we'll also be starting to unmask why this is so.

Hiding in the bedroom

Firstly, regardless of gender, almost all producers are freelance. I have not come across a single artist during this research who was actually employed by a record label or promoter. Under contract, perhaps, but not employed. In electronic music it is rare to be 'signed' to a record label in the same way that happens in the pop world – things are more precarious in electronic music (and also more libertarian, to be fair) because it is individual tracks that are signed, rather than an exclusive claim on the artist, and the revenue generated is usually split 50/50 between the label and the artist. Some artists do have a recognized affiliation with a label – they appear on 'label rosters', for example, and regularly play DJ sets at label parties and festivals – but this is not a formal contract of employment, or even service, and is usually non-exclusive.[11]

The size of freelance populations in general is notoriously difficult to estimate[12] and the music industries tend to rely on self-report surveys to generate statistics on the size and characteristics of the workforce.[13] In order to be counted, you first have to know the census is happening, but more importantly, you have to consider yourself to be part of the population that's being counted before you'll complete it. This is particularly compounded within electronic music because a large number of artists in the underground are what is referred to as 'bedroom producers'. This somewhat patronizing term is widely used in the industry to denote producers who make their music from home studios (often the corner of their bedroom) on a part-time basis, squeezing their creative time in between other paid employment, and particularly in the case of women, care-giving too – both of which are often full-time roles. I can't help thinking that the very term 'bedroom producer' is gendered, with connotations of adolescent boys shut in musty, dark rooms filled with decaying laundry, curtains closed against a sunny day, alternating making beats with playing video games. It's unlikely that these 'serious hobbyists' would regard themselves as bona fide producers worthy of standing up and being counted. Women are particularly reticent to define themselves as producers, so it's reasonable to assume they will be particularly under-represented among this population. One of the education and development organizations I interviewed for the project was set up precisely because of the reluctance of female students on university music majors programmes to associate themselves with the 'techie' side of things, as founder Liz told me:

> Most of the female first-year students were already amazing singers, songwriters, performers, and all of them when I asked them what do you want to major in [said] 'oh, probably performance, song writing, composing', and then I would show them [our] video … but what if you could write your music and perform it like this, or you could produce this track, everything is from you, they were like, yeah, I want to do that [but] I don't think I can.

There were several early-stage producers who took part in this project who started our conversations with apologetic disclaimers that maybe they weren't *really* producers, at least not yet, as Ruby told me: 'I always feel not good enough and I have this complex of thinking, ok, someone else does it better so I'm not as good … my music needs to be impeccable before anyone can be exposed to it, or maybe not impeccable but kind of nearly there.' This perfectionism went hand in hand with an assumption that it wasn't right to call yourself a producer until you could quit your day job and earn all or most of your income from your music, as Helen told me '… [that's] when professionalism comes, when you're actually confident to ask money for your craft'. Despite making and releasing music for commercial sale, I too have never completed UK Music's survey of musicians, because I do not class myself as a 'proper musician' as it's not my main job. As we shall see later, this is a problematic mindset given how hard it is to make money as an electronic music artist.

Probably the closest we have to reliable figures in electronic music specifically is the Digital DJ Tips Census which runs every year. It primarily focuses on DJing but always asks whether respondents produce – or want to produce – their own music.[14] In 2024, this self-report survey generated 15,000 responses worldwide,[15] and confirmed that:

> Just a handful of years ago most of you hadn't even tried [production], but [this year] a whopping majority of you said you really wanted to. Now an awful lot more have had a go. I think this is a useful trend among us DJs trying to differentiate ourselves from others, but also as a way of expressing ourselves creatively, especially when the basics of DJing are getting easier. (Phil Morse, Founder Digital DJ Tips, 2024)

The 2024 IMS Business Report[16] also found this bias towards production, with 85 per cent of artists surveyed stating that production was more intrinsically more important to them than DJing.

Data from the Digital DJ Tips Census shows '[DJs are] doing pretty well in life generally – [they earn] good money as a whole, but it's not from DJing. For [them], DJing is generally just a fantastic hobby'.[17] This hints at the fact that a certain level of income is probably needed in order to subsidize the DJing – a fact that almost certainly mitigates lower socio-economic groups' access to this occupation, with implications for people of the global majority who are disproportionately represented there. Denoting bedroom producers as just 'serious hobbyists' is problematic, though. If we measure these artists' success with a financial yardstick then, sure, they are more akin to amateurs than professionals, because when most people think of a 'professional occupation' they think of someone who earns their living from what is keeping them occupied.

But as we'll see later, those at the grass roots of electronic music earn little to no money from their craft and, as a result, they have other benchmarks of success within the underground scene – such as authenticity, and simply moving others with their music.[18] This is also part of the 'home-made' aesthetic in a lot of electronic music genres, as India told me during our interview: 'I got a little illegal cracked version of some software from my cousin when I was 14 … it didn't seem like such a farfetched or adventurous thing to want to do to want to start making beats, because [genre] is very DIY.' Being able to do – or knowing how to do – every step in the process yourself is a badge of authenticity and quality identifying you as a 'proper producer', as we shall see in Chapter 5. From this vantage point, bedroom producers are far from amateur, or unsuccessful. Almost all the women I interviewed for the project, for example, work from home studios, and yes, some really quite successful ones are set up in their bedrooms.

Notwithstanding the earlier observation about socio-economic disadvantage, having a home studio in one's bedroom is made possible by the fact that powerful music production software is within financial reach of a lot of people now, in the form of 'digital audio workstations' (DAWs). Visiting a professional (and expensive) recording studio is no longer technically necessary, plus the arrangement is one of convenience and cost, as much as anything to do with whether music production is one's hobby or occupation. As popular music scholar Nick Prior explains of the explosion in home production and the rise of DAWs, 'the new amateurs are threatening the very boundaries around professional and amateur, expert and non-expert, so central to modern social configurations'.[19] As the designations of hobby/occupation are made fuzzy by the technologies involved, as well the aesthetics and value-bases of the scene, we can start to see why counting 'how many people work as producers' becomes an unreliable metric.

Who's on record?

So, the population of women and gender-expansive producers is hard to estimate, first of all, because many may not 'officially' regard themselves as music producers. However, since they are still making and releasing music, then perhaps they will be more visible if we look at how many people are earning royalties and/or listed on the credits of the music itself.

Who's registering for royalties?

Royalties are collected as a result of complex intellectual property and copyright laws and rules that vary from country to country.[20] In order to claim what are known as your 'music rights',[21] you register with a collective rights management organization (CMO) for your territory, such as the Performing Right Society (PRS) in the UK. Most artists registered with CMOs also have an 'administration publishing deal' with a music publisher as well to navigate the complexity of collecting royalties on their behalf, such as Songtrust,[22] Sentric, or Ditto.[23] As the market is crowded and competitive, music publishers often offer further services to artists to add value to the deal, because they receive a slice of the artist's revenue and so have a vested interest in seeing them do well.

In the UK, 82 per cent of members of the PRS and 80 per cent of those registered with Songtrust identify their gender as 'male'[24] – and in 2019, women made up just 14 per cent of all music publishers' memberships,[25] as further evidence, perhaps, that there really *are* very few women making electronic music. But 20 per cent, or even 14 per cent, is not *none*. PRS's female membership, for example, now grows by 2,000 every year. These figures are for *all* musicians, though. They don't distinguish by genre, so the extent of *electronic* music producers is impossible to see. Using these figures also assumes artists actually register themselves for royalty payments. It is entirely possible that many feel they are too small and financially inconsequential to see any return, and so do not register. Speaking with Lia about the earning potential of her 12-year career to date, she told me, 'I think if you go into it and think, *right*, I'm going to earn loads of money, I'm going to be famous, I just don't think that works.' She paused, before continuing thoughtfully, '… and I don't know anyone who's *actually* ever done that to be fair!' So, not bothering to register tracks with a CMO or publisher because there's no point is a perception that is actually grounded in reality for most artists. Lia supplemented her income with other music-related activities (running a mixing and mastering service and offering DJ lessons), plus she had a day job. A familiar pattern across the majority of my interviewees and people I have met in the industry.

The reason why underground producers earn so little from their music is that they never sell or stream enough copies of their (digital) records to earn more than a few pence from the hours of effort they pour into making music. In my tiny and very short career as an electronic music artist, I have earned the sum total of about £20 from releasing eight tracks with record labels in the last four years, one of which included a two-track EP that spent a few days at No.1 in the Beatport Top 100 releases chart for the genre.[26] I wasn't alone in this. Helen told me she didn't recall receiving any money at all from her early releases: 'I never heard anything about money from them, so now I release by myself on Bandcamp, but it is tiny amounts, like a few pounds each time if I'm lucky!' Alice, who was quite business-savvy about her DJing career, simply accepted that she wasn't going to see financial return on the music she released. 'There is no money in it at all, but it's necessary for your reputation. So that's the payment I guess.' Kate told me how things had changed dramatically in the years she had been in the business and from the days of releasing vinyl:

> When I first started in the scene, it was like you could write a record and you would make enough money to literally last you for a year, you could buy a *house* with that money, whereas now you're not going to make any money off of a release, especially an underground dance music release, because it is so accessible and everyone is streaming everything basically for less than pennies.

Even the most successful dance tracks released by the women I interviewed earned them only a few hundred pounds a year at most, and even well-established artists found it hard to make ends meet and that DJ gigs provided much greater returns. Hayley told me: 'My biggest track so far made a couple of thousand, I think, and I can get that from doing one or two good shows.' This is because the bulk of music distribution is digital which, as we saw previously, means almost no earnings unless you hit the big time.[27] Music publisher 'Ditto' confirm this with their advice on how to earn money as a music producer[28] – streaming or download royalties from actual tracks made is only one of 12 strategies for earning money. But regardless of whether money is earned from selling or streaming the tracks, artists and producers are listed on the *credits* for electronic music, so perhaps that could be a good way to hunt out whether women are more visible there.

Who's getting the credit?

There are a few places we can look to see who is being credited on electronic music tracks – by hunting through releases for sale in online record stores, looking at the rosters of independent record labels, and looking through the official surveys of music creators undertaken by various bodies over the past few years. The Annenberg Inclusion Initiative do exactly that each year, counting up the numbers of women and non-binary folks that appear in various roles across top Billboard songs in the US.[29] Despite the survey being US-based and not focusing specifically on electronic genres, the annual

Annenberg report is the most-quoted source within the electronic music industry for the numbers of women in music production roles, for example the Facebook Group '2% Rising'[30] is named after the proportion of non-cis-male producers stated in the Annenberg research when the group was set up. The research has been carried out since 2012, and since then a total of 1,972 production credits have been analysed. In the period 2012–23 cis men made up a staggering 96.8 per cent of them while women took just 3.2 per cent of the share: a gender ratio of 30 men to every one woman producer. Non-binary people didn't even feature as producers, and women of colour have been just as scarce (less than 1 per cent), despite people of colour accounting for 49 per cent of the *artists* who featured in the Billboard Top 100 in 2023. Women do slightly better as songwriters in the Annenberg report – almost 20 per cent in 2023 – but these numbers were as low as 11 per cent when the annual count began. Fix the Mix,[31] the report produced by gender in music charity Moving the Needle, does identify patterns across a range of genres, though, two of which are the 'dance' and 'electronic' categories. The most popular 50 dance tracks across the major streaming platforms were analysed. Women amounted to only 4.5 per cent of named producers in 'dance' and 12.6 per cent in 'electronic'.

Surprisingly, 'electronic' was the most gender-diverse genre in the Fix the Mix report. But if you factor in the unique ways electronic music is 'self-produced', things make more sense. Pop or rock music, for example, is usually produced in a professional recording studio with a recording engineer capturing the band and vocalist's performance(s), a producer shaping the sound dynamics of the various parts, and a mix engineer harmonizing the balance between the elements and finessing the 'space' that the music takes up in the listener's head (through volume, editing frequencies, left/right panning, reverb, delay and many other aural effects). Each one of these roles is performed by a specialist – and often a different person – but this is generally not the case in dance, or electronic music more generally, as I noted in Chapter 1. As we learned earlier, many electronic artists make their music in home studios, or even while travelling, using DAWs – sometimes with just the software on a laptop and a pair of headphones if on the move. Importantly, this means that they are 'self-producers', to denote that they perform all the studio roles themselves. So, the person composing the musical ideas, arranging the track, adding effects and engineering the sound, and perhaps even singing is the artist themselves. Paula Wolfe[32] notes that this shift to the home studio has particularly favoured women, who no longer need to engage with the male-dominated space of the professional recording studio, often rife with masculine dynamics and in many cases posing a threat to safety, as I discuss in Chapter 4.[33] With this in mind, we might expect more women to be producing electronic music at home rather than engaging with professional studios. Even so, women claiming just 12.6 per cent of the production credits of the Top 50 electronic tracks in 2022 is still a low proportion, and that for dance is miniscule at 4.5 per cent. Yet, we know women producers are out there. Jacki-E can find them, and so can I.

So, on the basis of these reports then, we can say that the tiny numbers of women appearing on credits as producers of music is probably another explanation why people think there aren't any. Because, taking these statistics at face value, that assumption is generally correct. This picture is repeated in The Jaguar Foundation/SONY report based on UK electronic dance music from 2022. Identifying artists using Official Charts Company data, 95 per cent of the tracks included a (cis) man, in 78 per cent of cases as the primary artist on the track, and an over-emphasis on the designation 'featuring' when it came to the women. The main way women artists are featured on a track is when they are vocalists. This firmly positions women back inside their bodies, doing what women are safely allowed to do – singing sweetly and staying well away from any of that techie stuff that's the domain of the boys, as we saw from the example of Liz's music tech programme earlier, and will explore further in Chapters 5 and 6. Here, this over-emphasis on vocals and singing could suggest that women will be more visible in measures of performance than on production credits, as the following section explores.

Who do we see and hear performing electronic music?

To assess gender balance in performances of electronic music, I shall examine event line-ups and festival rosters – not all of these women will be producers, of course, but higher-profile bookings often come from having a catalogue of your own releases as an artist, rather than 'just' being a DJ, as Charles Audley, Director of Noisily Festival told me during the recording for the 'In the Key' radio show in 2019:[34] 'It's really important to have [producers] as an offering, far more important than just filling a festival with DJs, because I think it's inspiring, it's creativity, it's artistry …'

This is corroborated by Phil Morse from Digital DJ Tips, who we heard from earlier. He commented as far back as 2016: '… if you want to become famous, play outside your own town, tour the world, get added to big festival billings, and live the full-on "DJ lifestyle", nowadays you have to be able to produce music'.[35] In my own experience of programming the stages for Deevstock[36] – a small community-run micro-festival – we also feel the 'pull of the producer' when receiving applications from DJs wanting to play for us. There is something very special about experiencing someone playing the music that they have personally spent hours producing and honing for that ultimate dancefloor moment, a view also shared by Charles: '… it's important for us at Noisily to be creating a stage for these sort of people, that's what makes the festival so magic, because it is art … it's not just music'.

This idea that 'the art' is greater than 'just the music' is a discourse that feeds into the underground scene's ethic of authenticity I mentioned earlier – that people are in this scene for love first, followed by (moderate) fame and only then fortune. We can also see this hinted at in Lia's previous comment about newcomers having the 'right' mindset – for example, not even *expecting* to earn any money. Huge amounts of time, education and effort are poured into production by people who care about keeping the underground scene alive despite the precarious working conditions, very low pay, zero employment protection, and long hours of the (original!) gig economy. Working in the underground scene is hard work, even before you layer the need for ameliorative work by minoritized genders on top. The ideal of the 'romantic individual' who labours for their art unsullied by financial concerns is as old as the arts themselves and often used as a way for musicians to justify the fact that they earn very little for most of their lives.[37] This has been referred to in creative industries research as self-exploitation whereby creative workers 'take advantage of themselves' in ways that would be seen as completely unacceptable if these conditions were placed upon them by someone else – for example Uber or Deliveroo.[38] While elements of this are undoubtedly true, it does take rather a narrow view of reward, and is the epitome of the 'paranoid readings' I explained in Chapter 1. Read *reparatively* we pay equal attention to the real joy that was recounted to me by my participants – joy in what they do *despite* their self-exploitation, which is probably not the case for those driving cabs or riding bicycles to deliver fast food.

Who's in the clubs?

Data on performers in music venues is surprisingly hard to find. A 2018 survey by DJane Mag is the only attempt I can find to quantify how many women are booked as DJs at clubs, from small(er) venues to top superclubs, and it's a tiny number. Six per cent of the acts in the global superclubs were women in 2018 – and the same 15 women at that. Women accounted for ten per cent of the acts in the mid-size clubs, and a slightly rosier picture emerged in the smaller clubs – perhaps more cash-strapped venues – where women make up 18 per cent of the bookings. A work-in-progress study I'm currently involved in has sampled data from 16 mixed-capacity O2 venues in the UK over a three-month period in 2024 and found a similar picture looking at music as a whole – 80 per cent of the bands and artists appearing across 511 performances are either male solo acts, or bands fronted by men.[39] In 2023, tech company A2D2 cross-tabulated the names on the DJ Mag Top 100 DJs list with the numbers of gigs each played and in which countries they played them to ascertain who were the 'hardest working' Leaving aside the rather unhealthy, and perhaps macho, undertone of workaholism to this piece, what they found was alarming from a gender perspective. Although only 11 of the Top 100 DJs were female, trans or non-binary (11 per cent), they made up 40 per cent of the DJs playing the most shows (four out of ten):

> The average number of gigs for a male DJ was 13 in 2023, whereas the female DJ's average was 23, quite a considerable difference. This speaks volumes about their determination to make a mark in an industry historically dominated by males.[40]

This confirms the findings of the DJane Mag study of 2018 – that it's the same women getting booked over and over again without any trickle-down effect to up-and-coming artists. It could also be why the myth that female producers do not exist is so enduring, because audiences and industry player alike see the same faces over and over. It's also a concern because, yet again, it's the minoritized artists who are having to work the hardest in order to be seen. Ironically, the prevalence of these same few artists gives the impression that we've fixed the gender problem altogether and there's no more work to be done. As long-time producer and DJ Tess remarked drily during a conversation we had over coffee at a music conference, 'Oh, *no*, we haven't got a gender imbalance problem now, have we? Because [we've got] Nina Kraviz, and Honey Dijon. A woman, and a trans woman. Job done. Bye!'

Who's playing the festivals?

So, from the scant data on club performers it seems cis men dominate there. However, festivals are growing in popularity as the spaces where people go to immerse themselves in electronic music with opportunities for a far greater number of artists to perform, so perhaps things are more progressive there.[41] In the UK, venues are closing at a rate of five per *week*[42] due to cost-of-living crises, unfavourable licensing laws and the power of property developers to buy up inner-city land from financially desperate local authorities and town councils. Most of these are the small, grassroots venues where up-and-coming DJs and producers would cut their musical teeth – and small festival stages are where that is now more likely to happen. So, who's on those stages?

The biannual FACTS survey run by Female:Pressure from Berlin analyses the gender of performers at a wide range of electronic music festivals across the world. There were 175 editions of 110 unique festivals included in the 2022/23 edition, which published the latest figures available at the time of writing this book[43] and, of those, almost 30 per cent of acts were women, a considerable rise from 2012 when the FACTS survey began, recording just 9.2 per cent of acts that did not include a man across their dataset. The FACTS survey also shows that gender diversity across festivals varies by country and festival size. Portugal programmes the least diverse festivals (from a gender perspective, at least) with 85 per cent men across 13 festivals, and Slovenia has the most diversity on stage with 50 per cent male acts across 11 events. Sweden is a close second, with 52 per cent men, performing at 19 festivals.

The biggest festivals are the least gender diverse – Boom, held in Portugal, had women in just 10 per cent of its 123 billed slots in 2023, which was actually a *decrease* from the year before. Size matters when measured by audience numbers, too, with the biggest capacity events having the highest number of men on stage – Coachella in the US has over 100,000 festival-goers through the gates, so from a representation perspective, it's a serious matter that in the 2024 line-up, male acts outnumber female acts 2:1, with almost 70 per cent of the performers that people see under the bright lights being men.[44] The same pattern is repeated globally in Music Data Analyst *Viberate*'s 'post-pandemic' round-up of the top 330 festivals in 2022. Seventy-six per cent of the most-booked 100 artists were men, and there no women in the top three. One hundred and one of those events were exclusively electronic, and across all 330 festivals 40 per cent of the artists appearing were from electronic genres, which gives some sense of the importance of electronic genres to the festival landscape overall.

A visual representation of gender and festival line-ups comes from Book More Women,[45] who do a diligent job of blanking out the male acts from festival line-up posters with striking effect. Drawing on US data from top music festivals across all genres, their 2023 progress report found that across all festivals in 2018 there were only 14 per cent of acts that identified as women and non-binary, but this had risen to 28 per cent in 2023, with 25 per cent of the acts falling into the dance and electronic categories.[46]

These figures provide a clear reason why your average Jo Public doesn't think of women when they think 'electronic music', despite there having been *some* change when it comes to the gender of people that we see on stage at festivals. This is testament to the pressure that has been exerted on music industry organizations in recent years, both on-stage and behind the scenes. A longstanding player in that pressure has been the Keychange initiative, which invites music festivals and promoters to commit to achieving equitable gender representation on their line-ups. Keychange offer this rallying cry as part of their manifesto: 'Performers alone don't make up festivals or the music industry – [yes,] line-ups should be scrutinised; [but also] hiring policies of record labels should be examined; pay disparities corrected.'[47] High-profile ambassadors for holding large organizations to account are the Australian DJ HAAi[48] and the UK DJ Jaguar. who have 'inclusion riders'. Here's a section from Jaguar's detailed on her Foundation's website, which suggests the following diversity conditions artists can include in booking contracts:

> [Artist] has made the decision not perform on line-ups composed entirely or overwhelmingly of cis male performers. [Artist's]

participation is dependent on at least one other woman, trans or non-binary person, or person of colour, or member of the LGBTQ+ community being booked for this event.[49]

It's a controversial move, to be sure, and perhaps one that can only be made by artists with enough commercial clout to force promoters to comply. But both HAAi and Jaguar still run the risk that booking agents will simply refuse to book them – it's an admirable move to stand in your power and literally put your money where your mouth is because the pace of change is just *too slow* otherwise. This is a particularly clear instance of ameliorative work – huge risk shouldered by the minoritized individual for the greater good. It's both frustrating and inspiring. Jaguar is a black woman, too, so her marginalization is intersectionally compounded. What would be really powerful would be one of the 'big name' white cis-male DJs doing the same, but so far – to my knowledge – not one has.

These figures are poor as they are, but they also mask a subtler question of *where* the minoritized artists perform, in terms of times and physical location within the event. According to a study of UK festivals by Sky News, women occupy only 18 per cent of headline slots,[50] which are those where the biggest audience is expected. Of course, bigger crowds are drawn by more famous and respected (fashionable?) artists, so the process is mutually reinforcing, but generally headline slots are the peak-time dancing hours. For a standard night-time event, beginning around 9 or 10 pm and ending at 3 or 4 am, peak time is anywhere between midnight and 2 am. There are also popular slots around sunset if the party is happening during the day, and sometimes early afternoon can be a relatively popular time as festival-goers emerge from their tents after sleeping off the excesses of the night before. The final night of the party – the 'closing set' – can also be a highly prestigious billing, and is accorded responsibility and gravitas. You are trusted to *close the party*. It might come as no surprise that women and gender-expansive artists rarely occupy these slots – apart from the few 'big names' that dominate the scene.[51] Instead, they are temporally and spatially relegated to the sidelines. They appear on smaller stages, early in the day, or even all bunched together on a special 'female DJs stage' or a run of acts grouped together in, say, one afternoon, for example, because they 'go together well'. To paraphrase a sentiment from some of my interviewees, 'Er, guys, woman is not a genre for fuck's sake!'

This marginalization of representation is largely hidden in the statistics presented earlier, yet it significantly increases people's perception that all DJs and producers are cis-men – because that's what they see. But it can be changed. At Noisily Festival in 2023 there had clearly been a concerted effort to schedule more women at visible times (although still not the really top slots) and it was a delight to hear fragments of conversations among the dancers remarking how refreshing is was not to be seeing a 'sea of white dudes', as I heard one man say, and another remarking 'Man! These women bring so much energy to the party!' The 2024 UK Electronic Music Report confirmed this sentiment with around 80 per cent of respondents feeling that electronic music is where diversity and inclusion should happen. Yet everything I have presented thus far points to the fact that the industry is a long way from being that. For now, at least.

*Alright then … whose music do we **listen** to?*

By now you might be able to discern a pattern, as the picture is pretty clear. We can't find a decent number of women or gender-expansive performers anywhere. It's actually getting increasingly hard to blame those who claim there are no female producers in the face of such tiny numbers, but for the sake of completeness, let's look at the final piece in the score – how prevalent women, trans and non-binary artists are in the music that gets played on the radio and the music that we stream.

Linda Coogan-Byrne was one of the first to analyse the gender composition of domestic UK artists whose music is played on the radio, using 2020 data from Radiomonitor[52] that covered a range of music genres. A familiar pattern emerges to the story told by the CMO membership, production credits, club and festival bookings related earlier – only 19 per cent of solo artists, 18 per cent of songwriters and 3 per cent of producers that appeared in the Top 100 radio airplay chart of 2020 are women.[53] Cis-male solo artists represented over half of every single radio station's tracks – solo act women rarely get above 20 per cent airtime. National BBC radio stations did best – but 85 per cent of the artists whose music was played on flagship station Radio 1 were cis men. In rock and metal genres, a staggering *100 per cent* of the airtime is taken by cis-male acts – not even one mixed duo in an entire *year*. Dance music stations Kiss and Kiss Fresh came in at 15 per cent and 5 per cent all-female acts, respectively, which is actually pretty good when compared with the data from The Jaguar Foundation/SONY Report in 2022, which looked at electronic dance music in particular. In that study, 99 per cent of the 467 tracks played by the sampled radio stations were by acts that included a cis man.

The story is repeated for streaming too. The Jaguar Foundation/SONY Report alerted me to the fact that women's music is not streamed as often as men's. Up until December 2023, live global data from Spotify algorithms fed into analysis on the 'Everynoise' website,[54] and at last count, while 44.3 per cent of Spotify users identified themselves as female, only 23.1 per cent of Spotify streams are by female artists. Female listeners listen to more music from female artists than men do – 31.9 per cent against only 19.2 per cent. The Jaguar Report found that there are fewer women-made tracks included in streaming platforms' playlists, too. This data was largely drawn from publicly available lists on Spotify and only included artists where gender could be accurately attributed to the artist. Music by women and non-binary artists' comprised just under a quarter of tracks on specialist dance music playlists (23.6 per cent), and the Everynoise analysis shows that when 'listeners play their personalised "Discover Weekly" playlists, they end up streaming 19.7% from women artists which is 3.4% *less* than when they choose their music themselves'. This is a clear example of how algorithms can feed inequality by replicating and amplifying existing listening patterns, rather than challenging them. Editorial playlists do slightly better, but it's negligible – if listeners choose pre-selected music from playlists actively curated by Spotify staff, they end up listening to 0.1 per cent more music by women.

Drawing the line – decloaking structural inequality

To conclude this chapter, then, women and gender-expansive artists' music is not playlisted by streaming platforms, is streamed less times than cis men's and played *much* less on the radio. Cis men still dominate festival stages and, importantly, take a lot more of the top billed slots and main stages. This is made even more significant when we take into account the shift towards people now encountering electronic music at festivals more than in clubs – especially since the COVID-19 pandemic. Women are also absent on event line-ups in clubs, too, although the figures on this are very thin on the ground. In short, women and gender-expansive artists are not visible as performers of electronic music in the places we listen to it, and/or dance to it. They do not appear as producers signed to record label rosters or in music store charts, and are a tiny proportion of the technical credits on electronic music tracks. This means women, trans and non-binary people don't register themselves or their music with CMOs, and few use music publishers, which – especially at grassroots level – is partly because they are freelance, part-time 'bedroom producers' not earning enough of an income to even consider themselves to *be* music producers.

But they are out there, and the work of finding and platforming them is vital in deactivating the cloak that keeps them hidden – the myth that there are no (or very few) women producers. Finding music by minoritized artists is essential in order to change perceptions that there aren't any – as happened to me – but it takes time and effort. And it is usually left to the very people who are marginalized to do it, for no pay and often no recognition, while others take the glory. The identity tax effect is high and it's part of the ameliorative work that loads women, trans and non-binary people with *more to do* than their cis-male counterparts, compounding their disadvantage and making the playing field even less level, as I introduced in Chapter 1.

Explaining what we can do about this is ultimately the aim of this book. I'll be showing how the walls of structural inequality can be demolished by unsettling their foundations and taking a metaphorical sledgehammer to the various bricks that make them up, decloaking ameliorative work in the process. I know this is possible because the women I have been working alongside over the past six years are already doing it. It's important to note here that while ameliorative work is indeed an additional burden, recognizing women's agency and their power to resist and subvert societies' structures also avoids positioning them as helpless victims.[55] But it's my contention that these sisters shouldn't *have* to being doing this for, or by, themselves. Ameliorative work should not just be women's and gender-expansive people's work. In the next chapter, we start to examine this in more depth through our next myth that 'good music is all that matters' and that talent is all you need.

Chapter track: 'Keep Your Disdance'

Figure 2: Artwork for 'Keep Your Disdance' EP by Dovetail, reproduced with kind permission of Break Wind Productions

Source: https://breakwindproductions1.bandcamp.com/track/keep-your-disdance

'Keep Your Disdance' was the first piece of electronic music I wrote and produced that wasn't composed entirely of drag-and-drop samples. I started work on it at the same time as the In the Key project really got under way, and I feel the track title has resonances with the sheer extent of gender inequality in electronic music I have sketched out in this chapter, and the various practices and regimes that I'll be discussing throughout the rest of the book that effectively tell women and gender-expansive folks to back off and keep their distance.

The track started life as a practice project for the short online course in music production I was following through MPW (Music Production for Women) run by Xylo Aria. Specifically 'Keep Your Disdance' was a practice project for programming drums – learning about the basics of kicks, snares, the delight of clicking in random hi-hat patterns, and adding swing and movement to percussive elements to create a groove. I worked on it in bursts over the summer and autumn of 2019, using my laptop perched on my knees while sitting on the sofa, or in bed. I'd recently moved into my partner's little house already populated by him and his two children – so 'Keep Your Disdance' is very much testament to what you can do with just a laptop, a DAW and a pair of headphones. As the name suggests, I finished it during the spring of 2020 and named it after the social distancing rule that was propelled into everyday parlance by the UK's 'stay safe' guidelines during the COVID-19 pandemic – with a nod to dance, of course.

3

Good Music is All That Matters

I don't listen to music with my eyes

> I don't care what gender, colour, race, or anything else anyone is.
>
> I don't listen to music with my eyes, what does it matter what a DJ looks like?

This opening quote is a comment from the carnage that ensued on Facebook after I posted a question on an up-and-coming underground dance music organization's Facebook page in January 2020:

> Hey folks, how come there are so many white guys on your festival line-up? [Name] is such a diverse and inclusive party – what's going on?

As I sat on the edge of my bed that morning, and opened up Facebook on my phone, I saw the line-up poster and felt an icy jolt of fear. Across the two stages and three days of programming at the event, only three of the eighty-something acts were women, and only one artist was black – Asian heritage, to be exact. That was at least *76 white dudes* booked by an outfit who claimed to be true to the inclusive roots of the scene – where you could leave your hang-ups at the door and just party, no matter who you were, or where you came from. Whether I liked it or not, I was going to have to call this out and that undoubtedly meant trouble. I'd already had two DMs from women DJs asking me to speak out on their behalf because they were too afraid of the 'backlash' and of it looking like they were just miffed because they hadn't been booked to play. In the Key was also getting traction on social media – I was quite a high-profile player in the gender equality space for electronic music, especially since getting a piece published in hallowed clubbing magazine *Mixmag* and speaking at Amsterdam Dance Event. If I couldn't call this out, then who could? But I was quaking in my slippers, if not my boots.

By mid-morning there were hundreds of comments from angry fans, and a festival organizer who claimed to be mortally wounded by my 'accusation' – [name] was one of the good guys, keeping rampant commercialism out of the scene, championing good music and exceptional talent – *feeding the starving underground. A messiah of the rave scene!* There was outrage. I was attacking their precious festival as low-hanging fruit – I should be targeting the big guns, they were just as bad *and* they had the resources to do something about it. [Name] was struggling to survive, it was run on love – the founders' blood, sweat and tears. I should just go crawl under a rock with my vile attacks and stay there. Someone even made a meme about me.

With my rational researcher's head on, this was absolutely fascinating – just WOW. I hadn't accused anyone of anything! All I had done was ask why there were hardly any women or people of colour playing at the party. As a woman, however, I felt emotionally battered. Attacked, stripped bare and the target of hate. Even writing this now I feel echoes of a trauma response in my gut.

By early afternoon, I'd had to step away from the thread. I was physically exhausted from the extreme stress of being attacked, and repeatedly replying to the more measured comments, posting links to resources and arguments that explained *why* it mattered what a DJ looked like. I had a headache and had to take to my bed. By the end of the day, and before I could save the posts, the thread was deleted without trace.

Introduction

The story that opens this chapter shows how hard it is to raise the subject of diversity behind the decks because of the entrenched belief in electronic music that, with hard work and dedication, talent will rise to the top no matter who you are. The belief that the music is everything is so strong that my simple act of asking why a festival wasn't booking more women was met with hostility and dismissiveness. Because we don't listen to music with our eyes. Identity is unimportant. Representation is political correctness that jeopardizes the sanctity of 'quality'. As long as the music is good, and the party is true to the spirit of the scene, there is nothing more to say. This was expressed to me quite simply by the head of one dance music's biggest independent record labels during a conversation about how demo tracks from women were considered by the label: '… we treat them on the same terms [as men], we treat them on *musical* terms, how they look is not relevant to me … we will simply judge them on their musical terms'. On the face of it this seems to be a laudable aim – *the music she makes is all that matters* and not her appearance. But on closer examination, this kind of belief undermines attempts to increase diversity. We'll be excavating this as a myth in this chapter, by exploring a range of other myths that sustain it.

Peace, love, unity and respect

The first of these is the perception that dance music is immune to inequality because it was born in black underprivileged neighbourhoods, in gay clubs and as resistance to neoliberal politics. Detroit techno was black music born from the poverty of industrial decline of the car industry in the 1980s,[1] and New York disco was invented a little earlier by the gay community as feel-good music in resistance to persecution. Acid house raves in the UK were a revolt against neoliberal politics, increasingly stark individualization and economic inequality,[2] and the reunification of Germany in the late 1980s and 1990s brought people together to rave in all manner of abandoned buildings to put aside the differences of earlier generations and unite. These all provided diverse and inclusive roots for electronic music culture.[3] The acronym PLUR – peace, love, unity and respect – that originated from the US scene in the 1990s, is a poster child for this sentiment and continues to be a big part of US electronic dance music culture.[4]

But these roots have blinded those in the scene to creeping inequalities of many kinds, and particularly for those with privilege – namely the white, middle-class, cis guys who now dominate the scene all over the world.[5] What this founding story means is that there is a particularly strong belief among stakeholders that electronic music is egalitarian and democratic. The DIY roots of music production and recent developments in digital audio workstations (DAWs) enabling personal, home use for 'amateurs', introduced in Chapter 2, add further fuel to this, culminating in a myth which is a virtual truism in the scene: that talented people (and the good music they produce) will always shine through because dance music culture is, by its very nature, inclusive.

The myth of meritocracy

This leads to the second illusion that supports the view that good music is all that matters: that electronic music is a meritocracy. Like all art-based occupations, this industry runs on the belief that everyone has access to the same opportunities, that talent is largely something that individuals are born with and/or work extremely hard at developing and perfecting over time through selfless dedication to the cause. But as the rest of this chapter (and indeed the book) shows, this is not true. Minoritized genders in music have to work harder to be noticed and face additional obstacles before their creative output is seen as 'talent'. Climbing over the hurdles, going out of their way to avoid the obstacles, and running up a sloping playing field while being gaslighted that it's level, is ameliorative work that women and gender-expansive artists undertake. It's also testament to women, trans and non-binary people's resilience, ingenuity and determination to succeed, and is incredibly inspiring. But ultimately, it is still gender-driven work that cis men never have to do. We can see how this plays out in my story in the opening vignette. The fear and emotional and physical exhaustion I experienced from the backlash from speaking out. The fact that it took out an entire day from my schedule. This is ameliorative work. The incident sparked parallel discussions in the women's groups on Facebook, and I took heart from the fact that plenty of other people were feeling the same – sick of seeing white, cis-male-dominated line-ups while being repeatedly told nothing is wrong. But almost no one from those communities felt 'safe' speaking out in the actual furore. No one wanted the emotional and visceral angst of being attacked. What kept me (mildly) together that day were the private messages of support I received from people thanking me for putting my head above the parapet. They were tired of being shouted down, and told their experiences and views are unimportant and that good music is all that matters.[6] So, despite the gruelling experience, I also knew 'the sisterhood' had my back. I drew strength and solace from that and it was solid reminder of the power of having great networks.

It's not what you know, it's who you know

Networks and connections are vital to success in electronic music but they also sustain the myth that good music is all that matters because talent will always shine through. Networks and connections form between people who share the same characteristics, and they exclude others. If you don't have the right networks, your talent and hard work will never be seen. It's impossible to overstate the importance of connections and networks in the creative industries. In 1994, Scott Lash and John Urry's landmark text *Economies of Signs and Space* established what they called 'vertical disintegration' as a core organizing principle of the new cultural industries (as they were more commonly referred to then).[7] Instead of traditional organization structures where everything is owned in house, all the people in these new cultural industries were independent, coming together around specific projects (such as making a piece of music or a film, or putting on an event) and offering their services according to supply and demand, with speed being of the essence. This nebulous, ever-shifting organizational form works best when key players have a set of personal contacts across the skillsets and domains the project requires, so that they can call them in quickly, safe in the knowledge that the product or service (and the provider) is reliable, comes at a good price, and so on. Lash and Urry illustrate this through the demise of the contracted (or even subcontracted) A&R man [sic] for record labels, and the decentralization of record producers and engineers. Each person in the assemblage brings their own groups of preferred associates, who in turn bring theirs. Enter 'the network'. As the saying goes – it's not what you know, it's *who* you know, and, importantly, whether who you know has sufficient social capital and market clout to pull strings to bring you success. As we will see time and time again in this book, it is 'market forces' that are the music industry's go-to justification for non-diverse offerings.[8] Explanations for male-dominated line-ups centre around the presumption that 'women don't sell tickets' and that putting trans or non-binary artists in the spotlight is divisive and will cost revenue as they fail to attract large crowds.

The making of a meritocracy: privilege, implicit bias and structural inequality

A few years ago, a DJ I met through the underground dance scene in my home town, was producing a podcast series called 'Lowering the Tone'. Each episode was a long chatty discussion between the host Meat Katie (aka Mark Pember) and other DJs he was mates with, or had met over his career in the electronic music business. They were all cis-gendered men, of course, but we'll return to that later when we look at the significance of networks in more detail.

The podcasts are highly interesting, funny, irreverent, honest and heartwarming romps through (cis-male) DJs' stories of how they made it in music, and the scrapes they've got into along the way. In fact, it was listening to the Lowering the Tone series that inspired me to create my own radio show for In the Key that I introduced in the Prelude to this book – people narrating their journeys through conversation is incredibly engaging to listen to and makes for great radio. One of the most significant takeaways from those hours of listening is very relevant here. Pretty much every one of the guests on the show explained how they'd spent years grafting as a nobody, until they finally 'found their sound' and hit success – or became as 'successful' as it is possible to be in a scene where no one makes any money and it's a struggle to get your music heard. They could only say they'd 'made it' after they'd learned enough, honed their skills, polished their talent, stuck at it and done enough 'time' to pay their dues to the gods of meritocracy. All while staying true to the 'right reasons' for being in the game (such as authentic commitment to the scene). One example from the series has stayed with me – a young white cis-male DJ who paused his eight-year-long career and residency in Ibiza to lock himself away to 'do the work'. We'll call him Liam.

> So, I thought, If I really want to make this, or nearly make this, or make this my living, I need to do *work*. So, I took myself out of the game for two years and I slogged. I wrote tunes, I perfected my craft, I honed my sound and *I came back ready*. One of my tracks was picked up by [famous DJ] and that was it. I was off.

Liam is practically being an influencer for meritocracy here. It's a heroic 'great man' story of hard work, sacrifice and pluck. I heard similar stories everywhere – on conference panels, in conversations with every stakeholder I met, and in my own interviews with producers. Here are producers Naomi and Tess telling me what advice they would give to aspiring new producers:

> Do it because you love music cos you will have to put a lot of time in, it's not like something you can do occasionally, like you have to put a *lot* of time into it. So to be able to do that, you have to literally be obsessed with it and love it, because otherwise I don't think you'll get very far. (Naomi)

> I think the main thing for me is the kind of work ethic, you can't really stop, not in an unhealthy way, but you've just got to keep plugging away at it and not expect something to happen overnight. (Tess)

I am not for one minute suggesting that these accounts are untrue. I'm sure that today's successful and elite *are* talented and *do* work hard – that's not in question. But is merit enough? It's certainly romantic to see Liam (quoted earlier) as 'naturally' talented and a 'grafter', floating to victories all by himself just by being great and working hard – because it feeds the illusion that if he can do it, then we can too. His throwaway remark at the end that his track was so good that it was just 'picked up' by a prominent DJ who was willing to give it exposure by playing it in his sets probably hides multiple connections and activities that led to this happening, as well as it being a decent piece of music. The fact that Liam, and perhaps his manager and agent, almost certainly knew the 'right people' to contact and share his music with is likely to be a significant part of the story – and not just the fact that the music was good. Was it *only* Liam's merit-worthy hard work that led to his success? For example, in a fascinating piece of 'big data' research, data analyst and academic Milán Janosov and colleagues put forward some pretty compelling evidence that many iconic musical successes have more to do with *luck* than with the artist's special talent.[9]

Demeriting meritocracy

Meritocracy is nicely defined by gender scholars Jean Clarke, Cheryl Hurst and Jennifer Tomlinson as 'a ubiquitous, uncontested, seemingly natural, or 'common-sense' account that is resilient to countervailing evidence'.[10] Questioning why cis men still dominate senior positions in universities so stubbornly, the researchers analysed how leaders' talk sustains the veil of meritocracy by 'invisibilizing' gender. This either means pointing to successful women and saying, 'Look! They've all made it', in order to claim the problem is no longer a problem, or showing how numbers of senior women *are* growing, so there is no more work to be done. We can see this happening in electronic music – the small rises in women and gender-expansive artists on production credits, and appearing at festivals that we saw in Chapter 2 is evidence for some that things are working, and there is no need for systemic change. The prominence of a handful of women, trans and non-binary artists headlining events is enough to fuel rueful statements (from cis men) that 'things are now going the other way' and 'women are getting a bigger slice of the pie than the men', even in the face of the overwhelming evidence to the contrary I presented in Chapter 2. Minorities who are able to behave like the majority, such as childfree women, with competitive traits and no caring responsibilities, for example, appear to be making great strides for their gender (or race or sexuality and so on). But the reality is that they are only able to do so by fitting themselves into a system built to favour the dominant group. Techno superstar Charlotte de Witte confirmed this in a panel talk I attended at Amsterdam Dance Event. Charlotte is one of the A-list headline artists who I showed in Chapter 2 are working way harder than men to retain their space in the Top 10 rankings. An audience member asked her how she managed to work so hard. She replied that she was doing so while she had the 'luxury' of being single and not being a mother. With no relationship or caring demands on her, she was able to fulfil a punishing schedule of global travel and multiple appearances, often on the same day in different countries – just like the guys. The difference is, of course, that the guys continue to be able to do this when they become parents if they choose, something we will look at in more depth in Chapter 4.

Where women with caring responsibilities *do* make it up the ranks, Jean Clarke and her colleagues found evidence of behind-the-scenes individual adjustments and informal arrangements that no one else sees – important accommodations that level the field for these women, for sure, but equally, because they were 'exceptional' this means that nothing is done to actually change the norm. From the outside, the system appears to be working because women are rising up the ranks 'by themselves'. Belief in meritocracy continues unchallenged. Likewise, when gatekeeping decisions are made in electronic music, from the outside it appears that the sole criteria on which those selections are based is 'good music'. Never mind all the networking, lobbying, back-scratching, favour-calling, and micro-politics behind the scenes that is never seen.

This was a key reason why I *publicly* called out the festival on their gender balance in our opening vignette. After the event, I received an angry email from the founders calling me unethical for not contacting them privately about the issue, and for deliberately stirring up a hornet's nest on social media. I was grateful for the chance to respond, but my argument that these things should not be brushed under the carpet, or discussed in secret whispers behind closed doors fell on deaf ears. According to them, I had publicly shamed them and that was that. But public attention (albeit not shaming) was my aim – to show that the system *is* broken and meritocracy is *not* enough. Dealing with things informally, offline and in private, gives the impression that everything is working just fine because nobody sees the problems. This is a key cornerstone of structural inequality.

Structural inequality

Structural inequality refers to how resources are distributed in society in ways that favour one group over another, but are taken for granted as neutral and fair because people have forgotten their origins – like meritocracy.[11] In relation to gender, it is the way cultural and implicit biases, stereotypes, misogyny from (cis men's *and* women's) fear of women, habit, routine and downright mean-ness have become hard-wired into the operating systems of societies, which has the effect of making it appear that discrimination does not exist. How can it, when the systems are seen as fair? To uncover the bases for structural inequality then, we need to question how a veil of 'objective reality' obscures inbuilt biases towards men, consider what fuels those social processes, and how this leads to assumptions that 'good music is all that matters'.

Applying this logic to the evidence I presented in Chapter 2, the question shifts from 'Why are there no women producers?' to 'Why aren't women showing up across every measure we use?' and 'Where are the biases in our measures?'. Put simply, most of these measures involve some form of gatekeeping. They are not objective measures like the height of a tree or the temperature at which water boils when at sea-level, they are the result of all manner of social processes. The top-selling music and sell-out gigs that the available statistics are mostly compiled from do not happen by accident – so what we are actually measuring are the outcomes of these social processes – particularly ones that are legitimated by economics. Almost all the statistics presented in Chapter 2 are driven by market forces– music sales, the selling of tickets to gigs and festivals, and the commercial return on maximizing streaming income, for example. This is how success is defined, even if that's less the case at grassroots level. Ultimately it is market forces that determine who gets seen and heard, who gets regarded as 'the best' and makes it into the top slots, rankings and award nominations: *who has merit* – and crucially who does not. These statistics show us who gets *chosen* because their music sells and/or they are 'marketable'. But that's a very biased process. Someone makes a *decision* who to book for an event, who to sign to their record label, or what tracks to compile into a streaming playlist. As that person is highly likely to be a (white) cis man, it's also highly likely that (white) cis-male interests, connections and networks will drive what talent looks and sounds like. The more white cis-male music we get to hear, the more white cis-male music comes to stand for *all* music.[12] If the bias in these systems is not called out, the illusion of meritocracy thrives. But it is unlikely to be called out by those who have sufficient privilege for the issue not to affect them.

Privilege

One of the best metaphors I've seen for privilege was a free-text response in a Gender Diversity survey I was involved in running for the industry in 2020/21.[13] When asked 'has your gender ever advantaged your career?', one of the responses was this: 'As a white cis man in the music industry, I don't think I would ever notice that – *it's like riding a bike with the wind at your back.*' This is a perfect metaphor, because the only time you ever really notice you have the wind behind you is when you turn around and try and bike, or run, the other way. When I was a long-distance runner, I would often feel great on a morning seafront run, clocking up an unusually fast time with ease, only to turn round at the end of the promenade and realize 'Wow! It's windy!' as I puffed and chugged my way back – much slower and with a lot more effort. My easy breathing and speedy time were the product of my environment, not my hard work or a sudden newfound talent as a runner.

It is privilege that makes it so hard to challenge people on their (lack of) diversity actions, because no one likes to think they are privileged or that their actions (or mere existence) disadvantages others. Indeed, when we are challenged on how our privilege advantages us, research clearly shows that we tend to quickly jump to defensive responses pointing out the hardships *we* have faced.[14] But regardless of those hardships, we are all also privileged to some extent and in different ways. As a cis-gendered woman I never have to deal with the intrusive curiosity, downright hostility or violence that trans people face. Likewise, as a white woman living in a majority white country I can walk down the street without worrying that people will eye me suspiciously, or shout abuse (or worse) because of my skin colour and dress. Socio-economic status is also a significant source of privilege in underground music, as I noted in Chapter 2, and as DJ and producer India explained to me during our interview:

> A huge luxury that's completely overlooked, I think, is that a lot of younger producers come from middle-class and upper-class backgrounds have the *time*, your parents aren't busy surviving or you're not busy surviving, you have the time to explore [music production], and also to get into the industry I think that's why record labels and such are filled with a lot of privately educated people, because they're not having to pay rent as soon as they're able to contribute to their household, they can take an unpaid internship. You have to be privileged in order to take an unpaid internship, and that is your access to a lot of these jobs in media and music.

Taking an internship, or locking yourself away to practise, like Liam, who we encountered earlier, is not available to all, even though it seems it is. We hold these beliefs about all sorts of things because of our upbringing, and – as we shall see later – because we tend to hang around with other people like ourselves, so we never see the world through others' eyes and with others' bodies.[15] And because we rarely question how our privilege eases our paths, it feeds implicit, or unconscious biases – beliefs about the nature of life, the universe and everything that we never question, and are often not even aware we hold.

Implicit bias

From a psychological perspective, our unquestioned beliefs are important ways we classify and make sense of an overwhelming world. But they are also the basis for stereotypes, such as the kinds of traits we automatically associate with different genders, certain races, or the abilities of people who are disabled, for example. These stereotypes feed into actively biased behaviours that we are often not conscious of and therefore do not intend.[16] This is known as implicit (taken for granted) and/or unconscious bias (unaware), and it's ubiquitous. For example, the UN Gender Norms Index covers 85 per cent of the world's population across 91 countries, and has found that in 2023, somewhat astonishingly, almost 9 out of 10 people hold some kind of bias against women.

We should pause here for a note of caution. Implicit bias not only arises from and feeds stereotypes, but can be a highly convenient shorthand excusing the perpetrator for their actions – in other words, if they stopped for just one minute and actually thought about what they were saying or doing, they'd probably realize they were being a dick. In this day and age, we have the ability to educate ourselves in milliseconds with a few clicks of a mouse – so claiming 'implicit bias' is often more accurately the metaphorical equivalent of putting one's hands over one's ears and singing 'la la la! I'm not listening'. If the issue doesn't affect you, excusing yourself by saying 'you didn't know' means you don't need to make yourself uncomfortable learning about other folks' disadvantage. Implicit bias is also claimed incorrectly in situations of quite clear explicit bias.

It is because of unacknowledged privilege, implicit bias and explicit prejudice, that people as equally talented and hard-working as Liam, who we met at the start of this section, don't seem to catch a break, no matter how hard they hustle, or how much promise they show. Implicit biases polish the illusion of meritocracy because they mean dominant groups do not even notice (or refuse to accept) anything is amiss. Maybe your music *isn't* as 'good' as others', but maybe that's because you haven't had the years of head-start that white cis-male privilege affords. Women and gender-expansive people face *so* many more hurdles, knocks to their confidence, exclusion, and unsafe situations that it is just harder for their talent to be recognized as such. They are required to *work* at strategies to overcome, work around and ameliorate their situations in ways that cis men do not. They are running into a headwind while the (cis, white) guys sail past with the wind at their back. As I explain further in the rest of the book, this 'wind' centres around differential treatment they encounter because of their gender. Fighting people's perceptions of you and/or second guessing their ulterior motives or hidden agendas is exhausting. Your working life is on at least medium alert all the time, as Olga explained to me:

> There are some things that I feel like you experience as a female musician that just get a bit tiring after a while … sometimes I wish I could just say in the first five minutes of a conversation, how would this go if I was guy? Like, can you just treat me the way you would treat another male singer, producer, or whatever?

The 'things' that Olga is referring to take many forms and are the subject of the remaining chapters of the book. Implicit assumptions from gatekeepers based on the way women look, and explicit judgements about their 'talent' being mediated – or determined – by their looks are dealt with in Chapter 4, where we also see how their careers become almost unmanageable once they become mothers. Chapters 6 and 7 deal with the ameliorative work involved in managing women's perceived incongruence in tech-heavy roles, which is constantly reinforced to them at every turn because of the historical and enduring association of men with technology. Chapter 8 recounts stories of how women are just urged to be more confident in the face of unsafe situations in the course of their work. In all these chapters, we will see the creativity, resilience, ingenuity and strength these artists exhibit, as well as recognize the difficulties they face. We will celebrate the ameliorative work that women and gender-expansive people do, as well as lament it – but for now, what's important is that there *is* extra work to be done if you are a minority gender in music and so it is a fact that it is way harder for your talent to shine than it is if you are part of the majority. But this work is trivialized, un-noticed, or disregarded *as work*. In the previous quote, Olga meekly tells us that she finds the treatment she receives from men to be 'a little bit tiring'. Language to minimize what is actually far more significant. This is illustrated by this exasperated voice note a producer sent to me after she was dropped from a prestigious record label despite pulling in big crowds at the label's parties:

> Its excuse after excuse about why my music isn't quite right … after they sit on it for months. All I see is [male DJs'] dull shitty tracks coming out on repeat and they tell *me* I just need to work harder, put more hours into perfecting the tracks. But the thing is I play those tracks already at *their fucking parties* and they go OFF [people love them]. Dance floors literally go *insane*. So there's clearly nothing wrong with those tracks. [SIGHS]. At the end of the day, it doesn't matter what I fucking do does it … cos I'm not one of the *bro's*.

We've covered a lot of ground in this chapter – and through it you might have been feeling seen and validated, or uncomfortable and challenged because you've never really noticed, let alone thought about, this stuff before. If you're not an academic, there are also a lot of 'big ideas' here that might feel overwhelming to get to grips with. I hope I'm explaining them in an accessible way, but if this is you, please do feel very free to take a break and ruminate before continuing – treat this as a kind of chapter 'half-time' pause. Just minus the oranges and team talk.

Guys like us: homophily and homosociality

'Bro culture', along with 'sausage fest', are terms that have become shorthand slang for the male dominance of electronic music, denoting a back-slapping, in-group mentality that male artists use to propel each other forward, sharing (but also gatekeeping) opportunities which they overlook when insisting that opportunities come only to those who make good music. It comes about by building networks that often start at a young age and form on account of what's known as 'homophily'. Homophily is the tendency to gravitate towards people with whom we share similarities in order to form friendship groups and networks.[17] With the explosion in social media and the algorithms that control it, this process has been greatly accelerated and we now come into contact with fewer and fewer people who are 'not like us', unless we make the effort to seek them out. This is exactly how 'bro culture' happens.

Boys form bands, go to parties together, then carry those friendships into adulthood, where they are introduced to more people like them by their friends and the process replicates into what is known as 'homosociality' – the tendency to form all-male friendship groups with shared similarities. The US musician Benn Jordan has used his privilege and his platform to critique how this happens from a white, cis man's perspective on his YouTube channel, and also in conversation with Xylo Aria, in her MPW (Music Production for Women) podcast series. Both are excellent and insightful discussions.[18]

Often we don't even notice we are doing this, and we all have homophilic tendencies. I've already mentioned the comfort and support I draw from the women and gender-expansive artists groups I belong to on Facebook, for example. When I attended the first conference of global women in music organization 'She Said So', on returning to my Airbnb apartment on the first night to write up my notes, I was shocked to realize that despite the opening reception being filled with women and gender-expansive people from all sorts of countries, backgrounds, ages and sexual identities, I had pretty much only engaged with other white middle-aged women from the UK. In a room where you don't know anyone, you search for similarities in others that will allow you to connect, and in so doing, alleviate the discomfort you feel. That's a totally natural part of making friends, but it's also a red flag for diversity, because without conscious effort to ensure otherwise, networks converge to be more and more homogenous over time. As an example of how this happens, my DJ sets now include more music from marginalized artists than they do cis-male artists – because I am now following more of these artists on my record-store and music-sharing profiles. Indeed, after a few months of interviewing people for this project I noticed that I had very few black and brown women's voices in my dataset at the time because they were outside my network.[19]

This is important for our discussion of meritocracy because if dominant groups become homosocial, their judgements and decisions cease to be neutral. Because everyone in the group is similar, they cannot help but reproduce their own tastes, preferences and, crucially, their own interests. Data scientist Milán Janosov and his colleagues undertook a thorough analysis of the DJ Mag Top 100 over its 22-year history and found that mentorship was one of the biggest predictors of success for rising stars in the industry, for example.[20] Seeing as 90 per cent or more of the DJ Mag Top 100 are men, we can see this is as evidence of the power of homosociality on artists careers. And because they are in a majority, the rules, norms and standards they set are taken for granted by the rest of society as if they were objective truth. What is judged to be merit-worthy by 'default' is therefore more accurately only what the dominant group define as merit-worthy. Musician and researcher Emma Hooper explains the importance of this process forcefully in her analysis of how 'the vast majority of the time, [cis-male gatekeepers] are looking to promote something "good" in their own terms and according to their own tastes'.[21] The claim that good music is all that matters starts to crumble when we realize that.

British artist Grayson Perry shows in his book *The Descent of Man* how white, heterosexual, cis-gendered (usually American) men are society's 'default', positioning other masculinities as deviant, or abnormal. Caroline Criado-Perez's 411-page book *Invisible Women: Exposing Data Bias in a World Designed for Men*,[22] is crammed full of instances where seemingly gender-neutral and often mundane words, objects, situations and occupations are shown to be driven by white cis-male, or masculine concerns and/or favouring these men and their proclivities. And music is no exception. The keys on a piano are spaced to comfortably fit male hands because it was men designing the instruments for other men to play. This means that women – whose hands are on average an inch shorter and half an inch narrower than men's[23] – are immediately at a disadvantage when it comes to judgements about the fluidity and expression with which they play – yet this is hidden because *everyone is playing the same piano*.

In intellectual property (IP) law, too, we can see the influence of men's interests in determining what has value: there are many examples of women's traditional creations that are not protectable under copyright law – for example, textile art, fashion and cooking/recipes – whereas the more traditionally male endeavours of technology, science and design are all subject to patent.[24] And where there is IP, there is income – without ownership, there can be no royalties. Since those who are able to legally protect their creations and earn money from them are more visible, they are much more likely to be regarded with respect and accorded prestige than people who are denied access to these same routes to recognition. Once there, the prestigious folks become a critical mass, their creations define a field, cemented by an agreed-upon standard by which quality of work is judged. Those who produce this work, and do it well, are the 'talented' ones – thus talent can never be regarded as separate from the interests of the people who are doing the defining. The sickening twist in this tail is that, as creative industries researcher Natalie Wreyford explains, this is so 'prevalent and embedded in the creative industries that [it is] seen as legitimate even by those who benefit least from it'.[25]

Criado-Perez illustrates this with a 2015 example of a UK A-level student's complaint that all of the 63 set works on her music syllabus were by men, and the exam board's reply: 'Given that female composers were not prominent in the western classical tradition (or others for that matter) … there would be very few composers that could be included.'[26] This was despite there being 6,000 women listed in the *International Encyclopaedia of Women Composers* at the time. The problem wasn't that there were no women – but with the fact that none of these 6,000 were deemed to be noteworthy, influential, or field-defining enough in the history of music because of the implicit biases, cultural and aesthetic preferences of the men who made the decisions. She also cites the results of now famous 'blind' auditions experiment published in 2000 by

Claudia Goldin and Cecilia Rouse where musicians applying to play with the New York Philharmonic Orchestra were auditioned with a curtain separating them from the assessors. Fifty per cent of those selected were women, against a previous record of almost none when the assessors could see the musicians play. Beyond music but equally illuminating recent research has shown that men and women use different implicit criteria when they are hiring staff for jobs in STEM areas:[27] men look for evidence that candidates can work long hours as a key criterion, whereas women favour problem-solving ability. The result? Men select more men to shortlist – because they perceive women less able to work long hours, presumably because of imagined childcare responsibilities.

The bias associated with names has been revealed in hiring practices too. A 'big data' study of recruiters' searches of candidate profiles views showed that women's profiles were 7 per cent less likely to be considered for male-dominated occupations, and minority ethnic candidates 19 per cent less likely to be viewed overall, despite being equally qualified as white applicants.[28] In my own interviews, Sharon gave me an example of the power of removing identity from the equation when she explained to me how a huge A-list DJ played her tracks at one of the most iconic underground music clubs in the world:

> … he didn't put my name on any of the track[lists] … just blanked it out unknown, and then got people coming up to him saying, 'where is this track from??', 'who has done this track??', and he was like, 'I'm not going to tell you,' and it wasn't until 18 months later that he put [the first track] out on [his record label] that people realized it was me. Cos, he said, 'you are an amazing musician, people have got to understand that and they can't pigeonhole you into what they think you are.'

Sharon is one of the lucky ones: her long pedigree in the industry as a DJ meant that when she moved into music production, she was taken under the wing of a key gatekeeper in the scene. But, irrespective of that, this story shows that when people don't know who made the music, they almost certainly judge it differently. This is supported by results from experimental research at the University of Portsmouth currently in progress at the time I am writing this book. When asked to describe the anonymous artist behind a specially created AI-synthesized instrumental electronic music track, almost all of the participants described a man. As we will see in Chapter 5, this is particularly important for women where gatekeepers doubt their skills and in some cases are suspicious whether the artist even made the music herself.

In electronic music this 'taste arbitration' largely comes down to technical prowess. Being a skilled sound designer, audio engineer and often mix engineer too is as – if not more – important to being a 'good producer' than great songwriting and arranging of music. This is because electronic music is generally made to dance to, so the quality and originality of the *sounds* and the all-important 'groove', as well as the way the music creatively fills the space in a club, or headphones, is of particular importance. With electronic music this is achieved by a process called sound, or audio, engineering, which, along with electronic music production in general, is a very technical endeavour. Technologies of this kind are not things girls and women have traditionally been encouraged to learn about and practise. But as I discuss in Chapter 7, more expressive and accessible technologies of music-making are starting to emerge which might lower barriers to entry, especially benefiting women who are actively socialized *out of* technological pursuits from a young age. Furthermore, perfectly good music can be produced by arranging pre-made sounds (called samples) and even full loops (mini musical sections, like percussion or basslines and so on). Software design has advanced so that complex sound design and audio engineering tasks can be performed using presets or simplified controls or even be automated, which means an in-depth, 'techie' mindset is arguably less necessary for making music than it used to be. Yet being able to create your own sounds from scratch and/or use analogue hardware (such as synthesizers) to make your music is still prized over laptop-based digital approaches, because these are skills valued by and fiercely protected by 'bro culture'. Any attempt to simplify music production or make it more accessible is lambasted as deskilling – music made with simpler technologies may well not be regarded as 'good music' for these reasons. Yet it is also plausible that encouraging people into the occupation gently and on more familiar terms would give them the impetus to dive further into more advanced and detailed engineering education as a second stage. Nadine, who was now a proficient producer and a rising star with industry mentorship, told me how she'd been put off starting to produce music for years because a male friend told her how vital it was that she learned to 'do it properly' from the outset: 'he used all these complicated words, like side-chaining, and compression and stuff and said I had to know all that before I got started. It put me right off because I'm rubbish at maths and it sounded hard and not very fun!'

Outsiders: the ameliorative work of getting connected

So, we can see from the previous section that homophily – and particularly homosociality – is how strong networks of people with power come about in order to be able to impose their worldviews as neutral and default. We can also see that this results in a skewed view of what good music is, who makes it and how it gets made that challenges the claim that 'good music is all that matters'. As I noted at the start of this chapter, networks are the lifeblood of the creative industries, and networking was an oft-repeated tale among the artists I interviewed. Alice had managed to establish herself as a successful DJ and producer in the UK a matter of 18 months through effective networking. She played gigs most weekends and had several releases on record labels already, and told me how that had happened: 'It's basically through connection – networking, networking, networking, it's all about networking and getting yourself out there, and opening your mouth. Speak to people and say I'm a DJ, I'm a producer, who are you?' Importantly, Alice saw this as a proactive behaviour:

> If you have a particular label you want your tracks to be released by, then contact them. I was playing in Cyprus in Ayia Napa last April and I met the event organizer there, and he had a connection who owns a record label and he introduced me to this guy, and he said he would be happy to release my tracks ... so this is how that came about.

She went on to offer advice to newbies entering the industry:

> ... we have to be brave enough to go out there, [have] the confidence to go networking, go to events, go to club nights, go to the festivals, find the owners, the managers, the stage managers, whoever of importance ... Go and talk to them, give them your business card, *have* business cards [in the first place], do the marketing.

Alice's advice is sound. 'Personal-contact networks' have long been recognized as vital to popular music entrepreneurship with advice on how to form networks centring on 'find those who you feel an affinity with' or 'look for common ground in others'.[29] The Musicians' Union (MU) have found that just over a quarter of women musicians say that not knowing anyone in the industry is a major career barrier, and is the third highest reason for not being able to progress a career.[30] Yet the idea of being able to form networks just by 'trying hard' is itself an illusion. In research on the TV industry, Professor Jonathan Morris and his colleagues found younger entrants struggle to get a foothold because their networks are not yet developed, and the groups they need to access were simply closed to them.[31] This is particularly exacerbated for women in film[32] and in electronic music; building networks will usually mean assimilating yourself into 'bro culture' somehow. But this is easier said than done when you are an outsider. Music researcher Freida Abtan sums it up beautifully in her account of how she got into electronic music in Canada: '[It] is as awkward as trying to make friends with the schoolyard boys in the first grade. Even if each is friendly when you meet them one-on-one, you are not invited to the monkey bars when all the boys are there.'[33] I've seen this in action when I have been in clubs. During a DJ changeover, it is customary to engage in celebratory back-slapping, high fiving, hugging and fist bumping. But when a woman takes to the stage she is often pretty much ignored. This may not be intentional, but it further cements a feeling of exclusion. Artist and researcher of DJ culture Rebecca Kill sums up DJ changeovers as holding the potential for 'some quite unpleasant moments ... fraught with misogynistic microaggressions. Sometimes it's rudeness, or not talking at all. Sometimes it's more patronizing.'[34] These feelings of exclusion are not trivial, and they are not inconsequential. A sense of belonging at work has been found to be a significant factor in reducing anxiety and depression.[35] Poor perceived person-career fit has been shown to be an antecedent of burnout.[36]

But Frieda Abtan goes on to explain why this is important beyond 'just' feeling included. She recalls from her teenage and adolescent years how boys seemed to be invited to join bands and hang out to do music without any necessary skills or expertise whereas girls were only allowed in the crew if they were dating one of the boys, or were already very talented. Crucially then, '... boys were invited to make music before they had the necessary skills to be successful at it [whereas] girls were only invited if they ... had pre-existing extensive technical knowledge'.[37] But how do you get that pre-existing knowledge when you're not part of a 'garage band' group that learn and experiment together? Emma, who worked for a music tech company explained to me how she has been put off from learning to make music at all because of the dynamics she sees in the workshops she runs. 'I don't know what the stuff does!' she said, shrugging. 'It just makes a lot of noise, which is cool, but everyone else seems to *know*, and I can't be bothered to look stupid.' Heather summed up the 'head start' boys have when we were talking about how it felt to start her music production degree course after she'd already been DJing for several years: 'Obviously you're surrounded by a lot of boys, and they're all young boys ...,' she said. 'I ha[d] a little knowledge about production [but] all these young boys? *They already knew what they were doing.* It didn't make me feel anything bad, it's just because of my less[er] knowledge I felt a bit left out.'

Interestingly, Heather not only saw it as being 'obvious' that she would be outnumbered by boys, but went on to attribute their prior knowledge to the fact that these lads had simply worked harder, and with a more singular focus than she had, and not to the fact they had been living and breathing music together since a very young age – the illusion of meritocracy in full swing. She also minimizes her feelings of exclusion as 'not that bad' – and just feeling 'a bit' left out, when as we have seen, forging strong ties is so vital for success in this industry. This illustrates an entrenched tendency to minimize exclusionary experiences, but also demonstrates how strong minoritized individuals are at rolling up their sleeves and getting on with it regardless.[38]

Opportunities to 'play with the lads' are also harder to come by for women and gender-expansive folks, meaning it's simply harder to get access to the practice, inspiration and means to make 'good music'. Evelyn explained to me how she had to wait until all the guys were 'wasted' from drug-taking at the end of the night before she could have a go on the turntables – 'it wasn't that they were like, "oh, you can't play on it", but they'd just be getting [high], playing around, playing around [one after the other] and

I would have to wait till quite late until they'd all finished and there was a space for me to get on ... *cos I didn't know what I was doing*'. Clearly none of Evelyn's friends thought to show her or help her know what to do, even in a group of men she was left to get on with it by herself. Interestingly, Solar, a non-binary artist explained that once they had cut their hair and were able to 'pass' as a man more easily, they were welcomed into 'bro culture' far more readily than they had been when they identified as a woman: 'It was quite a shock to be honest,' they told me. 'The guys were suddenly just *great* – inviting me to collab[orate] with them, for studio sessions, or to come down to their nights and guest DJ, record mixes for radio shows and stuff …. When I looked like a girl that never happened to me. Not once.'

These examples also show how a lot of networking happens in the club, so that's where you need to go – partying with the promoters and probably going to after-parties too. This means long hours – which may be fun – but are nonetheless also 'work'. It is part of what creative industries researchers Ewan Mackenzie and Alan McKinlay call 'hope labour' – effort expended in the hope that paid work or opportunities will come from it in the future.[39] But attending raves and nightclubs as a woman, trans or non-binary person, walking up to cis-male promoters and giving them your number is fraught with dangers that just don't happen to cis men. Here's what Esther told me when we chatted about getting booked as a DJ:

> … as a woman I don't want to go on my own to the gigs, [mates] don't always want to come and I don't always feel comfortable going to an all-night gig on my own where I know no one, at the other end of the country, just to meet a promoter who might or probably won't book me anyway. And when you get there you've got to find the guy. Well, where the hell are they? Usually you've got to ask strangers and very often you get in a situation you really didn't want to get into. You ask someone 'Do you know who the promoter is?' but then you get a leering bloke next to you with his beer and saying 'oh heellllo …'

What Esther is describing is called 'supporting the night' and involves buying a ticket and attending the event, preferably with friends who will also buy tickets. It's a quid pro quo arrangement – help make the promoter's night financially successful by swelling the crowd and you'll be in with a shot of getting booked to play at a future party. But as we can see, this is far easier for cis men to do than for women. So again, its cis men who are more likely to be booked for events, and everyone will just assume that this is because their music and DJing are 'good'. Furthermore, 'supporting the night' is likely to be exceptionally risky for trans women who face considerable threats of harassment and violence in public.[40] No matter how anxious or nervous a guy is about networking or 'putting himself out there' he is highly unlikely to be afraid for his safety or of being taken as giving off an intention that he wants a sexual encounter (unless the night in question is a gay night, perhaps). Esther continued, exasperated, to explain how this is simply unacknowledged by the gatekeepers in the scene:

> I don't *want* this, I don't want *any* of it. And I don't think that's understood at all by promoters. I remember going to [radio station]'s DJ training event, and a lot of their panel discussion was about how to get more women into music, and it was very, very good, but they said this thing about getting booked – and their thing was 'go support the nights you want to play at'. I wish I'd opened my mouth then and said what I've just said to you, *That it's not that straightforward!*

Conclusion: Good music is not *all* that matters

In this chapter we have seen how women and gender-expansive artists face very real challenges that do not affect cis men to the same degree, or at all. Fears for physical or psychological safety, and the dynamics of exclusion make it much harder for those in a minority to form the networks that are vital to sustain their careers in electronic music. These networks are essential in order to make the right contacts and get involved with the right promoters, record labels, collaborations and so on – not only for getting opportunities to make, sell and perform music, but also for learning how to do so in the first place. Making good music, and getting the opportunities to get your good music in front of the people who matter is contingent on these things and is disproportionately harder for minoritized-gender artists to do.

Even when women and gender-expansive people do manage to forge networks, this has traditionally meant joining the boys' club and learning the rules of 'bro culture' on their terms – unless explicit efforts are made to accommodate those who are not cis men. This is harder for minoritized individuals to do because homosocial networks solidify norms, practices and standards in their own image. What talent 'is' and how good music becomes considered to be 'good' is in reality a reflection of dominant groups' interests, yet appears as the norm, as the default setting, and therefore apparently attainable by all. It's simply harder for 'outsiders' to be seen as reaching those standards due to implicit bias and sometimes outright discrimination – further evidence for this will unfold in the remaining chapters in this book.

Thus, meritocracy is rigged and talent cannot rise evenly and equally to the top. Talent is contingent on identity – on who you are, because who you are impacts how others treat you and who you can engage with. Hard work is *not* all it takes, or rather it is harder work for some than others, because they do not have the wind already at their back. 'Good music' as judged under these conditions is likely to be easier to make, and get accepted by the dominant group, so the kinds of music made by the dominant group therefore become 'good music'. Unless there is a diversity of people making music, 'good music' is therefore the music of bro culture. and so paying attention to 'good music' above all other considerations will not result in greater diversity, it will result in a system that continues to favour music made by cis-gendered men. Good music is *not* all that matters and in the next chapter we shall be examining further evidence of how the playing field is not level for all genders in electronic music.

Chapter track: 'Almost Like'

Figure 3: Artwork for 'Almost Like' by Dovetail, reproduced with kind permission of DaCosta Records

Source: https://www.beatport.com/release/almost-like/3386452

'Almost Like' is released on DaCosta Records, which is owned and run by Louise DaCosta, who I met when I interviewed her for an In the Key radio show in April 2021. As part of the conversation we chatted about the style of music she likes to release on the label and how she enjoys releasing music by new producers. After we spoke, I decided to ask if she'd take a listen of a track I'd recently made that was sitting on my computer waiting for me to pluck up the courage to send it to a label for consideration. Much to my delight she loved it, and agreed to release it and I've included it in this chapter because that's the value of making connections and having contacts right there in action.

The track's vocal pays homage to my favourite song by Depeche Mode with me whispering a line from the track 'Somebody' throughout – *All the things I detest I will almost like* – for no other reason than I always thought this was a great hook for a dance track and it was fun to use my own voice despite the fact I am no singer! I also developed my sound engineering skills on this one by manipulating a stock sample in my DAW into the saxophone/trumpet sound that appears in the second half of the track.

4

But ... Nobody Discriminates!?

The value of being 'hot'

> 'Yeah, but how does she *look*?' he mused as he considered the contract in front of him. Deborah frowned as if she were puzzled, but knew exactly what was coming.
>
> 'You, *know* ...' he laughed, '... is she *hot*? You know what this business is like! It's gonna be much easier to sell her if she's marketable, and a much bigger risk if she's not. Am I right?'

Deborah is a media lawyer specializing in the music sector, advising clients on their rights and ensuring that they collect all the royalties that are due to them through the production and performance of their music. Record deals, management deals and dealing with copyright infringement are some of the negotiations she carries out. Deborah is very much at the business end of being an electronic music artist. The previous quotation is just one instance of what she regularly hears in the course of her work negotiating contracts on her clients' behalf. In this case she is dealing with a middle-aged white guy at the management company considering signing one of Deborah's female clients to their roster of artists.

Deborah carries out this work for clients of all genders, but she only hears stuff like this when she negotiates on behalf of women. No one had ever asked her what her male clients looked like, let alone suggest their appearance was a factor in their decision to enter into a music contract with them. The talk there was almost always about numbers of social media followers, Spotify plays and the kinds of gigs they were already getting. What she told me upset her most about the exchange above was the fact that the guy she was negotiating with clearly saw her as complicit in the knowledge of 'how this business is'. His wish to know if Deborah's female client was 'hot' before he considered the terms being put to him was just a run-of-the-mill fact for him – and he assumed Deborah thought so too, even though she was also a woman. Deborah also told me how gatekeepers were less willing to 'take a punt' on early-career female artists, compared to men, and less likely to accept evidence of popularity. 'The message I get is very much that it's *them* who were doing the artist a favour by taking them on because they feel they are taking a risk,' she told me. Women don't draw in crowds, or sell tickets, apparently.

All of this leads to greater 'push-back' on the terms Deborah draws up for her female clients than she experiences when negotiating on behalf of men, where the exact same clauses are routinely accepted. Since protracted discussions equal expensive legal hours, this is not a metaphorical identity tax, it is a real, financial burden. It literally costs more money for women to manage the legal side of their careers than it does for men.

Introduction

Deborah's experience contradicts of the idea that 'all that matters is good music' as I discussed in the previous chapter. It is clear evidence that even if meritocracy does exist in this industry, what constitutes merit differs according to your gender – and probably your race, age, sexuality and many other characteristics too. The idea so clearly illustrated in the opening vignette is exactly that. Women need to be 'marketable' (read: attractive) beyond the music they produce. Women are treated less favourably because of their sex and/or ascribed gender. In this chapter I'll show how women, trans and non-binary people are indeed discriminated against, and what is being done about that.

The merest hint of an accusation that there is gender discrimination in electronic music, however, is met with an indignant 'I don't know *anyone* who would discriminate against women!', which is then usually followed up with stock lines such as '… everyone has the same chances, it's just that there aren't any women producers, there aren't any gender-expansive headliners, trans people never send us their demos for consideration … [insert any other myth here].' Yet this immediate concern with how a minoritized artist looks is one of the clearest sources of unequal treatment I have encountered during this research. On the one hand, you have to be attractive enough to be a viable, 'marketable' proposition, yet on the other, the more attractive and feminine you are the more you more will face accusations that you lack talent and technical expertise (addressed in Chapters 6 and 7), and the greater the likelihood of harassment, as we shall see later in this chapter.

One of the reasons for the puzzled sentiment 'but ... nobody discriminates?' is that when we think of discrimination we usually think of intentional and blatant negative treatment because the person is gay, trans, black, has a disability, or is of a particular gender, for example. This is what is known as 'direct discrimination' in the UK and the EU[1] and it is only a fraction of the story. More common, and often harder to detect and establish, is 'indirect discrimination', where (in this case) conditions of employment or market opportunities appear to be neutral but disproportionately disadvantage one group of people over others.[2] Being 'marketable' as a route to securing a contract with a management company means very different things depending on your gender, as we shall see, and is beautifully summarized by one of the contributors to The Jaguar Foundation/SONY report:

> There is an unspoken economic value that is attached to non-males and it pisses me off so much because I think people will book you and pay you well if you are something that will feed the appetite of the male gaze.[3]

Lawyers like Deborah fight hard on behalf of their female, trans and non-binary clients to ensure they get deals as fair as the men. She told me that she often didn't pass on all the extra costs from drawn-out negotiations to her female clients because '... it's simply not fair'.[4] Access to favourable contracts is an important cornerstone of making money from your music career as I introduced in Chapter 2. If women struggle to cut the same deals as their male counterparts it's a clear disadvantage. If you don't make good deals, with good royalty percentages, you won't earn good money – it's as simple as that.

The UK music industry already has one of the largest gender pay gaps among companies with more than 250 employees,[5] with the latest figures showing that women earn almost 40 per cent less than men at the major record labels.[6] However, we know almost nothing about gender pay differentials in the smaller music businesses that make up the majority of the scene, and currently have no way of comparing the incomes of freelance electronic music artists of different genders other than notoriously unreliable self-report surveys. I have found it impossible to obtain concrete data on costs, fees, pay and other financial indicators of how men, women and gender-expansive people are treated in electronic music. Despite my own and my university's assurances of commercial confidentiality and anonymity, none of the organizations that I've contacted were willing to share even their aggregated, anonymized fee data for artists, for example.[7]

What we do know, however, is that 'market forces' are regularly cited as being behind the commercial decisions to treat women and gender-expansive artists less favourably – for example, preferring to allocate headline slots, peak times and central locations to the cis men at festivals and clubs because they 'sell more tickets' as we saw in Chapter 2.[8] Likewise, it is the subtext of our opening vignette – pushing back on standard contract terms because it is too risky to offer women, trans and non-binary people deals equivalent to the more lucrative offers that 'safe' cis men receive. Market forces that have as much to do with how women and gender-expansive people *look*, it seems, as they have to do with how they sound.

Dressing up and dressing down: the ameliorative work of managing appearance

Women and gender-expansive people exert considerable effort in paying close attention to how they dress as part of their personal image strategies. Lauren, Sharon and Ines all work with stylists to ensure they have a coherent brand, for example, and Nelly just wears 'black, all black' because, as she told me, laughing 'That's just my thing!' Rarely, however, have I encountered artists who deliberately choose to play up their sexual attractiveness in the ways we saw demanded in the opening vignette. Exceptions to this are those who leverage the fact that social media content of their faces, or bodies with plenty of skin showing (particularly if videos), receive far more interactions than other material. 'If it's an important post I know I need to do the whole tits and teeth thing,' Tyla told me, sighing. 'I'm so not that kinda person and it grates, but the difference is massive when I do that.' It matters little whether this is because users *actually* prefer this type of content or because social media algorithms (particularly Instagram) are programmed to deliver this kind of content to users' feeds more often.[9] Since algorithms learn from the data they encounter, it is likely to be a self-perpetuating spiral which is problematic from a gender perspective, amplifying the need for artists to present themselves through bikini-clad photos or at the very least, as smiling, engaging, wide-eyed versions of themselves, which reinforce traditional gender stereotypes.[10] Often the series of images is supplemented by a caption that says 'Here's a picture of my face so that the algorithm will show you this post to tell you about my upcoming shows', or 'Here I am on the beach looking hot to announce the release of my new album'. The more women artists strategically – and therefore perfectly sensibly – present themselves in this way, the more common these kinds of images become. This would not be a problem if femininity and hyper-sexuality were commensurate with perceptions of being an amazing DJ or music producer, but they are not, as we shall see more fully in later chapters. At the intersection with race, artists also told me how they realized how often they straightened their naturally curly, black hair for photoshoots and gigs, because even in electronic dance music, being authentically black was not acceptable, especially as a woman.

Unfortunately, looking too much 'like a girl' has negative consequences that require a good deal of work to manage, particular in the early stages of an artist's career when they haven't yet established a solid reputation. 'I would literally dress like a boy. I covered every part of my body', Kate told me about her early days in the industry. 'There was nothing you could obviously tell my gender from. I had long hair, but I didn't wear makeup. I was doing everything in my power to draw attention away from the fact that I was a woman, and it's kind of heart-breaking.' The reason for Kate's denial of her femininity was the fact that once people saw she was a woman, all the stereotypes were invoked and people would just, as she put it 'expect me to be shit'. Likewise, Olive explained that when she started her career, she was an 'underground DJ who would dress down. I tried very hard to be one of the lads and to hold my own, and to be able to mix as well as them technically, that's what mattered to me.' This was essential for Olive to do back in the late 2000s in order to avoid accusations that she was talentless, and one of the 'new breed of "female DJs",' as she described them, '… women who would just DJ topless, which was actually a thing and it was awful'. She went on to explain how exasperating this was: 'I'd spent years learning how to be at the top of my game, in my craft, and you've just got these women with their boobs out just taking it all away from us.'[11]

Topless DJing was part of a trend for 'model DJs' when digital DJing became commonplace. Digital equipment arguably simplified the skills needed to be a DJ, and certainly made it a less performative occupation. With no need to select and slip vinyl records out of record sleeves, flip them on and off turntables, manipulate them and move the needle of the record player, the activities of the DJ became harder for the crowd to see.[12] As a result, models and celebrities – most famously Paris Hilton – were paid huge sums of money to 'DJ', which consisted of pressing 'play' on a CDJ (digital music player) and then pretending to mix music. Solar told me how they lost their residency at an upmarket boutique club to a 'model DJ', which was what motivated them to learn production skills as a differentiator. Beyond losing bookings, the trend had unfortunate repercussions for all women DJs, particularly bona fide artists who were attractive. The industry's faith in women artists' abilities was (and to some extent still is) so fragile that even now, attractive women are still accused of being fake. Emily recounted being trolled during an online livestream set, when she wore a 'sexy, feminine top,' as she described it. 'And this guy wrote "she is probably is there because of her Dad's money, and she looks like Paris Hilton" … It broke my heart.'

'So now I wear big T-shirts and dress like I am now, with no make-up,' Emily went on. 'I do that on purpose. I don't *want* to be sexy I want to be cool.' As with Emily's explanation, often this dressing down was expressed as a desire to look cool, or simply be 'comfortable' while DJing. Others referred to the ubiquitous underground DJ's 'uniform' of T-shirt and jeans as androgynous, detaching it from their gender. Naomi insisted that the reason she wore baggy T-shirts instead of tighter ones was because 'I just feel more relaxed, and it kind of affects your mindset, like your mood, like if you're more relaxed. So I tend to wear jeans, trainers and a baggy top.' It's not that I don't believe Naomi's reasons – I'm sure that this is exactly why she dresses down. But my response is to ask *why* should she only feel relaxed when she wears what are ostensibly men's clothes to perform in?

It is not only dress and make-up that my participants spoke of toning down. Lia, Heather and Katarina all said they had received advice from more experienced male DJs to dance and smile less to look more credible behind the decks in order to be taken more seriously (by men). Excessive dancing in video footage online draws sexualized and misogynistic comments in their droves. Comments on visible nipples, large breasts, body shape and physical attractiveness are everyday occurrences when women artists are featured online. The documentary *Underplayed*,[13] directed by Stacey Lee, includes hard-hitting stories of the debilitating online abuse faced by Scottish artist Nightwave after her 'Boiler Room' set was aired on the online Boiler Room TV channel. I have even seen ridiculous accusations that one producer was 'bouncing on a dildo' on her chair while she gave a demonstration of her new track played live on a drum machine.

Beyond the crude, sexualized and misogynist trolling, it is common to see way more skills-focused critiques on women's content too. Accusing artists of 'just standing there dancing for Instagram' while the music plays, of not having their equipment plugged in when they are giving studio demos, of 'trying too hard to be one of the boys', and just generally being 'talentless bimbos' are a tiny fraction of the comments I've seen on Facebook over the past few years. It is rare to see this type of feedback on cis men's content, and certainly not in this quantity. Moira, the communications manager of a major dance music platform, explained to me how hard she was finding it to get women, trans and non-binary artists to agree to be featured in online content because of the amount of abuse they feared they would get. Yet this kind of positive representation she also told me 'is what the industry desperately needs if we are going to change people's beliefs that all producers are white men'.

This is part of a long history of men keeping women out of the public eye – not allowing them to speak, or demonstrate intelligence and skill. In Europe, this dates back to at least the earliest Roman and Greek societies that we know through the stories written about them.[14] As feminist historian Mary Beard sums up, 'even when they are not silenced, [women pay] a very high price for being heard.'[15] A price that is even higher for black artists, as Zara remarked in a depressingly resigned manner: 'If you raise [racist issues] then you're problematic, and of course because you are woman and you're *black* … oh God here we go.' She rolled her eyes. But as we saw earlier, it is not even necessary to do or say anything controversial. Merely appearing in public in a role socially designated as male will attract misogynistic abuse. The fear of this is quite understandably enough to dissuade artists from being visible and, importantly for our discussions here, this kind of treatment discriminates because of gender. It simply does not happen to cis men, who can happily post about anything they like or publicize their expertise without attracting ridicule and threats of abuse and death – even if they bounce about and show off their nipples.[16] The discrimination is compounded further when we consider how this kind of abuse is sanitized through language like 'trolling', which refers to mythical folkloric characters rather than the very real violence that such actions enact. Every time I have heard this topic raised on social media or on conference panels the remedy is the same – that the person suffering the abuse should rise above it, not let it get to them, focus on the positive, and so on. Is this really the best that we can do?

Managing the symbolism of the body itself

Although our bodies give off impressions that we can't do much about, their *representation* is something that women and gender-expansive artists go to great lengths to manage beyond their dress. This can most clearly be seen in the intersections between gender and age, and particularly in relation to the curation and circulation of images that appear online. I remember Yvette, Ines and Angelica being particularly fastidious about how they looked in the selfies we took together, adding filters that erased signs of their age, rendering them flawless, even though we had been in clubs dancing for several hours. Tess told me a story of being at an event with other women artists that was being livestreamed and how she was quite shocked at the extent the other artists curated and controlled their image, insisting on poses and camera angles that showed them in a particular light, for example. Initially I was surprised and a little disappointed that these women were being so complicit in their oppression – because I would put money on the fact that stuff like this never even crosses cis-male artists' minds, let alone takes up their time and energy. But when you pause to think about it, this behaviour is actually completely rational, even strategic, in an industry obsessed with (women's) youthful appearance. It is aesthetics-based ameliorative work because women and gender-expansive artists are operating in an image-saturated world. French philosopher Jean Baudrillard predicted this in the 1960s when he wrote about the idea of 'hyper-reality' and 'simulations', both names to explain how representations of places, people and things come to be more real than reality itself. In a hyper-real world, it matters little what artists *actually* look like, when their fans – and, importantly, gatekeepers – almost always only see photos and videos of them on social media. And, of course, these representations can be – and are – manipulated, creating what Baudrillard called 'perfect copies of things that have never existed'.[17] Importantly, these simulations are experienced as 'real', which fuels this process even more as people try to keep up with ever more *un*realistic image expectations.

All of this matters because appearance is usually how other people form instantaneous first impressions of us and is strongly related with implicit bias.[18] For example, Zara explained to me how her black skin resulted in career-limiting assumptions:

> When my agent has asked why promoters haven't booked me, they say they think I play grime, or rap, or other types of 'black' music – but I have never played that in my life! They've made up their minds that I can't be suitable for their event just cos of how I look, without even listening to what I do.

Nelly explained how she had been refused access to the stage as a DJ even while wearing an artist wristband, because she was not only a woman, but a brown one who was also larger-sized. 'I don't look like your regular DJ, I guess!' she joked, but her humiliation at having to fetch her manager to convince security of her identity was clear. Disbelief that you are the DJ is common for women when they are also younger and petite, such as Kate, who we heard from earlier, whose gender minimization strategy was also driven by the fact that, she 'looked 13 for several years' of her career. Naomi, Katarina and Emily also told me how they'd been refused entry to clubs where they were booked to play. 'Once I had to show the guy my Facebook page before he'd believe it was me,' Katarina said. 'My face is on the bloody poster outside your club, for God's sake!'

Another example was from India, who noted how she felt sure her lighter black skin had made her passage smoother in the industry than it had been for her darker-skinned friends.[19] Conversely, Aysha, Nelly, Genevieve and Loretta all told me how their mixed-race heritage meant that they were often on the receiving end of mistreatment from black communities for not being 'black enough', but neither were they 'white enough' to be accepted in white-majority environments. Apart from the racist misery of never feeling they belong, this mattered because, as Loretta told me, '… people don't know how to pigeonhole me, which means I always have to convince people I make the kind of music I do'. Others told me how they felt they didn't look 'queer enough' to play queer parties, or felt pressure to conform to an androgynous image to justify being non-binary, for example never wearing make-up, and wearing their hair short. Similarly, a transgender contributor to a panel on safety in nightlife spoke of her anxieties around 'passing well enough' in 'straight' clubs where she is booked to play – one presumes in order to avoid transphobic abuse. Queer studies researcher Saiorse O'Shea gives powerful accounts of the experiences of 'passing' (or, more accurately, not passing) in their work,[20] ending with the poignant statement '[p]assing is what I am expected to work at – not for my sake but for yours'. The body is read by others in ways we'd rather it wasn't – and often by ourselves too, as the next story describes.

The world's biggest bingo wing

It was 2018 when I had my first experience of an unsanctioned photograph of me DJing making its way online. In it, I am sporting what (at the time) I regarded as the World's Biggest Bingo Wing.[21] Dimpled with cellulite and hanging down from my upper arm it was captured for all eternity by my friend as I waved my hands in the air (like I just didn't care[22]). The picture itself is wonderful. An artfully blurred depiction of a joyful and exhilarated dancing DJ, but looking at it, all I could feel was *sickening horror* at the abject and out-of-place flesh dangling there, mid-swing.

> *DJs do not have bingo wings.*
> *They have tight, toned 'celebrity arms' like Amelie Lens and Nina Kraviz.*

I was relieved it had been sent to me privately by the photographer after the event where it was taken. Shamefully, I knew what I was going to do. I opened up my photo-editor software and smoothed the skin to erase the dimples, trimming the flesh to a more acceptable size. Not too much, but just enough to curate the kind of arm I regarded as appropriate for a woman in her late 40s. I still feel shame when I tell this story because doing so made me a bad feminist (in my book) – by erasing signs of perfectly normal, ageing female flesh, I was contributing to the very culture I abhorred. Yet I still did it. Unfortunately, in the meantime, my friend had uploaded the original to his Facebook page and unbeknown to me, the host of a radio show I was due to do a guest mix for that week had already downloaded it from there to use for promotion. The wing had taken flight and escaped despite my best efforts. I couldn't bring myself to ask the guy to replace the image with my new slimline version. It felt such a petty and shameful thing to do. I was certain that, as a bloke, he wouldn't understand, and would think me horribly vain. Instead, I sucked it up and made two decisions. One, I was going to get some proper, professional press shots done, and two, I would always DJ in long sleeves, no matter how hot it was in the club – something I kept up for almost three years.[23] There would never be a need for me to airbrush pictures of me again, I would make sure of it.

Until there was. Only a few weeks later I received the files from the photoshoot I had with a photographer friend. We'd had the most fun afternoon with her snapping away as I posed in a variety of outfits, dance music blaring to get us in the mood. I was so excited to see the results but, again, all I felt was disappointment. Who was this old woman trying to look cool? Why had my friend taken photos that made me look so *wrinkly?* I wasn't even sure that I *was* that wrinkly, to be fair – but, regardless, this was not the look I wanted out there in the world. Once again, I opened up the photo-editor and carefully smoothed over just the right amount of lines and creases to erase *just* a few years. To help myself feel better about what I had done, I also lightened and applied some effects and filters to the photos to give them a more obvious 'cool edge' – gritty, grainy, washed-out or mysteriously shadowed, black-and-white and retro-filtered.

By now you are probably thinking 'Yeah, she actually is just horribly vain', but hear me out. Career-wise I'd gone from a place of just playing some tunes and not really caring if I was any good or not, to realizing that I actually *was* quite good. Being taking seriously as a DJ had begun to matter to me – something that I hadn't anticipated at the start and was now showing up in the way I wanted to be seen as a credible player in the industry. This self-governance is what I call 'embodied patriarchy' – we *feel* the fear of not conforming to what we have learned is expected of us in and through our bodies. It compels us to adjust ourselves – whether behaviour, attitude or appearance, even when no one tells us to.[24] The gendered visual culture of DJing is probably something to study more closely for my next project but here it's enough to note that there is one, and I felt it's force as soon as I started DJing in bars, clubs and festivals in front of people who didn't know me. My wrinkles, flabby arms and signs of ageing didn't really bother me in everyday life, but suddenly here I was in this image-conscious world and I didn't want to be seen as *old*. Never mind that the grand-daddies of electronic dance music *were* all old – with paunches, grey hair and wrinkles to prove it, but of course, that's acceptable because they're men. When women age it's a different story.

Getting older in the electronic music industry

So much so, in fact, that Evelyn asked me to edit out the conversation we had about ageing in the industry from our podcast recording altogether, even though all she did was mention that she was in her mid-40s:

> This is the thing with age … as you get older you look older. It's not that you can't still do [the job]. But it seems more acceptable for say, Danny Rampling to be out still there, whereas would a woman in her fifties be still acceptable to be seen out there on the decks? It would definitely have a bit more of a debate going, I think.

Nothing controversial or offensive there whatsoever, we might think, but in a public sphere Evelyn didn't want to be heard even *talking* about age.

Dance music culture researchers Prof Alice O'Grady and Prof Anna Madill[25] are two of the only academics to have studied older women's experiences of underground club culture, finding that they have complex decisions around appearance norms to navigate in order to strike the right blend of visibility and acceptance for the particular event they are attending. As older women on the dance floor, my friends and I resonate with this, usually getting at least one or two well-meant, but pretty patronizing hugs and comments from younger clubbers: 'Ahhh, you're such an inspiration! I hope I'm still raving at your age!' they beam, while at other times we are looked at askance for daring to even be there.[26] But as Esther remarked during our interview, when older women DJ it's seen as a novelty – even if it is perhaps an inspirational one. 'It's held up as being like a fish riding a bicycle,' she said, '… it's a gimmick.' She gave the example of a video that went viral '… it was a Japanese woman in her 70s, a DJ, but the comments weren't "How good is *she?*"', it was about the fact that she was doing it at all, and that's wrong.' This is definitely an age-meets-gender effect too. At the time I'm writing this, video content from an older cis-male artist called 'The Last DJ' is currently sweeping social media to great acclaim.[27] In his 70s, he sits in ordinary domestic environments with a notepad and pen, programming and playing techno music from a small, simple synthesizer. Although the comments on the music – and him – do address his age, they do so out of reverence and respect for the fact that he is making great tunes, rather than applauding the fact that he is doing it at all 'at his age', as in Esther's example of the older woman DJ earlier. These ageist attitudes appear to have concrete consequences on women's decisions to continue in their careers, as evidenced by the Musicians' Union, who found women's representation in the industry 'significantly declines with women making up just 26% of musicians aged 55 to 81 or older'.[28] This is likely to be a choice older women artists make at least partly because, as Lauren put it, 'there is a perception that [women] have a "shelf-life" that doesn't apply to men in the same way'.

The implications of this exit include reduced ability of older women to earn income from music, lower likelihood of reaching the upper echelons of successful DJ/producers, and a general sense of defeat, or being pushed out. We should take care to remember we can also see this reparatively, though. Moving into adjacent careers where they are more valued (or working for themselves), women and gender-expansive artists can earn more than they would through music – rather than a 'leaky pipeline', this is more akin to what economists have called the 'vanish box'.[29] Like a magician 'disappearing' their assistant who returns unharmed later in the show, women who exit are often moving to something better, rather than being 'leaked out'. This was recounted to me by several older artists I spoke to, who had chosen to move into education, consultancy and sound therapy and were much happier for it. Nonetheless, this does still remove older women from the industry, which means they are no longer there as role models for new entrants to the profession, or society at large.

At the other end of the spectrum, Zara and Grace commented on how they felt 'lucky' to look younger: 'I feel fortunate that like I have my genes in my favour,' Grace told me, 'but I'm very much aware of that fact. People think that I'm like 20s, maybe early 30s, it's a big compliment and I'm very grateful for that because I think it works in my favour for what I do. But I don't feel comfortable talking about my age either.' The very fact that Grace sees others' low estimation of her age as a compliment is telling here. 'Age is a fucked up topic,' she concluded, going on to explain what was happening to friends who were either older, or who *looked* older: 'They approach their art in a different way. Some of them don't even show their face or they create their characters instead … people never know who the human behind the creativity is, and that's so sad.' As the words of the 1933 song by Al Dubin and Harry Warren remind us, it still seems to be the case that as a woman you must simply '… keep young and beautiful – if you want to be loved'.[30] Or, in this case, booked, or signed.

Like Grace, India was also grateful for her youthful appearance, saying she 'gets ID'd every day, I look 17 but I'm 30'. As well as recognizing (and being thankful for) looking younger, she nonetheless told me: 'I play with my age on social media to confuse people and make age not a thing.' But she also recognized this was borne out of fear because of the 'unofficial expiration date women are given' and that 'older women just disappear', as Lauren noted earlier. Similarly, Loretta had been in the music industry since she was a teenager, and had made the move into music production and songwriting after being told by her agent she was 'getting too old' – in her late 20s. Likewise, Ines, whose childhood dream in the 1990s was to be a pop star, eventually gave up trying because she became too old for the business to even be interested in her. Something that was compounded by race, as she told me, 'at that time nobody was interested in an Asian girl, even if she *could* sing'. Nancy told me she had felt 'too old to start' learning to produce music in her mid-30s, and talking about Jennifer Lopez' acrobatic performance at a recent sporting event, Hayley summed up what she saw as the only acceptable way older women can maintain their industry presence. 'Part of me was thinking *this woman is in badass shape, this is so cool* … But then I was like, NO! this is fucking *bullshit*, you're telling me that the only option we have if we want to be 50 and still performing is to look like we're 25? Is that what we're telling the world?' But, of course, if you do look 25, you might look *too* young and the bouncers won't let you into the club to do your job, as we heard earlier.

Body-clock watching: pregnancy and motherhood

An important way that age matters for many women in this industry (as elsewhere) is through the decision to have children. For cis-gendered women, this showed up as fears around how to manage an unpredictable, potentially tired and cumbersome pregnant body while DJing on tour, often in the middle of the night.[31] However, all my participants who spoke about motherhood (whether wanting to be pregnant themselves or not), worried about the effect that taking time out of their music career to start a family would have. Nancy explained how this 'negativity creeps in, of like, *you're going to end up DJing late at night on weekends, and how's that going to impact family?*', and both Naomi and Tess worried about maintaining career continuity. 'If I take that much time off I'm probably going to get forgotten, and it's whether I can stay in the limelight,' Tess explained, a concern echoed by Naomi: 'I've got this fear like if you come out of gigs for like five months people think you've stopped the career, or you don't want to do it anymore, cos they're not seeing things going on.'

Lauren had been involved with founding a group for mothers in music after she heard young women discussing career aspirations: 'They were feeling that they had to choose between a career and family life,' she told me. 'It was like "I'm going to try my career until I'm X age and then if it doesn't work out, then I'll build a family", and I'm like, *Whoa just a minute, this is not right*, and this is not a question that any man would ever ask himself.' Jane and Tyla also voiced fears about wanting to have children in the future but also just not seeing how that could ever work. This is despite some of my participants also telling me how motherhood had been a positive influence on their career. 'There's a lot of benefit to doing it post-children and being in a much more grounded place,' Nancy told me. She went on to explain: 'I probably would never have had success pre-children because of being in such a negative cycle – I was taking too many drugs!' In a similarly positive vein, Lauren explained to me how she believed that having children had enhanced her career:

> My creativity has been fed so much by my pregnancy, my motherhood, my children, way more than it has been blocked by it. It can be absolutely exhausting, but the juggling act is what I've perfected the most, I'm just way more clear in why I'm doing what I'm doing, and how I'm doing it …

These are less-heard examples of how mothers accommodate the 'juggling act' to positive effect. But there is no getting away from the fact that the industry needs to do more. Lauren questioned why there is never childcare at music events – particularly daytime ones. The absence of childcare, and any presence of children in the music workplace, is a problem, as Olive explained: 'You're hiding it and you're making it more of an exclusive men's club again.' She was telling me how her DJ partner had recently given birth and they planned to take the baby with them: 'We'll be doing a festival tour together and the baby will be with us, the baby will just be there beside the stage,' she said. 'Sending that signal? You're taking away one of the biggest barriers that women have in returning to work is that DJing is not considered an environment for a woman with a child.'

Olive's observation is well grounded because the industry is in no way, shape or form set up to deal with the demands of parenthood, and especially mothers.[32] Thinking about birth mothers, Carmen told me how the minute she told her manager she was pregnant in the early 2000s she found herself 'dropped from her record label like a hot potato', and recent public judgement of A-list DJ Amelie Lens' decision to continue performing well into her pregnancy[33] evidences how the world is not ready to see pregnant DJs, let alone accommodate them and support their career breaks. Once children arrive, whether a birth mother or not, the conflict between continuing to work and not being there for your child has been recounted to me in heart-wrenching terms. This is not exclusive to the music industry, of course, but in the 'regular world', when you are employed (and not freelance), there are usually statutory entitlements to maternity leave, crèches, flexible working schemes, accommodations made by employers for parents doing the school run, and so on. I have heard stories of booking agents and promoters arranging long-haul flights home from gigs that mean the artist misses their child's birthday, for example – and all of this is before we even begin to consider the potential financial hit that artists must take if they slow down their gigging schedule. I'm sure men also face similar challenges but we don't really hear about them if they do. Figures from the Musicians' Union's 'Women Musicians Insight Report' show that responsibility and effects of parenthood are differentially experienced by gender. Twenty-nine per cent of mothers cite 'family/caring commitments' as barriers to their music careers, against 18 per cent of all other respondents. Mothers are twice as likely as fathers to report childcare difficulties as something that prevents them progressing their careers.[34,35] In fact, only 23 per cent of the 5,867 respondents to the survey said they had any caring responsibilities at all,[36] and, likewise, only a handful of my interview participants actually had children – even the older ones. This surely suggests that parenthood and a music career don't (yet) mix.

Conclusion: Showing up and 'you do you'

This chapter has shown that, contrary to common assumptions, discrimination is rife, and the claim that nobody discriminates is a myth. We have covered several different ways that women and gender-expansive people face disadvantage just because of their gender. The penalty for being a mother in music is real, for example, whether you *are* a mother, or even thinking about how you might become one. Disadvantage that is not about *parenthood* per se, it is linked to gendered expectations about *mothers'* roles and behaviours. Likewise, age is a tangible negative for women's careers in ways that don't exist for cis men. Whereas older men are revered in society, ageist treatment of women and the cult of youth in society mean getting older is a limiting factor for women,[37] particularly manifesting through the additional work required to maintain a 'timeless' look for their bodies and especially their faces through poses, filtering and curating hyper-real representations that work to reinforce the illusion and increase the pressure on others. This is discrimination that is felt and acted upon at the level of the body: minoritized genders have *so* much more work to do than the majority – cis men – in order to fit in. But, as we have also seen, looking too young compounds others' assumptions about lack of skills and ability that we will look at in Chapters 6 and 7, and this is something that is harder to influence. Along with skin colour, body size, and gender, these more immutable attributes such as 'looking young' speak in ways that are often beyond conscious control – and they result in unequal treatment of women, trans and non-binary people in the ways we have seen in this chapter. To at least try to deal with this, we have seen how artists either dress like men, and downplay their femininity to gain respect, and/or use a strategy of 'tits and teeth' to gain traction on social media in a digital attention economy programmed to reproduce gendered stereotypes – and who can blame them? The likes, shares, follows and plays that result indicate (rising) star status. The market forces that mitigate women's involvement in the industry – for example, 'Will she sell enough tickets?' – can only be exploited by playing to gender stereotypes and behaviours.

But it's way too bleak to conclude that the only way to close gender pay gaps, and redress the cis-male domination of the electronic music industry is to engage in sexist strategies that reinforce the kind of attitudes we saw in the opening vignette. Artists *are* rejecting misogynistic cultures and presenting themselves differently – Billie Eilish is a case in point, deliberately dressing in ways that hide any hint of sexual identity and gender. But why should women have to hide away, non-binary people look 'androgynous' and trans people work so hard to 'pass'? This is another form of erasure, of denial of who one is and how one chooses to present, in ways that almost certainly never apply to men. A way to reclaim this situation then – to read it reparatively as I outlined in Chapter 1 – is to celebrate that women are carrying on being women regardless – bold, sexy, cute, butch, camp, or *however they choose*, and that is A-OK. They are owning their space in this industry, no matter what the cost. Showing up how *they* choose to produce and perform music as skilled artists who deserve their place no matter what they look like. It is these dynamics that we are going to examine further in Chapters 6 and 7 – considering how women and gender-expansive people navigate the myths around gender and technology. In the next chapter, however, we stay with the theme of discrimination, because there are other ways that the claim 'nobody discriminates' reveals itself as a myth. Sadly, these arise from precisely the 'positive action' activities that have been instigated to try to *solve* inequality in the first place.

Chapter track: '1984' (with Shawnonymous)

Figure 4: Artwork for '1984' EP by Shawnonymous and Dovetail, reproduced with kind permission of Diesel Recordings

Source: https://dieselrecordings.bandcamp.com/album/1984

1984 is a collaboration between Canadian musician and producer Shawnonymous, and myself. Shawnonymous is also my cousin. He sent me the stems for this track, because on listening to it I could 'hear' the bones of a faster, clubbier, breakbeat version, so I set about reworking the parts into the version that was released with Diesel Recordings in 2022. The original was much slower and with more of a dubstep sound ('9 Teen 80 Four', available here: https://shawnonymous.bandcamp.com/album/9-teen-80-four).

I've chosen this one for this chapter because of its dark and ominous vibe and vocal sampled from a reading of George Orwell's dystopian novel *Nineteen Eighty-Four*. It focuses on the operation of power. Perfect for the dynamics described in this chapter, I feel. It was my first (and, so far, only!) collaboration with another musician and we were delighted that the record label chose to ask some heavyweight breakbeat artists to remix it – you can also hear these versions on the EP I've linked to at the top of this box, and the Perpetual Present remix propelled this release high up in the record store charts because it was so popular. I've also chosen to use this track for this chapter because Diesel Recordings have been receptive to my music and asked me to remix a couple of tracks in order to increase representation of women producers in the breakbeat scene, which is a particularly male-heavy one. They don't make a song and dance about doing this; record label boss Sylwia, who DJs as Bassica, just quietly gets on with it which, as we'll see in the next chapter and Chapter 9, is exactly how to bring about real change for the 'right reasons'. In my opinion, Diesel are one of the finest breakbeat labels in the scene and I'm honoured to have been welcomed into their fold.

5

Positive Action Is Just Not *Fair*

Jumping from the Trojan Horse

We gather around Charlotte in the small DJ booth of an empty London club one dark, chilly night in January. Charlotte is a drum and bass DJ, and we are a diverse bunch of women and gender-expansive folks, there to learn or improve our skills as part of a 'female DJ course' where both students and instructors are from minoritized genders in music. Charlotte, a very petite and feminine woman, is our instructor for tonight's session. She's standing on a box so we can see her and so she can reach the DJ decks which are always positioned too high for even average-height women to use comfortably. She's excitably waving her arms around: and is a little fireball of infectious energy telling us a story.

'I'm currently on tour as warm-up for [high-profile male artist],' she told us. 'And I know that as soon as I walk onto that stage and put on my headphones, people will have made up their minds about me. How can *she* be the warm-up for [headliner], WTAF??' We laugh as she mimes the 'incredulous' faces of the crowd. 'I can see it in their eyes … "*here we go, bloody diversity booking*", they're thinking. And maybe the promoter did book me because it looks good for [male headliner] to have a woman playing his show – who knows? I mean they aren't going to book me unless I'm actually good, are they? But, *who cares anyway!?* Cos the thing is, I know I am in a perfect position to blow them all away. It's *good* that people don't expect much from me.' By now we are hanging on her every word.

'… because the crowd are there to see [headliner], not me,' she continued. 'They expect *them* to be amazing, cos that's why they're there, that's why they've paid through the nose for tickets. So, when

I fire up the decks and rock their world, it's *me* they will remember because I made such an impression. They're not expecting to see a tiny woman like me dropping absolutely filthy bangers! It's me they'll look up on SoundCloud and 'insta' when they get home, and me they'll tell their mates about: "This bird I saw at [male artist's] gig last night. She was insane!"' We laugh again at her impersonation of an excitable male fan. 'It's me who wins!'

Charlotte's words have stayed with me ever since – instead of seeing negative attitudes and potential 'tokenism' as disadvantage, putting her on the back foot and decreasing her confidence – she helped us see how being 'the only one in the room' can also be a career-boosting advantage. Like the Trojans jumping out of their horse to invade Troy in Greek mythology, she smuggles her brilliance in her pint-sized feminine form to unleash when people least expect it.

Introduction

Charlotte's story sums up the experiences of positive action that I'm going to talk about in this chapter. Being booked as a token gesture to diversify the artists appearing at an event is sadly very common in the industry. We saw some evidence of this in Chapter 2 when we looked at the times and venues that gender-expansive and women artists are scheduled to play at festivals. Pushed to the quieter slots, and marginalized from the career-defining spaces, these artists nonetheless appear on the line-up and promotional materials, making the promoter look good for booking fewer cis men. This is often in response to a 'positive action' initiative, and these programmes are controversial, with a really mixed bag of effects that we are going to empty out and examine in the pages that follow.

Positive action ('affirmative action', in the US) is anything intended to increase representation and participation of marginalized groups in society. It is action that is taken to positively impact inequality and redress disadvantage, but it is often not seen as positive at all, including sometimes by the very people it's intended to support. Multiple initiatives have been introduced with the aim of providing additional support to women, trans and non-binary people in the music industry in order to enable them to compete on the same terms as the majority. The aim is to level the sloping playing field we excavated in Chapter 3, and rectify some of the disadvantages that women and gender-expansive artists face and that this book presents. Examples of positive action initiatives include the platforms and promoters actively seeking more gender-diverse content for their channels that I described in the previous chapter, and the all–women and gender-expansive courses, workshops and collectives I have mentioned throughout this book already, and I will say more about these and others in the chapters still to come.

The story in our opening vignette shows the power of positive action, as Charlotte 'blows the audience away' when they least expect it. But it also highlights some of the problems, too, many of which stem from the belief that positive action is unfair – discriminating against others who are not part of the minority. The eyerolls from the crowd because they presume Charlotte is a token booking just to satisfy the diversity agenda, a booking that has meant another, more talented, cis-male DJ had to be passed over because of his gender. This chapter tackles this myth, showing there is an important difference between positive action and positive discrimination.[1] In the UK, at least, positive *discrimination* is unlawful – choosing an artist *solely* based on their gender, age, race, sexuality, disability and so on is against equality legislation. Positive *action*, however, describes attempts to make up for the additional obstacles that minority groups face (such as all of the ones discussed in this book), but that's not how it looks to majority players and often to the everyday (wo)man on the street. The problem is that those in majority groups (for example, white, cis men) tend to view these campaigns and initiatives as preferential treatment that gives minoritized individuals an *advantage* that is unfair rather than believing they are corrective measures to a system that is already biased. It is a common perception that this advantage is unfair because it is based solely on the basis of gender and not because the artist is skilled or talented. That perception gives rise to beliefs that the artist is a token 'diversity booking' who only made it onto the line-up or roster because the organization needed to avoid having an all cis-male offering. This is the case in Charlotte's story. She earned her place on the line-up – albeit as the warm-up act – but she also suspected others regarded her presence as being decided by her gender.

Virtue signalling and ticking boxes

Fighting this perception (which is often unspoken as we have just seen) is a pernicious form of ameliorative work because one rarely hears direct accusations. Instead, women, trans and non-binary artists internalize this as a general suspicion that they may have been booked just because they 'tick the box'. It's for these reasons that many women and gender-expansive people publicly decry the positive action agenda, arguing it does more harm than good, seeing it as patronizing and undermining their hard work, skills and talent as artists. It is likely that women and gender-expansive artists who oppose positive action were also the ones who declined to take part in my study, but nonetheless, many artists I did speak to understandably expressed how they definitely didn't like to think their gender was the reason they'd been chosen for opportunities. 'I ask my manager to suss out their reasons,' Kat told me, 'see if they've even listened to my stuff and want me as an artist, or do they just want *me*, you know, as a black woman. I can never get away from that, but the right reasons need to be there too.'

The 'right reasons' were generally defined as either 'choosing people for their talent first, then think what type of human they are', as Naomi put it, or gatekeepers who were genuinely trying to make a difference in the industry. 'Why is there this view that you can't be good *and* be booked because you are a woman?', Alyson asked. She runs her own record label, and went on to explain: 'I'm not going to give opportunities to women who are shit just because they are female. Why would I put out shit music? But I do want more females on the label. I want good females.' By comparison, the 'wrong reasons' for engaging in positive action are when gatekeepers comply with requirements, usually under duress, and often by doing only the bare minimum. While the gatekeepers significantly benefit from their actions as an 'ally', this is really only virtue signalling – something which rears its head particularly around International Women's Day (in the UK) and Women's History Month, which is the US equivalent. On these days, almost every brand and organization comes out gloriously 'in support of women' to respect and celebrate their contribution and achievements. The actual effort involved in this messaging, and associated events, is usually done by the women themselves and represents a ramping up of ameliorative work for them at a time when *surely* others should be stepping up, as I discuss further in Chapter 8. The key to avoiding accusations of virtue signalling is to be seriously working towards change behind the scenes year-round, change that is actually making a difference and change that is made without shouting about it from the rooftops, as I set out in the manifestos at the end of the book.

What virtue signalling usually looks like is giving one place on a line-up, or some other opportunity, to someone from a diverse gender and/or race and considering that their work is done. They have 'ticked the diversity box'. One black, lesbian artist with a neurodiverse condition that I spoke with, even described herself as 'the box ticker'. She recognized that a lot of her opportunities probably came about because of who she was, not what she did. 'It does make me a bit sad,' she said, 'but I prefer to just get on with my job and feel lucky that I did at least get the chance at the end of the day.' Her use of the word 'lucky' shows how damaging this can be to self-belief – not attributing the opportunity she got to her skills and talent but to the luck of having been born the way she was. Feeling like a token undermines the confidence that women and gender-expansive artists are continually instructed to grow,[2] as we shall see in Chapter 8.

But to drag this back to more positive territory, it is probably through 'box ticking' that change will slowly happen. As I was writing this chapter, a glittering example of this dropped into a voice note on my phone. It was a producer telling me how she had been doing some ameliorative work by encouraging a well-established, but particularly 'bro-heavy', record label to do a little more work to diversify their offerings. She had suggested that they make it a condition that all guest mixes recorded for their radio show should include at least one track by a woman, trans or non-binary artist, and was pleased to inform me that this is what had happened. *Exactly* what had happened, in fact, because every mix since the inclusion clause was instigated had included *just one* track made by someone other than a cis man, and no more. She laughed as she told me the news, and I chuckled at the mental image of the recalcitrant 'bro' DJs grumbling as they searched for their 'diversity track' – doing the absolute bare minimum. But nonetheless we both still felt glee that no matter what the intentions, *this was progress. We were winning!*

The pitfalls of allyship

Motivations are important in this stuff because it is not until people in dominant groups *want* to do something about improving diversity that anything will ever happen. I have heard of artists lamenting they are now 'too white and too male' to get gigs, with one announcing he was leaving the industry altogether because he was fed up of getting passed over for opportunities in favour of people with minoritized characteristics. Never once have I heard these artists considering that perhaps their offering is now too stale to compete, or recognizing this is what life has *always* been like for women, trans, gender-expansive, gay, black, and other minoritized artists. Generally, those with the privilege of being majority players just don't see there is a problem because they don't face these problems themselves. Therefore, they regard the system as fair and perhaps have never even thought about inequality, let alone regard it as their problem to do anything about, as we saw in Chapter 3. So, being required by positive action agendas to address diversity is regarded as a chore, and unfair to other (white, cis, male) artists who are seen as losing out.

But this definitely changes when it becomes personal in some way. 'Guys often only start to notice things when they've suddenly got skin in the game' was a great comment from a participant in an online discussion during a webinar I facilitated. Niall was an example of this. He had initially reached out to me for advice on how to diversify his record label's roster because he now had a daughter. He was now up close and personal with how his daughter's life chances might be affected by discrimination, bias and misogyny, and he wanted to do something about this in his professional capacity. While some might be cynical of his self-centred motives, he nonetheless made the shift to 'male ally', as his privilege was revealed to him like the Wizard slowly revolving into view at the end of the film *The Wizard of Oz*, and with it a complete rethinking of how the world worked. Motives aside, this is progress. That label now has two women listed on their roster of 18, where previously they had none. It's great that they've made a start. Just so long as it's not also the *end* of their efforts too. The 'right reasons' need to be kept up.

This is important because once majority individuals and groups 'get woke', they usually swing into action to do stuff. Which is great, but it's also where things can get tricky and we start to see some challenges – what US organizational diversity researcher Karren Knowlton refers to as the 'promise and paradox' of allyship.[3] Allies from privileged groups are often vital because marginalized people lack sufficient power to bring about change by themselves – they are too easy to ignore, or are accused of furthering their own interests unfairly. The DJs who contacted me to ask me to call out the festival line-up in the opening vignette of Chapter 3 are a case in point. They weren't able to do this work themselves because of their vested interests *as* DJs and the fact they knew they wouldn't be taken seriously. They were asking me to use my privileged position as an industry outsider and knowledgeable academic researcher to help. They were asking for an ally.

A similar situation happened with another festival during my research, too, where I had a much more productive discussion about their poor gender diversity. This was Noisily Festival, who are happy to be named because that culminated in the founder having a public interview with me.[4] But after the conversation, I was offered a set at the festival myself. Since I am very much a 'nobody' as an artist, my immediate suspicion was that the offer was an enticement to stop my investigations. If I had accepted that set, I would have been abusing my position as an ally. Why? Because the important thing about allyship is that you are working quietly in the background to raise people up who are less powerful than yourself, and not for your own glory. 'Backstaging and spotlighting' *them*, as Karren Knowlton nicely described it.[5] But as she and her colleagues also note, this doesn't always happen. Because allyship is about power, that power can have negative consequences such as undermining gatekeepers' beliefs in the competence of the disadvantaged group – because they 'need' someone to speak up for them, for example. It also raises the spectre of questionable motives and virtue signalling that we saw earlier, and all too often aspiring allies themselves decline to advocate or publicly sign up to 'the Cause' for fear of backlash, or due to cancel culture. Being cancelled from bookings and partnerships because of accusations that they have skeletons in their closets themselves, whether true or not, is a common and powerful fear. Finding high profile cis-male allies to be the public face of anti sexual harassment campaigns has proven particularly difficult during my time working with industry bodies, for these reasons.

Novelty, not normal[6]

Being hyper-visible, feeling like you've been given a break for the 'wrong reasons' and so on, all require near-constant internal ameliorative work to fight feelings of inadequacy. I experienced this myself when I released my first EP. I'd contacted a record label to ask if they'd be interested in signing the tracks and they passed me on to their sister label, who agreed to sign the music as it was more their vibe. I was, and still am, extremely proud of these tracks – 'Keep Your Disdance' (featured at the end of Chapter 2) and 'Sea Organ' (featured at the end of this chapter) and I hyped up the release on social media as any good artist does. So, when the EP entered the Beatport chart at No.22 and kept on climbing, I was utterly overjoyed! Until, that was, I realized that people were buying the EP to help me get it up the charts, rather than because they liked the music. My elation and pride almost *instantly* changed to feeling embarrassed and ridiculous at being a novelty act. How could I have been so stupid as to think that people were actually buying the EP because they thought it was good? To this day I have no real evidence that any of that is true, but it doesn't really matter because of the effect it had on me. I had to pick myself up and dust myself down and convince myself that it didn't matter *why* people were buying it, it just mattered that they were. When it reached No.4 and then No.1, I had to accept that whatever the reason, a female artist was top of the Beatport Top 100 Breaks releases chart, and that was incredibly rare.

But the mental and emotional strength it takes to do this is energy sapping. It's hard to be at your creative best when your bandwidth is taken up with anxiety, fear and doubt. This also has real consequences for the empowerment and self-belief needed to confidently chase down opportunities, as we shall see in Chapter 8. But sometimes being hyper-visible means dealing with the consequences of downright malicious jealousy too. Aysha told me that at gigs where she was performing her music live (rather than DJing), she has discovered her equipment turned down by the (cis-male) sound engineers, or her microphone mysteriously muted when she had previously checked it was all working fine. Emily told me a similar story of sabotage to the DJ equipment she was due to use at a busy event: 'Every weird setting was set wrong, or switched to the wrong thing …,' she told me. 'There was *no way* it was an accident.'

These are responses that retaliate against the perceived unfairness of the artist being a position that they feel they haven't earned or don't deserve. This was often explained to me as 'the backlash' – majority stakeholders' outcries against the perceived injustice of positive action. The comments posted on women, trans and non-binary people's online content, and the outrage provoked by me calling out the festival's gender imbalance in the opening vignette of Chapter 2 are examples of this. Not wanting to alienate fan bases or upset the (white cis-male) majority has been a recurrent reason given why labels and other gatekeepers haven't publicly engaged in positive action initiatives. For example, Niall and Tim told me that despite the labels they represent genuinely wanting to sign more women and gender-expansive artists, they weren't prepared to run the gauntlet of angry accusations they felt they would receive if they issued a call specifically for music made by gender-diverse producers. Adeline summed this up about her label's positive action campaign, when she said '… it was *so hard* being like, how can you actively say look we want to have more females but then not upset anybody else? In the end we just went ahead and did it anyway and kept stressing the stats [about inequality] to say this *is* a necessary step to take.'

Although rarer, others spoke of competition between women as a result of hyper-visibility, especially those who had been in the industry for some time. Often these were expressed to me as a 'guilty secret' because women are presumed to always be in solidarity with one another, raising each other up and battling together for the common good.[7] 'I used to be quite competitive, which I am ashamed of now,' Jenny confessed. 'When there is only one place then you have to fight for that,' she explained, referring to the fact that event line-ups might only reserve one place for someone from a marginalized identity. Lia also told me how someone she had started her career alongside had turned against her over time: 'She said I was stealing her gigs, she didn't like that I was getting ahead of her,' and Sharon told me how her record label would 'keep the girls on rotation – we only got one gig in five because there were five of us. Everyone else [the cis-male DJs] played most of the time.' Zara recognized her competitiveness stemmed from being the only woman, or even the only black person, playing at an event 'is not a good place to be – but it had to be *me* who was on that line-up. Then I realized – why are we all having to fight for that one place? Something is wrong here.'

Competition between women, in particular (as opposed to gender-expansive people), is often attributed to individual characteristics such as 'bitchiness' and/or the behaviour of successful women who either refuse to support other women's progression, or actively sabotage them – so-called 'Queen Bees' – as the examples here from Jenny, Lia, Sharon and Zara show.[8] It is also a biologically essentialist assumption that lumps 'women' together as a homogeneous group regardless of systems of disadvantage that differentially impact women who are black, mixed race, trans, disabled, lesbian and so on. This 'blame the women' view conveniently sidesteps any question about why the environment they are in is so competitive in the first place.[9] Quite simply, if there were more places open for diverse artists – as there are for majority artists – the competition would be less necessary.

Furthermore, when you are a novelty – the only woman on a line-up or the only non-binary person in the studio, for example – all eyes are on you. You continually butt up against others' overt or whispered views that you are indeed a 'diversity booking', only included because of your gender, race, sexuality and so on. In response, minorities push themselves harder and are at pains to stress this when explaining their success because they have to justify *to themselves* that they deserve their place as well as everyone else. This is also ameliorative work. As early-career DJ Emily told me 'I am blonde and small so you feel like you have to really prove yourself, and when you're also standing there a little bit shy, I felt like people were *eating* me, you know? Like what the fuck are *you* doing there?' Ruby, who was also just starting out, but rising fast, recognized this pressure too: 'Yeah, you do feel you have to be that little bit better than the boys. There's just that bit more pressure I think cos everyone is *really* looking at you.'

When I started my own research this was one of the first things I heard from the women I was talking to – sitting in Olga's bedroom-cum-studio surrounded by keyboards, microphones, and a pile of washing, we chatted about how thoroughly she was learning to use Ableton Live – a popular music production 'digital audio workstation' (DAW). 'You just don't see women in certain roles,' she told me. 'So, to change [people's] perceptions when [they] see a woman in that role, I need to be really bloody good.' She has additional, ameliorative, work to do compared to her male counterparts who are less questioned, and less challenged on their ability than she is – because nobody assumes a cis man got there purely because of his gender. One way this manifested itself in my experiences was through the clear message I got from the instructors on my all-women and gender-expansive DJ course that we should avoid use of the highly illuminated (and therefore visible) 'beat sync' button on CDJs to automatically synchronize our tracks because to do so is low-hanging fruit for others to accuse us of not having the basic DJing skills of beatmatching.[10] Avoiding the sync button is even the name of an all-female DJ collective called 'Girls Don't Sync'.[11]

The harsh glare of the spotlight

The 'box ticking' attitude also feeds majority players' implicit biases that women and gender-expansive artists won't know what they are doing behind the decks, or in the studio, because they were put there for show, not substance. Perceived 'diversity bookings' were recounted to me cringingly by those who expressed them, such as Tess, who told me about a very strange warm-up set by a female DJ she'd encountered before she played her own set. 'I hate even saying this,' she started apologetically, continuing 'but her set was so *odd*, so out of place, and she wasn't even really mixing. I really think this was a diversity booking because she just didn't fit there and it just doesn't do us any favours at all.'

If a minoritized artist *is* put in a visible role by a promoter or record label just to 'tick the diversity box', it can do more harm than good, as Mona explained during our conversation about how gender norms affected her developing career as an artist:

> When I see women or trans non-binary DJs that aren't talented occupying spaces on high profile platforms I want to *scream*, because for me it perpetuates our problems. I had a discussion with [major online dance music platform] because there were some people playing who didn't deserve to play – and I mean they actually weren't mixing and

weren't even *trying* to mix. And when you see the comments section, people can be extremely nasty, so 1) you're putting this person in a position which means they're more vulnerable to these attacks, and 2) it perpetuates a stereotype that women can't DJ.

I have felt these same feelings myself when seeing women play at festivals and gigs where they make mistakes. It just feels like it gives people the perfect opening to roll their eyes and think the worst – that this poor person has just been slotted in, unprepared and perhaps not yet ready for the glare and pressure of the big stage. But it's precisely those accusatory feelings (even if they are not voiced) that contribute to this pressure in the first place. Because seeing women, trans or non-binary DJs is still a comparative novelty, there is a harsh spotlight shone on them in ways that cis men do not experience. Carrying the 'weight of the sisterhood on your shoulders', as I noted it in my fieldnotes, is the hard graft of ameliorative work. The burden is heavy but if you can carry it off the rewards are immense and radiate far beyond you as an individual artist. But if you buckle under the pressure the reverse is true, and *doesn't* happen to cis men. Abi, founder of a women's DJ collective, explains: 'People are like "She's shit, I've seen her and she's just shit …" and I'm like, well maybe she was just having a terrible day? She's probably knackered, like, give her a break! She's definitely far from shit.' In contrast I regularly see and hear cis-male DJs joking in group chats and on podcasts about 'shockers' of gigs where they've dropped the ball and performed poorly. This salience of gender above any other reason for a performance that's less than sparkling is a long-held notion in feminist studies – because gender is the very first way we identify other people, we have a tendency to attribute all other behaviours to that characteristic.[12] It's a primary mechanism of implicit bias in fact. No one is immune – not even a very woke, queer festival director who I had to pull up on this after a second female headliner in two successive years of his festival failed to show up sober for her set. He stormed into the tent where I was dancing: 'I'll give you something for your female DJs research!' he fumed, '[DJ name] is so fucked she can't even remember where she left her record bag. Same as bloody [DJ name] last year!!' After agreeing with him that incapacitating yourself before your set was indeed extremely unprofessional behaviour, I gently pointed out that perhaps the common denominator wasn't gender at all, but genre, since the genre of music both these artists played was notoriously made up of the hardest partying DJs in the scene (for partying, read: drugs and alcohol). He stood stock still in the middle of the packed 1 am dance floor, looking stunned. 'Wow. Yeah. You're right – I just jumped right in there with that assumption That's quite something.'

We will look at the extent to which gender-expansive and women artists' abilities are doubted much more closely in Chapters 6 and 7 but it's worth introducing here because regarding minoritized artists as 'diversity bookings' means they receive differential treatment as well as harsher judgements on their abilities and presence. Even well-intentioned interventions by majority players can easily slip into the territory of 'benevolent sexism' – discriminatory behaviours that are born of a desire to 'be nice' or 'do the right thing' but have actually been shown to cause damage to women's self-belief and intentions in STEM (science, technology, engineering and mathematics) subjects.[13] Much harder to challenge than hostile sexism, benevolent sexism is ambiguous, because the perpetrator usually means well and has the best intentions and probably never even thought how their words or actions might be perceived as patronizing or offensive[14] – leaning over to adjust the DJ equipment while a woman is playing is a classic, as this story from Tyla shows:

> ... when other [cis-male] DJs tell you how to use the equipment, or like come over and start twiddling things while you're starting to play your set and you're like, go away! Terrible. Here we go [rolls eyes]. I've actually got evidence of that on YouTube. A guy in the booth leans over and whispers to me, pointing, like 'that does that that ...' and you can see me go 'I KNOW', [mimes being stern] and say 'I know what I'm doing!'. You can actually see me say it on the video!

In my conversation with Tim, who was the artists and repertoire (A&R) representative for a large underground record label I felt this tension as he told me how he had recently introduced women artists who had submitted their music for consideration by the label to engineers to 'speed the process along a little bit'. He told me 'I can guide somebody *musically* if it's right or wrong, but I'm not going to be able to tell them to take off their kick-drum by 19hz or whatever so the bass cuts through, so I introduce them to somebody who knows that.' I can't decide if this is supportive A&R work to help upskill the women artists concerned, or benevolent sexism because Tim would probably not assume a man needed help in this way. It's probably a bit of both, and perhaps this doesn't matter if the end result is that the track gets released.

The complication arises because people consider they are doing things *right*, as Tess explained to me during our interview: 'People come up to me and say "it's amazing to see you, you're a girl and you're up there doing your thing, it's amazing!"' There is a complicated dynamic about visibility here – the well-meaning fan is sharing their delight, but also drawing attention to the novelty of Tess being up on stage rather than simple congratulating her for a fantastic set. Tess went on to explain, '... they think that it's a compliment to say that, and it *is*, but actually it's not ... and these are good open-minded people that still accidently make really sexist remarks'. Zara had a similar story to tell about reactions from the crowd to her set at a Spanish festival: 'They kept saying to the promoter, 'But who's the black girl?' They liked what I was playing but kept on with 'Who's the *black* girl, who's the *black* girl?' Maybe they just hadn't seen a black female DJ before ... but it all just sticks everything to who you are not what you've done up there.'

Yet intentional and positive representation of more diverse individuals is vital to challenge implicit bias and drive change, and so until diversity of genders is more normalized, it *will* be noteworthy that Zara is a *black woman* DJ behind the decks. It's further complicated by the warm fuzzies you feel when you hear these kinds of comments. After all, they are evidence that you are making a difference. I have not played a single gig without at least one woman coming up to me afterwards and saying how fabulous she thought it was to see a woman up there behind the decks – and an older one at that – absolutely smashing it (as they say). I've heard this a lot from others too. Hayley told me during our call how women come and find her in the crowd after her performance and ask how they can get into the business, learn to DJ or make music. Jacinda, a DJ of South East Asian heritage, told me 'there are always so many women down the front at my gigs looking genuinely delighted I'm not a white dude'. Seeing women, trans and non-binary artists on stage, and as the producers and artists on music releases, featured heavily in the origin stories of a lot of the artists I interviewed too, who were inspired by big names such as Annie Mac, Kemistry and Storm, DJ Rap, Grimes, Rezz, and non-electronic artists like Kate Bush and Billie Eilish. As Zara told me, 'I had some good people that were ahead of me who weren't white men, so that made me think it was possible.' Ines also saw women on the decks at squat parties when she first started going to raves: 'It was actually the first female that I saw on the decks, that got me really thinking, "I want to do that." Seeing other women doing it, I felt I resonated more with them.' And as Kate summed up of her idols, '... they looked cool, they played hardcore music, and you could just tell that their attitudes were just like they did not care, they were going to do what they wanted and how they wanted, and there was no men around telling them how to do it, or they should play this, or they should do it this way.' Kate told me: 'I still listen to that mixtape now and this was such a massive monumental shift for me in seeing two empowering women represent that music.'

This brings us back to our opening vignette – that being up there on stage, or visibly listed on the credits of the music you produce, is inspirational for others like you, and has the potential to change stereotypical views that the industry is a male domain precisely because you are 'out of place' and unusual. As we have seen, this is not without its costs to the artists involved but the fact that they are up there regardless is yet more evidence for the ameliorative and hope-filled nature of what they are doing.

Conclusion: Suck it up, representation matters

In this chapter, then, we have seen how representation matters because it inspires and empowers future generations of DJs and producers and over time it will normalize diversity in the electronic music industry. The fact that people are going to comment on the unusualness of the situation is probably something we just have to suck up until it fades away. I don't think anyone is surprised to see a female doctor or woman police officer anymore, for example. Like Charlotte, who we met at the start of the chapter, DJ/producer Alice made a compelling case for the fact that artists should *welcome* being booked 'for their gender, skin colour, sexuality, whatever …' if they suspected it was happening, because you at least had a foot in the door – 'and now it is up to you to make the most of that chance you've been given'. We shall see how this extends from individual stereotype-busting behaviours to what diversity scholar Karren Knowlton has called 'trailblazing motivation'[15] in Chapter 8, when I discuss the importance of women and gender-expansive collectives, and the details of positive action initiatives and organizations in more depth.

Normalization is important because it reduces the salience of gender as the go-to 'hook' on which to hang all kinds of accusations. Mistakes, unprofessional conduct, poor track selection, and any other less-than-perfect performances that might just be down to an artist having an 'off day' will no longer be attributed to their gender, skin colour, sexuality or any other identity characteristic if diverse identities are regularly encountered on stage and as music-making artists. To make this a reality, we probably just need to accept that, for now at least, 'diversity bookings' will happen, and there will be a compliance mindset among some gatekeepers who feel forced to engage when they'd really rather not be bothered with it all. Because it is only when minoritized artists are no longer so visible that they will feel less pressure, be held to less impossibly high standards, and be less in the blinding glare of the diversity spotlight. Normal, not novelty. And this will likely happen one or two artists at a time.

Until then, the majority (white, cis, male and straight) dudes – and some women and gender-expansive folks too – will continue to 'backlash'. They will rail at the assault on 'good music' and promoter/label autonomy to choose the best person for the job that we saw in Chapter 3 – even if they *are* all white, cis, male and straight. This is perhaps the biggest hurdle to positive action – that it is still overwhelmingly regarded as discrimination against the majority and unequal treatment that is unfair, rather than a necessary corrective to a system that is rigged. But the backlash is not an excuse to shy away from positive action – you can't cook an omelette without breaking eggs, as the saying goes. But we do need to be mindful of *how* positive action campaigns and activities are designed and communicated if we are to avoid doing as much harm as good. The manifesto in Chapter 9 sets out some ideas for how this can be done, and while it will never be perfect or straightforward, you'll be willing to navigate this terrain if you are genuinely wanting to bring about change, whether motivated by personal reasons or more altruistic ones.

So, as minoritized artists, we have to deal with our feelings of tokenism and do whatever it is anyway, and that's hugely inspiring work as well as being tough. Taking the hit and sucking it up now so that others don't have to do it so much in future is 'trailblazing motivation' for ameliorative work in action. But the trailblazers can't do it all by themselves and nor should they be expected to. The challenges of allyship are not a reason to abdicate real, meaningful responsibility for positive action, as we see so clearly around International Women's Day, for example.

Chapter track: 'Sea Organ'

Figure 5: Artwork for 'Sea Organ' EP by Dovetail, reproduced with kind permission of Break Wind Productions

Source: https://breakwindproductions1.bandcamp.com/track/sea-organ

'Sea Organ' is my favourite from all the tracks I have made so far. I made it fairly quickly when the owner of the record label requested another track to accompany 'Keep Your Disdance' – as they only release EPs that include two pieces of music.

I've used it as the track for this chapter because it's one of the tracks on the EP that made it to No.1 on the Beatport Top 100 Breaks Releases in December 2020 because my lovely friends, and extended music family all bought copies to propel me to the top of the chart, as I described earlier in the chapter. It's my favourite because it feels like my most accomplished composition to date. I love the way the arpeggiated melody swells and fills the space in the second half of the track, and it was largely made using my hardware synthesizer. It's called 'Sea Organ' because the burbling off-key refrain that rolls through the breakdowns (quieter portions of the track where the music literally 'breaks down' ready to build up again) are samples cut from a recording I made of the sound of the 'Sea Organ' in Zadar, Croatia. A concrete structure at the quayside with apertures that hauntingly 'hoot' in different tones as the waves wash through it.

Regardless of whether Sea Organ's success can be attributed to novelty rather than my musical prowess, it's a track that I think is actually really rather good, and that I am proud of.

6

Women Don't Make Their Own Music

Who's Your Engineer?

On a warm sunny afternoon, an eager music producer enters the 'Label Lounge' at a national music conference. She's excited, but nervous, as she enters the dimly lit space and her eyes adjust. She's here to have her music listened to by the artists and repertoire (A&R) reps from a selection of well-respected dance music labels. Tracks she has spent weeks, if not months, writing, tweaking, listening to again and again, getting feedback on, polishing and making as good as she can, hoping to impress at least one of these record labels enough to get them to offer her a contract to release it. Having the badge of a 'good label' behind her will do wonders for her career – maybe people will start to take her seriously. Once that happens, the bookings for DJ gigs will start to follow, and that's where the money is. She knows how it works, that's why she started producing her own music in the first place. Maybe she could finally give up her day job! The butterflies in her stomach flutter at the thought.

As her eyes adjust to the gloom, she looks around the room – 16 listening booths staffed by 16 middle-aged men, and one with a solo woman sitting at it. She's used to being on her own and it never gets any less nerve-wracking, but this time at least she isn't the *only* woman in the room. The event is 'speed-dating' style, where the wannabe producers visit each of the labels they're interested in. The more popular ones have several people waiting patiently in line for their turn. They look like they are all guys too. The label A&Rs don oversize headphones to listen to one or more of the producers' tracks and give them feedback. They are hoping to find the next big thing – new artists for the label, new sounds for the brand – their goal is to sign music today if it's good enough, or if not, give advice as to how it can be improved and/or encourage the producer to improve it and send a new version.

It's our producer's turn at the label she's most excited about impressing. She offers the regulation fist bump, trying to being confident. Smile, but not too much – it's been taken for flirting too many times. What are they thinking when they look at her? Is it just the music they are appraising? She'd already spent a long time deciding what she should wear that day. Be pretty but not too pretty. Make-up, but cool T-shirt and jeans. Definitely not the summer dress or shorts she'd rather be wearing in this heat. But she's already been told she's apparently 'the prettiest person that's sat down here today'.

The A&R offers her a pair of headphones, loads up her track, puts on his own and starts to listen. He nods his head in time with the beat and after a minute or so he looks impressed and raises his eyebrows at her. She swells with pride. 'This is *great*!', he mouths, and gives her a thumbs-up.

'Really great groove and crystal top end there, I love how the vocal floats in early – that's nice.'

She grins, and they listen together for a little longer before slipping off the headphones. 'The mixdown is really strong. No mud at all. Who made this for you?'

She deflates like a balloon, trying not to roll her eyes and sighs: 'No one. It's mine. I made it – including the mixdown.' He smiles patronizingly. 'It's OK, you can tell me – it's not a problem if you use an engineer, most girls do!'

'Nope, it's all mine – shall I show you the project on Logic [DAW]?' She tries to keep her voice light, but she's been here so many times and it's irritating. 'Oh, no, no need for that,' says Mr A&R, '… but maybe we can get you in for a chat with one of our producers – see what we can do for you.' She knows he doesn't believe her but she takes his card and private email – she'll just have to wait until she's in the studio with their people to show them what she can do.

Introduction

This chapter deals with the ameliorative work involved in constantly having to prove your skills and ability around the technologies of music production and DJing just because you are not a cis man. As the opening vignette shows, seemingly friendly and innocuous assumptions that someone else (that is, a cis man) must have made your music land hard for women and gender-expansive producers, chipping away at self-esteem and reinforcing implicit biases that men are more interested in technology than women, and better at getting to grips with it. You will learn much more about music production as the chapter unfolds, because it is the technology-driven dynamics of electronic music that feed the myth that 'women don't make their own music' and, instead, use what are called 'ghost producers'. Girls and women are assumed not have the interest, motivation, aptitude or skills to become proficient in the technologies that music production uses, and which I outlined in Chapter 1. Yet, interestingly, some of electronic music's first pioneers were women and trans people – for example Delia Derbyshire, Suzanne Ciani, Wendy Carlos, Daphne Oram, Pauline Oliveros, Mieko Shiomi and Iris Sangüesa.[1] Sadly, until lately, we had never really heard of these amazing people, and their presence hasn't moved the needle on gender imbalance at all until very recently.

The association of technology with cis-gendered men is dealt with more in more depth in Chapter 7, but here we will explore why it matters. Women and gender-expansive producers' work is consistently doubted by gatekeepers as we see in our opening vignette. This leads to patronizing behaviour, a lack of respect, lower status and assumptions that the artist is a fake, or just a pretty face to draw in crowds. This in turn results in minoritized-gender artists enacting the ameliorative work of rallying against being dismissed, having to work harder to convince gatekeepers of things that are never doubted in men, fighting against perceptions that they are just a 'diversity booking', as we saw in Chapter 5, and all the associated weariness, self-esteem damage and feelings of exclusion that come with this. This is on top of never feeling truly part of the networks that can equip them with the level of skill required because it's hard to infiltrate 'bro culture', as we saw in Chapter 3.

Ghosts and the machines

I first discovered there were ghost producers in electronic music when I was interviewing DJs for the earlier project about work and fun in the DJing occupation that I outline in the Prelude to this book. One of my interviewees decided he was going to 'lift the lid' on all the fakery and game-playing he saw happening in the underground scene – a scene that he believed should be based on authenticity and hard work, as we have already seen in Chapters 2 and 3. As well as things like buying followers on social media, he told me that some of my most favourite big-name DJs didn't write their own tunes, instead paying someone to do it for them who was then not credited on the resulting track. They passed off others' work as their own in order to be seen as a well-rounded artist with musical talent, which in turn earned them respect and kudos to be exchanged for bookings, record deals and other markers of success. Apparently, a large proportion of the early-2000s dance music tunes I *loved*, that kindled my adoration for this scene, were made by a bloke from Brixton and not by the famous artist I revered. I was horrified at this news and heard it confirmed by pretty much everyone I have interviewed since. Everyone seems to know someone that they have heard on good authority 'doesn't write their own tunes'. I'm usually let into these confidences as if they are a guilty secret and the whistleblower is visibly indignant as they tell me. Why? Because it cuts to the heart of what being an underground producer, in particular, is: musical and technical flair, dedication, hard work and honesty. People coming together to keep a scene alive that reveres authenticity and pushes back against commercial pressures and is community driven. Using a ghost writer is seen by most as a dirty business, as we can see in this story told to me by Lia, a DJ and producer who had just started her own mixing and mastering business[2] at the time:

> [A-list female DJ], for instance, the world's biggest DJ – she doesn't make her own music, and I was shocked more because she's a pianist like me, and I actually heard it from someone who's an artist manager, so they know what they're talking about, I know they're not lying to me. And I can tell when people use ghost producers because when they put videos on Instagram or Facebook, or whatever, it's always like a picture of the screen but the thing is with a ghost producer you're going to get the track sent to you, so you can easily open that up in [the software] and it's there on the screen, and it's playing … you never actually see her *make* any music.
>
> I understand it from the point that you don't have time to make tracks because you're touring constantly, but then I'm, like, you should just learn like everyone else has!

The very same day that I heard the story that opens this chapter, one of my favourite artists posted a screenshot on Instagram of a comment on one of her Instagram reels: 'Do you produce your own music [artist name], or do you pay ghost producers?' A deceptively innocent and polite question to an outsider, perhaps – but to an underground electronic music artist, this is inflammatory: the artist responded with a sarcastic 'This guy is trying to ruin my day already!' comment slapped over the screenshot. Challenging her (considerable) skills, calling into question her integrity and authenticity that she might be trying to sell music to her fans that she didn't make, and finally implying that she is paying someone to write music for her is possibly the worst set of accusations that can be levelled at an underground artist in this scene, and it happens to women with monotonous regularity. Gender-expansive people get this too, but the more androgynous, or hetero- and cis-normatively male you look, the less others doubt your production skills. We saw this hinted at by Solar in Chapter 3 when they reported they were welcomed into 'bro culture' more readily after they cut their hair and could 'pass' as a cis man.[3]

The important point here is that although plenty of cis-male artists are rumoured to use ghost producers, these accusations come as a result of some degree of evidence – true or not. Someone has heard from someone that someone they know gets paid handsomely for making tracks for Mr Big.[4] They are not levelled at the artist instinctively, just because of their gender. When confronted with good-quality music made by cis men, the A&R guys in the label lounge in the opening vignette would almost certainly never have questioned whether a cis-male producer did the work himself, and certainly wouldn't have then attempted to get him to 'C'mon, spill the beans' when he insisted the music was all his own work. It is also not only men who hold these views – the implicit bias around women not producing their own music is pretty universal, as Katarina explains, when she tells people she is a music producer:

> ... when you mention to people like you produce music, a lot of them actually can't believe it, like, '*Really*?', 'Really you? A woman? No, this is a *man's* thing, like you can't ...' and then they insist on listening [to the track] or are, like, we need to prove this. Yes, normally they are amazed, nobody can believe it's me.

We shall see why women (in particular) are so regularly doubted for their music production skills in much more depth later in this chapter, but before we do, it's useful to say a little more about what producing electronic music as a self-producer actually entails in order to question why using ghost producers is seen as such a terrible crime.

Production and career success

As I briefly introduced in Chapter 1, producing electronic music usually involves composing, songwriting, operating/playing the instrumentation and sometimes singing vocals, as well as engineering, producing and mixing the track. In other genres of music, these activities are the dedicated jobs of several people and usually take place more or less collaboratively in a professional recording studio.[5] In electronic music, this collapsing of roles means that the producer is more accurately a '*self*-producer', because they do all the activities and stages themselves, often at home. The properties of 'digital audio workstations' (DAWs) mean that a lot of the steps in making music dissolve into one another when traditionally they have been very separate stages. When you are writing your own music on a DAW, the character of the music (composition) often emerges in combination with the effects you can apply to the sounds you're using (mixing and production), and you constantly tinker with the overall balance and level of those sounds (mixing), frankly, because you can.[6]

Self-production is so widespread in electronic music partly because electronic music has grown from DIY roots,[7] as I explained in Chapter 2. It has also taken hold so firmly because there is no need to be able to play a traditional musical instrument (although many artists do), and partly because of the rise and spread of the DAW, meaning that electronic music production is within the reach of a wider range of people than ever before, as we have seen already – these whizzy bits of software allow you to undertake all the tasks that were traditionally, and still are, done in a studio by a whole team of skilled specialists. And because it is technologically possible to do all the steps yourself, an expectation has arisen that this is what *should* happen if you are a truly authentic and credible electronic artist.[8] At the same time, advances in digital DJ equipment have made it simpler to be able to DJ, thereby ostensibly devaluing 'just playing other people's music', resulting in the perception that anyone can be a DJ these days. As Loretta informed me about using a DJ controller, in comparison to the traditional vinyl records and turntables she learned on: '… God, it's so *easy* now. Even my Nan can do it.' My grandson calls me 'Disco Nanny', so you can take it on good authority that, yes, Nans can DJ.

Because of these factors, it has become increasingly *expected* that DJs will also make electronic music, rather than just mix and blend music made by others in a skilful and creative way – which has always been the traditional role of the DJ in a club. Like all role expansion, once a few people start doing it, others follow and soon the differentiator becomes a benchmark of baseline success rather than an additional skill, and gatekeepers start to prefer DJ/producers for their shows. We saw this in action in Chapter 2 with the 'lure of the artist' in relation to festival bookings and the advice given by Digital DJ Tips on learning to produce tracks in order to advance a DJ career.

Ruby was an early-stage DJ who had decided she needed to learn to produce from the outset, as she explained to me: 'Very quickly I understood that producing is important to differentiate yourself as a DJ, it's not about only the DJ skills and how you actually deliver the performance, there's also a certain value to creating your music and expressing yourself through production, and that's why I just started learning.' Others began through their DJing practice, like Jenny – now a prolific producer – who told me: 'I started doing my own kind of little edits and mash-ups,[9] and then I was like I really need to up my game'. This 'upping of the game' is nicely summarized by Suzie, another early-career but fast-rising artist, who summarizes the need for production as 'completeness': 'I think for me to be *complete* as an artist I need to have the production side. What I've been told by festivals and promoters is they want to book *artists*, you know? They don't just want to book DJs.' This 'need to produce' (and women's absence from production) was recognized as far back as 2011, when music researcher Rosa Reitsamer[10] conducted a study of women in drum and bass and techno scenes in Berlin.

So, it's not surprising that learning to produce music is an instrumental, strategic decision for DJs who want to progress their career. Because music production is complex and hard to learn (especially so if you are excluded from the boys' club), the need to do it can put pressure on DJs of all genders to employ ghost producers. That pressure can be internal or external. For example, an artist knowing they need to have music under their own name but having no desire or time to do make it, or, as Emily told me, being approached by a manager who wanted to supply her with tracks to release under her own name: 'I said, "Is it just like here's the track, put your name on it?", and he said "Yeah, basically you get no stress." But I felt like there was no soul in that, and I said sorry it's not for me.' Rachel also had a similar experience:

> I had one manager that told me he could 'put someone on the track', and I said, 'What do you mean?' I was kind of offended that even he would have said that because it kind of meant your track sucks so you basically need someone to step in and to fix it for you, which also is a form of ghost producing.

This pressure also comes from record labels, as Sharon told me of her early experiences with production at the start of her career in the early 2000s:

> [Party promoter and record label] decided they wanted to put an album out by us four girls [on the roster] so we just went into the studio with the engineers. I never questioned that. … I suppose in a way I didn't have time to actually make any tracks myself anyway, I'd [only] have that time to go into the studio with an engineer, put down my ideas and then come out with something on that same day.

The authenticity continuum: working with engineers vs ghost producing

Sharon went on to explain how her early tracks were written and produced, telling me that she was nonetheless always involved in this process, and stressing 'there would never be a time in the whole of my career that I wasn't in that studio making that track, I'd *always* be there. I'd make sure that I [was] sitting in that studio making the tracks [with the engineer]. Channelling my musical ideas through them.' Likewise, Solar explained that they 'worked with engineers', at least initially in their production career, but that they would 'get down musical ideas in a simple form in Logic [name of Apple's

DAW] first' so that the engineer had some raw material of Solar's own creation to work with. Others were more vehement that working with an engineer was a perfectly normal part of the process, particularly if you are a busy touring DJ like Kate: 'Of course I work with an engineer, and there's nothing wrong with that. Everybody does once they get to a certain stage. It's what's professional. They just don't say it. You don't expect a whole film to be produced by the actors, or the writers, so why think that for music?'

But Kate too was at pains to point out that she did the writing, composition, laid down the groove and had a good idea of the samples, sounds and other aesthetic choices that she wanted for the music before going into the studio with the engineers. Others explained working with more technically minded (and usually male) artists as 'collaboration', where their name is also co-listed as the artist of the track. This sense of professionalism-meets-collaboration is evident in Naomi's views. 'A lot of things out there that are successful come from a team of people,' she explained. 'Like, there might be someone who's written the piano melody, someone's written the bass line or created that, someone's made the drums, it's a team of people all coming together to make a really good result.'

What all of this shows is that ghost production – paying for a track made by someone you've never met to release under your own name – is more accurately the end-point of a continuum that all producers are positioned along at some point. The opposite end to ghost production would be undertaking all the roles listed earlier in this chapter yourself. An interesting exception to this is 'mastering' the track – which is almost always done by a third party – and often by the record label that has agreed to release the music. It's been explained to me as a sonic polish, necessary in order to get the right 'sound' for the label, or because the producer themself has gone 'ear blind' from listening to the track so much and can no longer make effective judgements. The skills of the mastering engineer are widely seen as involving particularly advanced audio engineering and some kind of magical ear that enables transformational aural wizardry. It's OK to use a mastering engineer, that's not fake. In fact, it's a taken-for-granted expectation, if not requirement, that you will.

In between the two extremes are all the various different arrangements we have seen earlier, from commissioning a track based on your own musical ideas, through sitting with an engineer in the studio riffing off one another, providing your engineer with a half-made track that needs technical know-how to bring it to fruition, to more collaborative relationships where all parties are named as artists on the track, and/or using a mix engineer to work on the final balance and sound of the music. Outsourcing some of these roles is seen as legitimate, and even necessary (such as mastering and to some extent mixing), but others are not. This happens according to what I have come to understand as a logic of authenticity. As we have seen, underground music, in particular, is regarded as *authentic* to the values of skill, talent, hard work, community – the 'right reasons' to be in the business. Using other people to make your music, even in part, does not fit well with this.

I have no way of knowing how many women and gender-expansive producers declined my invitation to be interviewed for the In the Key project because they use engineers to make the tracks that they release as their own. It's perhaps to be expected that the people I did interview were overwhelmingly the ones who do make their own music, and it's probably also no surprise that these artists get angry and frustrated when they find out other artists' boyfriends made their music, or become successful because they use engineers, or employ ghost producers. They are angry and frustrated because this makes life harder for them. They are competing with producers who have (what they see as) unfair advantage in being able to afford 'a team around them', as Naomi called it, or are shortcutting the system, as Lia lamented earlier: '… *Why can't they just learn like the rest of us?*'

But most of all they get annoyed because working with engineers and ghost producers feeds the notion that *all* women do this, themselves included. It fuels the myth that demands the ameliorative work that I explained at the beginning of this chapter – constantly pushing back against assumptions, and sometimes hostile accusations that the music you have spent days, weeks or even months working on is not your own work, and that you lack the skills and talent to make it on your own. This is hard to stomach when music is all you have ever wanted to do, and is your passion, such as for Celene who, aged 13, took herself to the local library to use the computer to make beats because she didn't have a computer at the foster home she lived in:

> I had won a little audio interface in a competition that came loaded with a DAW, so I plugged it in, and plugged in a mic and was sitting there awkwardly in the library, making music, recording me rubbing and tapping the mic and making kickdrums and stuff [laughs]. I always knew I wanted to be composer, or do something in music, since I was like … I don't even remember … for the *longest* time, I always knew that's what I wanted to do.

Likewise, Genevieve's dad made music for fun, so she asked him to give her a copy of his DAW and started to play around: 'I installed the software and started making beats when I was about 12 years old, but I had no idea what I was doing,' she told me, laughing. 'The songs were terrible but I was having fun, I was really, really having fun.' It was the same for India, for whom music production had just always clicked with her:

> It was just kind of normal [in my family] basically to make beats, it made sense, and it was mostly through my cousin … he was like the one who gave me the software when I was 14, and I just saw how

easy it was at his house, not easy but *fascinating*, it just made sense. The only thing I can ever say about making music and playing music is it just *makes sense*.

The joy and 'rightness' in Celene, Genevieve and India's memories was palpable. For them, music production was not a strategic choice, but an aesthetic calling, as we also see in Ines's recollection here: 'I just couldn't help but zone into the sounds and be fascinated. How *do* they get that sound, how do they manipulate that? How do they create that kick? So my curiosity got the better of me and it was a natural evolution to start producing music.'

But in order to follow their dreams and learn their craft, these artists have fought against all the odds that we have seen so far. They have slogged up that sloping field, day in, day out, to do what they love, and when they are in shooting distance of the goal? Some bro asks, 'Who *really* makes your music for you babe?' And this is problematic because when cis men use ghost producers or work with engineers, their behaviour doesn't spill over to *all* cis-male artists. Sure, they might be seen as less credible, inauthentic, and regarded in a derisory way – but this brush has tarred only them, and not their whole gender. The reason for this is that music technologies transgress feminine identities. When we think 'nerdy techie gadget geek' it is almost always a man that comes to mind.

The dance of the feminine

All of what we've seen in this chapter so far is fuelled by a seemingly unshakeable association been technology and maleness that has its roots in the social history of music itself, and in the history of participation in technological pursuits such as science, mathematics and logic. This is despite the fact that many of the pioneers of electronic music production were women, and indeed many of the early inventors of computing too, as I noted at the start of this chapter. Tara Rodgers' 'Pink Noises' project and resulting book from 2010, The 'Women in Sound, Women on Sound' initiative (WISWOS) led by Linda O'Keefe, and Johann Merrich's book *A Short History of Women Protagonists in Electronic Music* are great places to learn about these trailblazing artists.[11]

The reasons why these women and gender-expansive people's achievements have been under-emphasized, or downright ignored in the history of music technology has to do with the way certain activities have come to be regarded as gendered on account of the skills required to do them, as we shall see later. How this manifests itself today was hinted at to me during this research in quite complex ways. As well as erroneous assumptions that 'girls just aren't into tech' that we can see challenged by India, Genevieve and Celene's childhood experiences related previously (and discussed more fully in Chapter 7), there is also a more subtle undercurrent of assumption that comes from women themselves: that many lack the patience or focus to sit at a computer working and reworking the same short music loop, engineering and tweaking sounds for hours on end that is (apparently) required to make good music. 'I think as well, it's to do with the masculine and the feminine,' retired producer Evelyn explained to me by miming the 'caduceus' – the symbol for medicine – in the air as a metaphor:

> If you look at the caduceus it's a symbol that's like this, straight sword like this, so it's almost like the masculine sword, straight and to the point. Focused. And then the feminine energy that winds around it, we bring the beauty … we bring the kind of like aesthetics of things to the sword of truth, we kind of like do our hair or put make-up on and all this kind of stuff … it's like that's the dance of the feminine.

This feminine 'touch' was described to me by Alice in relation to the music that different genders produce: 'When I listen to tracks that are produced by women versus men the kind of feeling, or the feel of the track is a little bit softer with the women, and when with the guys, bam, bam, it's a bit more harsh, and it makes sense! We *do* usually like the softer stuff, no?' I am not at all sure this claim stands up to scrutiny, especially having spent time with hard techno and drum and bass producers who are women. But what's important here is that Alice (and others) have a *perception* of femininity around electronic music, even if that's not the reality. Several writers on gender in recording studios highlight how this 'feminine touch' is something to be mobilized for creative and career advantage in the course of their work engineering music for other people. Leveraging difference as a gender minority is one manifestation of this – selling yourself as something refreshing on the understanding that because you are not like everyone else, you will bring new creative ideas for the client (singers and musicians).[12] Other observations around the strategic value of femininity in traditional recording studios include niceness and emotionality – what engineers Sharon Jagger and Helen Turner delightfully call an 'economy of smiles'[13] – but also the ability to be tough with clients when they are not giving their best. One of Kallie Marie's interviewees called herself 'Studio Mom' for this ability to be tough but kind. Another interesting way it shows up is as a distinct aesthetic around making studios welcoming and 'homely' in contrast to the sterile studio spaces that are more usually encountered.[14] This is something I've noticed happening on social media with gender-expansive and women self-producers too – the sharing of photos of cosy, homely, studio spaces, with lots of plants, candles, squishy animals, fluffy cushions and so on to counterbalance the austere appearance of all the tech that is there too. I think this is important representation – associating different aesthetics with technology to 'soften' it – as we shall see in Chapter 7.

This feminine energy predominantly showed up in my research as performance, sociability, and emotional engagement in DJing rather than producing music.

Hayley referred to herself as a 'conduit of joy' when performing, for example, and as 'an embodiment of the divine feminine'. Helen, who said she'd never really noticed how male-dominated electronic music was, suggested that perhaps women were 'just carried away with performing music – there is so much excitement in just playing, just to interact with the audience. So I'd say it's just their choice [not to produce] probably.' Naomi, too, intimated that men might find music production techniques more 'natural' than women, because women might find the stark switch between DJing and production too hard:

> With DJing you're in the moment, you're playing, you've got a crowd in front of you, you're selecting your tunes as you go along, you're feeling the vibe of the crowd, going with it like that, and also you're with loads of people, whereas production is very lonely. I think generally, women are sort of more sociable? Production takes time, to get the track arranged, to do all the automation, editing, all the finer details, you might be spending a whole day, like eight hours, 10 hours, doing that, all by yourself at home. That's probably more naturally a man's thing?

Different wiring and lighter brains?

However, it is more common for the discourse around music production to challenge these ideas that men and women are 'naturally' better at some things and not others – as indeed did several of my interviewees. Any suggestion that men were better suited to making electronic music was either met with anger, or humour, but both expressing exasperation that these conversations are still ongoing.

> That is bollocks, absolute fucking bollocks. There is no reason, *no reason whatsoever*, why women can't make music just as good as men (Carmen).

> Are we *still going there?* You don't need a penis to make music. Be successful? Well, that's a different matter [rolls eyes] but production can be learned by anyone. End of. (Loretta)

The idea that male and female brains are naturally different from one another has long been contested in the so-called nature/nurture debate. Leaving aside the question of how such a binary divide deals with the brains of non-binary, trans or inter-sex people, the idea that different genders are just 'wired differently' is not the whole picture. Philosopher of science and psychologist Professor Cordelia Fine has made it her life's work to study the likelihood that female and male brains are different in these kinds of ways, which she recounts wonderfully accessibly in her books *Delusions of Gender* and *Testosterone Rex*.[15] She finds it way more plausible that tests designed to show brain-sex differences really just confirm that women are more likely to report traits that they consider others expect from them, and we can find this out by manipulating the context in which people take the test. For example, when men and women were paid to exhibit empathy in their responses to an experiment, and when men were informed that there was a scientifically proven link between sexual attractiveness and empathy, they exhibited just as much compassion and emotional sensitivity as the women did.[16] The same is true of logic and reason tasks – when women were asked to read literature that 'proved' they were just as capable as men at these skills, they performed as well as men on a spatial reasoning task. But when their pre-reading told them there were brain differences that prevented women from excelling in these abilities, they performed much worse.[17]

While cautioning that neuroscience has a 'seductive allure' that smuggles in sexist attitudes under the 'proof' of brain science,[18] using the concept of neuroplasticity, Professor Fine nonetheless efficiently demolishes the divide between nature and nurture in gender identity and expression. How we are nurtured shapes our actual physiological nature – our brains rewire themselves according to the way we are treated, and how we behave according to others' expectations.[19] Then we pass on those predispositions as instructions in genetic code to any children we might have. But, importantly, there is a difference between genes and the activity of genes, because genes can switch on or off depending on social and environmental factors, dramatically changing how we think and behave.[20] This fascinating science deserves far more attention than I can give it here (which is why Professor Fine has written two whole books about it), but what it means for our argument is that the way different genders are socialized around tech, and challenging the ways tech is reinforced as better suited to one gender than another, *really matters* if we are going to ever change inequality in engagement in technology-driven occupations.

In fact, Evelyn whose belief that men and women had fundamentally different energies I quoted earlier, went on to recognize this when she explained a little more where her beliefs were rooted. '[Music production needs] an ability to just cut everything off and really focus in,' she said. 'Women, we are much more kind of like this …' She paused to wave her arms wildly around before continuing. 'We're much more kind of like, we're dealing with *this*, dealing with *that* … I mean, some women *can* fully focus and forget about everything else, but most of us have got to think about a lot of things on a daily basis.' Her observation that women are pulled in many directions in ways that men generally are not is recognition that social expectations of genders are different. Reading between the lines here, Evelyn is suggesting that while men can lock themselves in the studio for hours at a time, uninterrupted and with a singular, obsessive focus, their wives and girlfriends are off cleaning the house, picking up the kids, dealing with life admin, remembering birthdays, keeping up with their friends, and so on. This resonates with Rebecca Farrugia's study of women DJs in the US, who reported having lives that were just too busy to allow them to devote whole *days* to music production to the exclusion of all else.[21]

Globally, women are responsible for 75 per cent of unpaid care work, which equates to some 160 billion hours and $10.8 *trillion* dollars of benefit to the global economy.[22] There is not a single country in the world where men's and women's shares of unpaid labour are equal, with ILO statistics from countries around the world making for stark reading.[23] The most recent figures from the UK on gender differences in unpaid work[24] show that in 2016 women in the 26-to-45 age group did over twice as much as men, spending 35 hours per week on domestic chores, cooking, childcare and looking after older adults, against men's 17. There was no age group where men and women's share of unpaid domestic and caring labour was anywhere near equal. Perhaps even more importantly, the cognitive and emotional burden of 'thinking about all the things' is disproportionately felt by women[25] for whom the *responsibility* for these tasks falls, whether they are actually doing them or not. Thinking about multiple things at once and task-switching leads to increased cognitive load that causes stress, depression, exhaustion and generally prevents women from being able to enjoy life.[26] None of this is conducive to the time and emotional energy that needs to be devoted to making music, let alone the hours of practice it takes to learn the craft. Women are not making music because they *can't*, but because they are socially required or expected to do far too many other things.

A quick scan of the magazines for sale in a supermarket confirms the ways hobbies and interests are gendered. The magazines are divided into 'Men's Interests' and 'Women's Interests' and the contents are sharply gendered, as I am sure you have noticed. Women's magazines are about home, garden, celebrity gossip, diet, cooking, beauty, textile crafts, watercolours and other such gentle pastimes, with light, fluffy colourful cover designs. The men's section is full of darker, sharper designs – publications that promise competence in cars, model trains, endurance sports, weight training, fishing, sport and, yes, computing and music production.[27] But the *character* of those gendered hobbies deserves closer inspection beyond the subjects – something that I had never noticed until I read Caitlin Moran's acerbic and hilarious book *How to be a Woman*. While men's magazines encourage specific pursuits that are laser-focused on specialized topics, women's hobbies seem to be unendingly broad. Instead of directing women's attention to fine-grained and well-defined singular activities – like fly fishing, or collecting clocks, women's hobbies simply relate to 'lifestyle' – they are not encouraged to develop a singular passion like men, but are actively encouraged to want to do a bit of everything. And when the bits of everything get too much? They can read about how to balance it all, while men quietly sit in their home studios for eight hours a day making music.

Conclusion: A social problem

In this chapter we've seen how the fact that different genders are socialized to appreciate and feel suited to different hobbies and interests runs alongside beliefs that they also possess fundamentally different 'energies' that make them better suited to some things and not others. We've also started to consider that this may be a product of the environment we live our lives surrounded by and that this gets encoded into our brains, leading to a self-fulfilling prophecy that 'girls just aren't into tech'. This is the topic of the next chapter. The socialized differences between genders leads to associations between women and sociability, relationships, caring and a 'homely approach' to work, life, and perhaps music production, as we saw in the example of the producers who leverage these 'feminine touch' qualities for career success.

There is *absolutely* nothing wrong with this, of course, but it does also cement gendered associations with things that are less techie. Because women are less associated with technological work, those that are present – including foundational pioneers – have been downplayed in the history of electronic music through a web of power dynamics and social barriers that we'll examine more closely in the next chapter. Everyone has heard of Kraftwerk and Brian Eno, but how many have heard of Wendy Carlos or Daphne Oram? It also means that when women and gender-expansive artists are technologically proficient music producers they are viewed with suspicion that they are not the authors of their own work, or that they have needed to work with engineers. And when they do work with a team of creatives, it's assumed that this is due to a lack of skills and perhaps more importantly, interest or aptitude, rather than a positive creative choice.

What arises from this chain of assumptions is a readiness on the part of record labels, or artist managers, to suggest to early-stage artists that they should use ghost production services, or studio engineers, and this is heavily gendered. Women, trans and non-binary people are more likely to be offered the 'easy way' to reap the benefits of having a catalogue of their own releases than cis men. The need to be an artist with original compositions (beyond 'just' being a DJ) is no longer optional in the digital age, as we have seen – so the choice can sometimes be seen as stark. For a woman who has not been raised to believe she can succeed with technologically clever stuff, indeed actively socialized *away* from such pursuits, the thought of having to learn how to produce music can be incredibly daunting. Who can blame her for accepting help when it's offered? Except it does little to change the status quo and casts aspersions on those who *are* battling to upskill themselves and make it under their own steam. It's a complex dynamic, for sure, and one we are going to dig a little deeper into in the next chapter by examining how assumptions that girls just aren't into tech have come about, and what can be done to change that record.

Chapter track: 'Fall Away'

Figure 6: Artwork for 'Fall Away (22 Mix)' by Dovetail, author's own artwork

Source: Listen to it at https://soundcloud.com/dovetail_uk/fall-away-22-mix

'Fade Away' is an unreleased track that has gone through several iterations but began life as 'Garafia', named after the province in La Palma where I recorded the birdsong that twitters throughout this track. It's a good track to use in a chapter to challenge the pervasive assumption that women don't make their own music because every part of it has been 'made' by me. All the instruments and sounds, apart from the birdsong, were generated from samples cut from the sound of a squeaky gate I recorded on my phone while out on a walk in Scotland one January. Small segments of the squeak have been stretched, reshaped, bent and re-pitched to form all of the song. I added the vocal later from a sample pack I have, because I felt something was missing, and from there the track was renamed 'Fall Away' as that's what the vocalist is singing.

I felt delighted and accomplished producing this track. Experimenting, twiddling unfamiliar settings through a process of trial and error and generally getting lost in the creative process was so rewarding. I played an earlier version of it during a 'New Year's Day recovery' set over livestream during lockdown and felt myself swell with pride at a friend's comment in the chat box: 'What, you made this track? The one that's playing now? Really? That's awesome!' I don't know what he expected my music to sound like, or perhaps he was surprised that I made something that sounded good but, either way, the validation and affirmation of having my creative efforts recognized and appreciated was incredibly motivational. I can only imagine what it's like to be constantly doubted in the way our opening vignette retells, and how much strength you need to continue to plough on in the face of that.

7

Girls Just Aren't into Tech

'I wasn't raised like a daughter'

I think part of my story I can thank my dad a lot for, my dad kind of brought me up in way where he treated me as though I was his son – which is probably why I ended up studying engineering. He was a supervisor of elevators, like installing elevators into malls and things like that, so he was always doing electrical technical stuff and I'd be there with him. I was carrying the tool box and helping him install the lights and things like that, which was funny really ...

[Dad] was always on his computer. He's been producing [music] for many, many years, like back when it was MS DOS, with the curved computer screen and the dial-up tones on the computer? And one day he brought home a CD-ROM for his music that he'd produced, and I said to him, 'Can I install this on my computer?' ... because I was *always* on the computer ... So I was just exposed to technology, electrical and sound, so I was exposed to all of that when I was younger.

My dad didn't really treat me like his daughter but in retrospect I'm very grateful for it. I think having exposure to technology and electricals and sounds and things when I was young gave me the space to drop down this kind of barrier towards it, so the longer you wait to do something the more resistance there is.

Genevieve, early career producer and DJ

Introduction

Our opening vignette for this chapter is from early-career producer and DJ Genevieve, telling me how she got into music production. Our interview conversation was quite late on in the In the Key project, and by then I had become used to hearing stories like these. I found it heart-warming how many parents and teachers were out there trying to break gender stereotypes and help their girls have different aspirations in life. But I also found it alarming that it seems to take a wholesale upheaval in parenting norms to inspire girls and women to take up electronic music production. How come making electronic music was so solidly associated with men and maleness that parents had to raise their daughters as if they were sons? Why can't girls be girls *and* do techie things?

In this chapter we are going to examine how these stereotypes show up in the world of music, music production and particularly music tech, and why they are so engrained in society and inside our individual heads. I'll also be showing the ameliorative work that women, trans and non-binary people are doing to disrupt these assumptions and how the future looks bright (pink).

Raised like a boy

'Personality-wise, I'm kind of like a guy,' Nelly joked, when we chatted about her entry into the music industry. But this was more than a joke – almost every person I interviewed told me a story about having a non-traditionally gendered upbringing in some way. This was the first pattern I noticed in my data and it didn't take long to emerge.[1] It usually took one of three forms (often within the same story) – either being a self-confessed 'tomboy' and hanging out with boys as a child; preferring and being encouraged in 'non-girly' childhood pursuits; and/or having one or more parent who actively transgressed traditional gender norms during their childhood.

Naomi's passion as a child was motorsport. She described herself as 'a bit of a tomboy' and told me how she was 'always out on motorbikes, [and] just always was involved in more male stuff' when she was growing up, as this was what she did with her dad. Likewise, as a child, Nancy told me she always wanted to be a Formula One racing driver. She wanted to challenge the fact that all she saw on her TV were men: 'I was watching all the racing car drivers, and going, why are they all guys? Why are there no girls doing that …?' She remembers always being very good with drills and building things and I got the impression she'd never really thought how 'unfeminine' (as she put it) all this was until our discussion. 'When I had my first car, I went on a car mechanic course so I wouldn't be one of these girls that couldn't change a tyre,' she told me. 'I've obviously got an energy there of, like, I can be a bloke if I want to, I don't want to be some helpless woman that needs a bloke to help her out.' Zara just 'wanted to be under the radar' as a teenager and told me 'the best way to, kind of, not draw attention was just to be more boyish, I guess, and in order to do that it just meant playing football every day'. Relatedly, Tess never understood why she was made to play football in a different team to the boys, just because she was a girl – something that made her increasingly angry as she grew up. 'I just always hung out with boys,' she explained, before adding '… weirdly'. She mused that perhaps this tomboy-ness meant that she hasn't found the technology or the 'bro culture' of electronic music as intimidating as others might. Words like 'tomboy', 'helpless', 'weird', 'unfeminine', and 'I can be a bloke' all show how deeply these gender stereotypes are rooted in Naomi, Nancy and Tess's psyches – in *all* of our psyches – because these words all indicate a belief that they have transgressed what's expected of them as girls in some way.[2] Dealing with feelings that you need to manage this constant transgression – that you are not the way you *ought* to be – is depleting ameliorative work.

Aysha told me she'd been a 'fan of technology from a very young age, building instruments and stuff from scratch', because she'd always seen her dad confidently and competently fixing things. 'I think it's in my DNA,' she said, '[my dad] always fixed things, no matter what it is. I kind of have that in me too, [and for] technical problems everyone calls on me, hey [Aysha], can you help me out here?' Mona was a self-confessed science nerd '… as a kid I used to ask for microscopes for birthdays and Christmas and stuff like that, like, building little circuits and stuff'. She connected this to the fact her father was a doctor and her mother an engineer, and she went on to study a degree in mechanical and electrical engineering herself.

It was mothers, rather than fathers, who played a major role for Carmen and Hayley. Carmen described her mum as 'a total revolutionary feminist in the 1970s', while Hayley explained she was 'raised by hippies', and especially her Mum. Carmen's mother steadfastly refused her young daughter's pleas for a doll and instead, Carmen reminisced, '… she'd just buy me cars all the time and tell me to build something out of a box. It drove me mad!' But as an adult, Carmen considered that her mum had been 'absolutely brilliant' for breaking her gendered play expectations. Carmen's mum also bought her a computer in the early 1980s, but not for playing games on, like everyone else. 'I got a Dragon 64 which you could only code on, so to make a pretty pattern I'd have to sit and write binary basically for about three hours'. Carmen is convinced this led her to realize that you could control computers to make beautiful things. From there it was a short step to computer-based music.

Hayley learned from her mother that '… you truly *can* do anything', which she was repeatedly told as a child. She credits this feminist determination as the reason why she stuck at music production, even though she didn't feel she had an aptitude for technology, and was the only woman on her course of about 250 men: 'I thought, this is *really* hard for me and this isn't natural, and actually I'm having a really difficult time of this. ... But had it been like 50/50 [gender split] or whatever, I would have been, like, this isn't for me. But because there were no women there, I was like *fuck this*, I *have* to learn this!'

This was not a typical response to being part of a tiny minority in the music classroom, with most of the people I spoke to commenting on how uncomfortable it was and not very conducive to either confidence or learning.[3] For artists who did not have access to stereotype-busting childhoods, the learning curve appeared to be very steep and difficult – for example, Rachel who found it hard to know how to begin self-teaching through watching YouTube videos, and Olga who spent weeks trying to learn how to use her DAW by sitting reading the manual on her own.

But even for girls raised by transgressive parents, or who felt 'naturally' drawn to male-coded pursuits and techie things, actively pursuing careers in these areas still felt hard. Hayley told me how she felt she would never have *naturally* gravitated to a production career from her roots as a classical pianist and composer because she didn't see role models there, which, as we have seen from earlier chapters, is the result of a range of factors that combine to keep minoritized genders hidden from view. 'I had never seen myself physically in that role, so it didn't even occur to me ...,' she explained. But because of her feminist upbringing she questioned this and thought '... what else am I subconsciously not even thinking I could be?!', which was one reason that spurred her on. Mona explained how, despite loving science as we saw earlier, the way her engineering degree was taught made it one of the hardest things she's ever had to do. Esther noted the importance of sheer determination too, and how overcoming inbuilt conditioning around gender bias is a conscious choice: '... *we* have to *choose* what women are doing in order to break the pattern,' she urged. This is perhaps the first kind of ameliorative work that new DJ/producers have to do – the 'catching up' work from simply not being a boy socialized into these kinds of activities. It is to this inbuilt conditioning that we turn next, looking at why music tech in particular has come to be seen as *so* masculine. As Olive commented to me during our interview: 'It's the fact that computers have traditionally been gendered as boys' toys, and girls have been separated from that, that playing on computers is a boys' activity from that primary age ... *that's* the thing that needs to be addressed.'

The gendering of music, technology and music technology

The way that music and technology have been constructed as male pursuits boils down to the way social power genders our bodies and their sensations.

Specifically, what we assume to be men's and women's skills are differently valued within what I call a 'gendered economy of the senses'.[4] Men and masculinity have long been associated with the so-called 'higher faculties' of sight and hearing because in antiquity, these were the ones associated with cerebral thought and even with presumed purity of the soul. This was because sight and hearing are the senses that most fool us into thinking we are separate from the world around us – because we cannot see light or soundwaves entering our bodies, these senses appear to give us an objective impression of a world 'out there'. Objectivity – that prize of cool rationality – was a masculine preserve.[5,6] Sensations associated more with flesh, such as smell and touch were deemed to be the domain of the messy, unpredictable and subjective bodies of women.[7] What we see and hear is 'out there' rather than experienced 'within' us, like taste or touch that require us to put things in our mouths or bring objects into contact with our skin in order to feel them.

The masculinization of sight and hearing thus provided the perfect justification for men to 'naturally' be better at ' "distance activities", such as traveling [sic] and governing, while women were made to stay at home'.[8] As anthropologist Constance Classen nicely puts it in her history of the gendering of the senses, 'men were deemed to use the sense of hearing to listen to weighty discourse and lectures, while women employed their hearing for frivolous gossip and love talk'.[9]

Hearing and sight were also regarded as senses that could be more or less faithfully reproduced through audio recording and photography, which further added to their status as objective faculties, and further aligned them with presumptions about masculine identity.[10] We can see this in the way manufacturers were quick to position women as passive consumers of the radio, interested only in its potential to bring the family together. Men, on the other hand, were targeted in advertising as the ones who would make the purchase and/or be interested in tinkering with the equipment once it arrived.[11] At the same time, this new industry in hi-fidelity music equipment in the 1950s (stereo systems, speakers and especially headphones), was sold as a way for the man of the house to carve out a space to enjoy high-quality music away from the hustle and bustle of the rest of the home.[12] As music researcher Helen Reddington notes in her book, this gendered marketing was supported by so-called 'expert' opinion claiming that women were not capable of properly understanding music beyond its capacity for surface entertainment.[13]

A sensory divide then emerges between women, whose primary concern is with the domestic, cohesive function of bringing the family together in everyday listening around the radio, and men, who are positioned as serious connoisseurs of refined audio, shutting themselves off in order to enjoy music. This feels like a pretty strong training for the hours of focused attention that we have seen is important in producing electronic music. This certainly holds true for my own socialization into loving music. Although from a young age I was transfixed by the smell of vinyl, and the dancing needles of the meters on the front of the amplifier,[14] my earliest memories of music recall that the expensive hi-fi equipment in our living room at home was very firmly my dad's domain. Sure, I was a young child to be kept away from fiddling with delicate and expensive things, but my mum also behaved very gingerly around it – in fact, I even recall that she had her own tape player that was separate from the main equipment. It wasn't until I was aged about 13 and given my own second-hand record deck as a Christmas present that I was free to play music as often as I liked – until then I had to ask if I could use 'Dad's stuff' and had very much learned to be afraid of turntables and records – my fear of scratching the record and damaging the player's stylus (needle), in particular. Nonetheless, I also absorbed information about what the 'graphic equalizer' did and how to adjust the sound coming out of the speakers (now shortened to 'EQing'). which I thought was super-cool. I was certainly seduced by these technologies, but there was also no doubt in my mind that *good quality* music equipment and technology in general was a man's thing. My grandfather went to night school in the 1950s to train as an electrical engineer and throughout my childhood, I witnessed him build an electric piano for my gran to play, and construct his own computer.[15] Before I was born, he even built a DIY TV, which is a firm fixture in our family's folklore. Although I felt free (and encouraged) to buy and *play* music, the 'high' end of audio stuff always felt out of bounds, and not just because it was expensive and 'delicate'.

As I grew into my music-obsessed teenage years, this was cemented by the fact that I only ever saw men (albeit effeminate ones) playing the synthesizers and drum machines in the electronic bands I loved. It was serious, nerdy, *achingly cool*, and in complete contrast to the frivolous pop and singing that I saw women engaging in. This didn't stop me desperately wanting a synthesizer[16] but I was also put off by the assumption that I needed to be able to play the piano to use one. I had given up music as a subject at school because we only learned about classical music composed by dead men, which was taught in such a *boring* way. No one had ever explained to me that synthesizers and drum machines were actually not that hard to use, didn't require musical training,[17] and that the keyboard was often just used as a trigger to make cool sounds. It never occurred to me to try and find out how they worked. I simply accepted that I would never be able to make electronic music because (a) I didn't play anything other than the recorder, (b) I couldn't read music and (c) it was all very firmly stuff that boys and men did – because that's who tech was for. In her lovely research into the gendering of music instruments, musicologist Veronica Doubleday reassuringly ratifies my teenage experiences when she says that 'it may be hard for girls even to *imagine* playing an instrument that is culturally assigned to males'.[18] That said, she does note that in nineteenth-century America the piano, harp and guitar were deemed appropriate for a woman to play because they all allowed her to keep her 'female allure' through the facial expressions they permitted. As long as women could smile sweetly and look gentle and pretty, the instrument was generally OK. However, the only really '*natural*' place for women in music-making was as singers, because of the voice's sensory origins within the flesh of body.[19] Hurrah! Finally something we are allowed to claim technical expertise over? Sadly, not. The very fact that singing relies on the *body*-as-instrument (rather than a complex bit of external technology) means that the skill involved in vocal performance is downplayed.[20] This has been echoed in electronic dance music culture, where tracks with female vocals – especially uplifting, more melodic ones – have traditionally been seen as 'girly' – so-called 'handbag house' – and less credible as artistic output.[21] So women *can* be skilled in that which involves their bodies, but the value of those skills is less than the technical prowess of men.[22] Music researcher Helen Reddington also notes how women's voices are subject to a process of ventriloquism as male studio engineers and other gatekeepers take control of how they sound in final recordings.[23]

This all plays out in relation to the kinds of music projects that men and women get involved in producing, as music education researcher Victoria Armstrong explains: 'Male composers are the do-ers and creators of large-scale works – works that require significant technological knowledge of instrumentation and compositional technique. Women, on the other hand, are historically associated with small-scale works (such as songs and works for solo instruments) intended for relatively private, domestic performance outlets, and these are considered not to require such extensive technical knowledge.'[24]

So, where do all these associations and assumptions come from?

The gendering of music and music-technology is part of a broader pattern where men dominate fields of science, technology, engineering and mathematics (STEM) and allied subjects. According to the UNESCO Global Education Monitoring Report in 2024, only 35 per cent of STEM graduates are women, which hasn't changed in ten years.[25] Figures for female participation in STEM careers are as low as 16 per cent in Japan and 14 per cent in India, despite these countries being seen as tech powerhouses.[26] Women hold only 26 per cent of the (highly paid and prestigious) jobs in AI and related disciplines, meaning that they have little say in how the algorithms are developed that are increasingly coming to define our day-to-day experience through digital platforms. Stop reading now and search

Google Images for 'electronic music producer' or ask an AI image generator to show you what a DJ playing to a crowd looks like, and you will see what I mean. Overwhelmingly male, overwhelmingly white. Technology and its artefacts are not neutral and in the following sections I'll give a brief overview of how that's come to be, a story that starts with biology and society's enduring association of cis women with the reproductive capacities of their bodies.

Until fairly recently cis-gendered women had little control over their reproductive lives and, indeed, in many parts of the world this is *still* not available to women living in poverty, practising certain religions, or living under anti-abortion regimes. Cis women spent – and in some places continue to spend – much of their lives either pregnant, giving birth or breastfeeding. As breastfeeding was a crude form of birth control, because a new pregnancy is less likely to occur while a woman is lactating, mothers fed their babies very regularly. Women's firm association with their bodies thus tied them closely to the domestic sphere, living private lives, behind closed doors, while men went off unencumbered to explore, fight, debate, invent, build nations and take up space in the public domain.[27] In short, women were excluded because it's hard to take up public office, study, engage in research or do anything much at all when a baby is attached to your breast.[28] While child-rearing is now much less prominent in many women's lives, the associations with domesticity and the private realm endure and the stereotypes remain.

Importantly, all of this reproductive and domestic labour was, and still is, vastly undervalued in comparison to 'men's work' and is seen as inferior, despite the considerable skills required to manage a home, family, village, and so on.[29] In order to cement this position, men of science went to great lengths to prove that women were 'only' fit for domestic and family pursuits because their *brains* were made differently, which was why they were certainly not suited to the things men wanted to keep to themselves. These ideas have never really gone away with the 'brain differences' hypotheses continuing to manifest in contemporary neuroscience, as I noted in Chapter 6.[30] Given how ostensibly visible and *valuable* men's pursuits were (colonizing foreign lands, discovering scientific breakthroughs, running countries, waging wars and so on), the line between 'different' and 'inferior' becomes almost non-existent. Women were prevented from studying at universities, holding public office, being in control of their own financial affairs, owning property, voting and so on[31] because it would be an utter waste to allow them access to these institutions on account of their second-class brains – so the argument went. Yet these are all the things that are necessary in order to realize one's potential in education, as a scientist, inventor, entrepreneur, politician, public figure and, of course, performing musician. Without access to these resources, women's position as intellectually inferior when it comes to science, technology, engineering and mathematics becomes self-fulfilling, and the achievements they *did* realize were brushed under the carpet.[32] The legacy of this is still stark today, visible in the gendered character of STEM subjects where we began this section.

Impacts of the 'masculine coding' of music tech

In his book on popular music and digital technology, cultural sociologist Nick Prior nicely summarizes the cumulative effect of the historical gendering of technology and experiences like the ones I described earlier from my own childhood. Electronic music's 'identification [with] gadgets seen as "boys' toys" and hegemonic masculinity is a potent sociological force that marginalizes women's presence and participation … in the studio, as well as consumer magazines, in the instruments industry, … Internet forums, in the classroom as well as the music shop.'[33] Conversely, and more positively, the stories that I opened this chapter with show how with some crafty and skilful deliberately transgressive parenting, this marginalization can be greatly reduced. But this needs to follow through into formal education, beginning with the school classroom.

Learning and education

The first impact of the cultural biases and associations outlined earlier results in girls and women actively opting out of music tech education at a young age, for example, the most recent figures (2022) show that only 25 per cent of the students enrolling on A-Level music technology courses in the UK are female.[34] In 2020, Jude Brereton, an academic music researcher from the University of York, and her colleagues published a comprehensive round-up of facts and figures about women's participation in music-related education.[35] In their own survey of 57 girls in UK secondary school education (aged 13–18) who were currently engaged in some kind of music practice already, they found that although over 80 per cent had heard of the role of 'music producer', less than 40 per cent of the girls were interested in a future career in that area. The numbers for engineering-related roles were way smaller – only 4 per cent were interested in audio engineering and 7 per cent in the role of mixing engineer. Indeed, the researchers found that only half of the girls were interested in a future career in the music industry *at all* – which the researchers put down to off-putting perceptions of the music business. For my step-daughter, this aversion was an actual, physical recoiling when I asked her, aged 14, if she'd like me to show her how to use my DJ decks. When I held out my headphones to her as she walked past where I'd set my equipment up in the living room, she actually swerved her torso and made a face 'Oh God! No thanks …,' she responded, clearly repelled. Her eyes were wide as she turned away from the equipment as if avoiding something of great danger.

This is not just confined to young women either. Nancy, a long-standing DJ told me: 'I still don't know what half the buttons do on my DJ mixer. It's a girl thing, isn't it?' She laughed, before explaining, '… you're just scared of buttons and getting it wrong and making a mistake and effing it up, and then, err, how do I turn it off again?' This is in part to do with the appearance of the equipment, as I will explore further in the next section, but it's also a result of what academic-musician Mavis Bayton calls the 'socially manufactured physical, mechanical and technical helplessness'[36] that girls learn from a young age.[37] Evidence of this was given to me by several of my participants who were involved in education. Lauren, a producer and teacher who runs music workshops for primary-school-age children, observed this pattern: 'It tends to be the girls want to sing or play the keyboards, and the boys want to do drums – they want to do more of the *noise* making, and try the synthesizer. They are not afraid of all the buttons.' Evelyn, a veteran of the industry, ran DJ workshops for young adults and explained to me what she observed:

> … the boys could almost not wait for you to finish what you were saying, they just wanted to jump on the kit and play. Whereas the women were totally different … they would listen to you, listen to what the kit is, what the buttons do, the cross fader, the up faders, or the EQ, before they touched anything.

Likewise, Hayley, who runs music production bootcamps for women and gender-expansive people alongside her own career as an artist, sees this as something that it's necessary to overcome: 'just touching the buttons is the hardest part but that's how you're going to learn … it's like almost like there's a precious …,' she trailed off as she tried to find the right words, 'like, some kind of unwritten rule, or even like, the stuff is going to burn you if you touch it?!' Suzie, a newer producer, explained this as a process of 'unlearning what you've always been told, you know? Don't touch, be a good girl, that sort of thing. You've got to forget all that and push through it.' Part of this can be attributed to a more general ethic of bravado and 'swagger' when learning music technology, as musician and educator Isobel Anderson explains in her podcast.[38] She calls for a normalization of making mistakes and experimentation that would make it less risky for everyone to just have a go – removing the fear of mucking things up.

Language

As Mavis Bayton notes in her discussion of women and the electric guitar, women's aversion to 'the kit' of music production is often reinforced by 'technical language [which] is often used as a power strategy in a mystifying way to exclude women'.[39] Of course, every branch of science, and every activity, has its own technical language that is necessary to convey specific attributes of the process. But the way technical terms are bandied around as if anyone who is anyone already knows what they mean is how technical language becomes a tool of exclusion. Victoria Armstrong's studies of behaviours in music education classrooms shows how this starts young, with teachers simply using more technological and computing terms with boys than girls.[40] Isobel Anderson also discusses how emphasis on technical terminology and software processes in the classroom eclipses the *artistry* of music production which tends to lead to formulaic and uninspiring compositions from everyone, regardless of gender.[41]

The terminology was something that I found particularly difficult to penetrate when I started learning to DJ, let alone produce music. It was a foreign language. How can you teach yourself how to use equipment when you don't even understand the words that are used in the instructions? Simple things like 'gain', for example. What was a 'gain knob'? When I twiddled it, it turned the volume up but for ages I was under the illusion that it must be doing something subtly different because *surely* gain couldn't be as simple as just how loud the music played? But that's exactly what it is. Gain is just another word for volume – a 'science-y' one that refers to the accumulation of audio signal. But because no one tells you this, you don't know, feel stupid, and are very reluctant to ask about it, assuming, of course, that you actually have someone to ask. And once we get into music production itself? Sheesh, that really is a different land of side-chaining, knee-hard compressors, gates, envelopes, mud, limiters and all manner of geeky stuff.[42] Importantly, it's not actually *that* hard to learn once someone explains it to you, but the smoke and mirrors around it all are convincing. At the same time, audio engineering terms, for me at least, are highly seductive because, despite being unfamiliar and anxiety-provoking, they are quite frankly, very cool.[43] And that's what you want to be too, but it feels a million miles away because you are constantly reminded that you are an interloper, and you don't fit the music producer mould in body, mind, action, or in what you see and hear about music producers and music production.[44]

Using gendered pronouns to routinely refer to music producers as men, guys, bros, and so on, is a case in point. It is a constant reinforcement that anyone not using the pronouns he/him is excluded from the conversation, as I explained back in Chapter 1. Nelly also pointed out how women – historically at least – tend to be labelled in sexualized or patronizing ways in promotional materials for events and music releases: 'I played an all-female event recently and I actually had a word with the promoter as they used some language that was a bit too gimmicky for me,' she explained. 'They meant well, but I had to speak to them and say, "You've got to change that". Because you don't see *The lovely Carl Cox* and *The sexy Paul van Dyk* on flyers, do you?'

But language is also gendered more subtly. Electronic music is full of metaphors that smack of fight, physical force and aggressiveness. Tracks are referred to as 'bangers', or 'bombs', and line-ups are 'killer' or 'fire'. DJs playing together have 'battles', and good performance as a DJ is described as 'smashing' your set. In production, bass is referred to as 'pumping', sounds 'attack' and are 'gnarly, twisted and fucked up', and finalizing the track – the final skilled finesse – is called 'mastering'. While we need to be careful to associate these kinds of words with masculinity per se, they do have connotations of testosterone-fuelled blokey-ness. Many of the names of music production equipment also have a whiff of 'Grrrr!' about them too: software synthesizers called 'Massive', 'Maschine' and 'Collision', virtual studio plug-ins named 'Infiltrator' and 'Decapitator', 'kill' switches for removing bass on DJ mixers, and so on. Even the less obviously gendered words like 'Omnisphere', 'Blackhole', 'Ozone' and 'Antares' are overtly futuristic in tone (no doubt to signify their cutting-edge programming), which is resonant of sci-fi geeks – who are, of course, archetypally male.[45]

The impression of the equipment

Names aside, the things themselves – both in software and hardware versions – look like deadly serious futuristic machines full of complicated-looking knobs, sliders and dials, and are overwhelmingly black in colour. The kaleidoscopic range of equipment, gadgets and *stuff* – and importantly how it looks – is a major contributor to the maintenance of the assumption that tech is 'not for girls.' Quite simply, these objects do not look like things women would own and operate, or that anyone could be *playful* with. After my grandpa died, my gran installed a handmade curtain of floral material to cover up her home entertainment equipment because it was ugly and 'manly', and I would suggest that my step-daughter was repelled by my DJ equipment primarily because of the associations she had about the way it looked. This was also noted by the artists I interviewed who worked as music educators as I mentioned previously.

Sharon explained to me the effect of this on her own career. One of the first women DJs in her scene, she had spent years working with engineers, as we saw in Chapter 6, before learning how to self-produce her own music, mainly because of the way it came across to her:

> Twenty-four years ago, you can imagine going into a massive big studio, and there's producers in there, all boys in there, and there's all these buttons so you're like, wow, what do these actually do? Cos you used to go into the studios and think that you've got to have the whole kit, all this and that …. you'd have to have that synth over there, and that synth, and there's like 30 or 40 thousand pounds' worth of stuff. That's

where it was at 20 years ago, and now it's like Ableton, couple of little lessons and off you go. I thought it was going to be a lot harder than it is, I probably should have started earlier really …

The impression that the aesthetic of music tech gave to Sharon, coupled with the engineering-heavy, masculine language that surrounds it, is a strong signal that this world is not for women and girls, or indeed anyone who lacks the socialization to feel comfortable with technology. And what's significant here is that because of this impression, many of the producers I spoke to thought music production was going to be *too hard* before they even tried it. Once they had a go, however, they realized it wasn't anywhere near as terrifying as they imagined, at least not at a basic level. But that's not the message that the world of music tech communicates.

This was certainly my experience the first time I opened up Ableton on my laptop, which is the DAW I use, and thought 'Ugh, where do I start?', but after my first lesson I was blown away by the sounds I could create and how familiar and intuitive the software felt.[46] I was used to using the Apple programmes GarageBand and iMovie for podcast and video production, and many of the concepts and actions were the same[47] – I was learning that I didn't really need to know all about the complicated audio-engineering terms and ideas in order to make some pretty decent-sounding music – to me at least! I *was* super keen to learn about synthesis, compression, MIDI, audio effects and so on, and felt that this would be absolutely necessary for me to feel like a 'proper' music producer (more about that in Chapter 8 when we look at confidence), but what's significant here is that these things are seen as a barrier to entry if you have been raised to regard technology as something that is not for you.

As so many of the controls on the software are automated and intuitive, to begin with I was encouraged to just play around with things and hear how they sounded as I changed settings and twisted virtual dials with my mouse. As we saw earlier, that doesn't usually come naturally to women and gender-expansive people who have not been brought up to actively experiment with things, and it certainly felt uncomfortable for me. I wanted to know what everything did and how to use it before I even moved a single dial, as we saw earlier with Olga, who read the entire Ableton manual before she even sat down to use the software. But several of the elements from my track 'Keep Your Disdance', featured in Chapter 2, were the result of just playing about and thinking 'ooh yeah, I like that!' as I experimented with various controls. It didn't actually matter that I had no idea what I did or how to do it again – although that was, of course, frustrating! Tyla, an early-stage producer whose career was really taking off when we spoke also described her 'have-a-go' attitude, something which several of the artists I interviewed talked about doing in the long days of the COVID-19 lockdowns because they were not able to go out playing DJ gigs:

I just thought, well, 'how hard can it be?' [laughs] kind of naive, *so* naive, But also, the less you know about something, the better. Cos when you know more, you're like, oh my god, I've bitten off way more than I can chew here and I'm never going to be up there with those guys that I've been aspiring to be like for years.

So perhaps it's only in the over-thinking of whether you're 'doing it right' that you feel the sting of your outsider-ness. It's only when you lift your head from being absorbed in what you're making – from having fun playing about – that the canon of gendered convention fires at you with full force.

So, what are women doing to fight back and change the tune?

But this is meant to be a story of hope and positivity, right? We've heard quite enough about the problems, so let's shift to appreciating how are women and gender-expansive producers are pushing back against the bias, and changing the tune around music technology.

Showing up as a producer and a woman

Sarah Sommers – aka 'The Bimbo Princess' – does this better than anyone else I have seen in this industry. A live techno artist from Berlin, Sarah's dedication to her aesthetic is utterly astounding. She has customized every single aspect of her (very) technical set-up in hot pink and 'girly' motifs, dismantling the interfaces, spraying the pieces pink, and applying decals.[48] Sarah herself is the epitome of hyper-femininity, with a curtain of long blonde hair, manicured fingernails, tight pink clothing and skyscraper heels. If Barbie made music producer dolls (which in fact they do) then Sarah Sommers would be the living version.[49]

Sarah forcefully shows how masculine-coded music tech is. Because we are not used to seeing racks of synthesizers, drum machines, mixing desks and keyboards in neon pink and spattered with sparkles and unicorns, it forces us to question the ways things more usually are when we see videos of music producers online – hetero- and cis-typical dudes in jeans and T-shirts in front of a sea of black, sombre, serious gear. Things associated with little girls are generally pink, sparkly, saccharine-sweet and involve baby animals or people. It's cutesy, trivial, frivolous and, above all, definitely not serious play at all. It's for these reasons that so many people detest this aesthetic – we train our little girls to be all of those things when we buy them this crap, so the argument goes. But why should such flights of fancy and playfulness be derided as more trivial than the boys' action toys, guns and sports-themed playthings?

'What's *wrong* with having gendered preferences??' lamented Emma, during what I'd best describe as an impassioned rant. 'There's *absolutely nothing wrong* with having those gendered likes, and if you can use tech within that? Use the two together? That's really cool. I don't think we should look down on it, and that does happen to a lot of women's interests – they're never deemed as worthy.' Emma works for a music tech company and we were talking about devising music-making toys that would appeal to girls. Our conversation took place just after International Women's Day (8 March, in the UK), and she was describing how a company she follows had posted some Instagram content about computer programmable charms for bracelets for girls to learn coding. However, because they were pink, plastic, probably sparkly, and hyper-feminine, there had been a backlash in the comments, as she explained. 'Some people, mostly men actually, were like "this is really lame! It shouldn't be so gendered! Women just don't want to do all this [tech stuff]", and I was like, to be honest when I was a five-year-old I'd have bloody loved it.'

I would contend that not only is there nothing wrong with smuggling in tech using traditionally feminine associations, but that it is essential to do so. It's the only way we are going to debunk the enduring myth that tech is not something that girls can, or want to, do. Carmen, a producer, singer and certified music-tech trainer deliberately resisted toning down her hyper-feminine aesthetic for this very reason. She explained to me that she is on a mission to 'put the glamour into geek' and to show that you can be attractive and conventionally 'sexy' in your self-presentation and still be an excellent technical practitioner.[50]

Mona also took this approach: 'I admit that when I DJ I probably dress in a more "provocative" way but that's because I like to,' she explained. 'When I see these criticisms of people dressing in a provocative way, they only centre on *women*, and for me it stems from this misogynistic viewpoint that you can't be all, like you can't be talented, you can't be beautiful, you can't be intelligent, like it has to be one or the other.' The complexities of this appearance – authority/sexy/credible – dynamic are well laid out by the cultural critic Mary Ann Sieghart (2021) in relation to politicians. She sets out the exasperating intricacies of how anyone apart from cis men has to navigate a constantly moving set of expectations about what it is and is not appropriate to look like in their role. This necessitates inordinate amounts of effort, time and expense in curating *just* the right look, buying and wearing *just* the right clothes, which is all ameliorative work men never have to do. Mona summed this up angrily: 'Yes, I dress in a sexy way when I DJ, but I also have an engineering degree and I also am a sick DJ, so *don't you dare* tell me what I can and cannot do.'

Carmen explains what the payoff is of showing up as her sexy, feminine self, and how her technical knowledge actually insulates her from getting hit on: '… you start talking about compressor ratios and that kind of thing, and they're like, 'My God! she actually really knows what she's talking about!' So very quickly you're disarming a situation that may have potentially gone dodgy.'

Likewise, Grace explains that once cis men realize that you know your stuff, they are more readily accepting of you:

> The majority of time if you are a girl and you walk into a studio and you explain that you sing and write and produce, as soon as you say 'produce', like, no one takes you seriously, they just look at you and they're, like, 'Ohhh, *you* really produce?'. [but if] we start our dialogue off from the nerdy music-production side, it's not like that, it's very much, like, 'Oh yeah? Let's get into this!', it's very, like, equal when it starts from there.

This is a heartening counterbalance to some of the side-effects of putting yourself out there in this way that we will see in the next chapter, such as unwanted sexual advances (or worse), microaggressions and mansplaining.

In sum, showing up unapologetically as a woman will challenge the situation that Victoria Armstrong puts forward: that girls only don't want to engage with music tech because most 'techie' things transgress their developing feminine identities – or at the very least don't affirm them in the same way that technology and being a gadget geek affirms masculine identities.[51] Dismantling the whole pink, sparkly, unicorns-and-princesses, ponies-and-dollies assault on girlhood is far too big a project for the music tech business to tackle alone, so why not use it for advantage as Sarah Sommers does? The Bimbo Princess is successful, living proof that music tech and computer programming can be pink and sparkly *and* that you can make tougher, more industrial techno sounds with it.

Making music technology less masculine

> I think a lot about how all these programmes and these machines – I mean literally all of them – are made by men, and I do think that there is a difference in how [men and women] intake information … and I think it's going to be easier for people who are like the people who are making this gear to learn it.

This is Hayley, an artist who teaches women and gender-expansive people how to use music tech. Her words confirm what researchers have also found to be true: that men more readily sequence, use logical steps, and control processes in music production than women, who prefer more expressive, faster routes to making nice-sounding music and learn through dialogue and social interaction.[52] Nathalie explained this nicely in her account of how she worked with sound: 'I like melodies and I like to feel different sounds playing with each other and *communicating* somehow.' In contrast, generally, men's preferred ways of engaging with music making are rooted in engineering and mathematics and greatly favour the digital approach of step-by-step programming.[53] It stands to reason, then, that if men design the software and machines in the ways they like to execute tasks, it will be harder for anyone else to become proficient because they are going against the ways they have been socialized to want to learn. As we saw in Chapter 6 through feminist psychologist Cordelia Fine's work, over time our environments and repetitive behaviours wire in new neural pathways which result in physical brain changes that are passed on in our genes. It is not inaccurate to say that men and women's brains like to learn differently – but this is because of the experiences they have had, which includes the equipment they have had to learn to use. This all takes up additional time and energy for those who don't fit the mould. Heather told me, 'I have been putting in twice the hours, in my own time, to learn the basics – you know just to know how to work the stuff?' She was laughing as she spoke, but also hanging her head in frustration. Evelyn also recognized this, explaining how 'it just takes us longer … to just really focus in and just almost like *drill* into learning this stuff, probably because the software is made by men. It's men making software that we then have to get *our* heads round – *if women were making software it would be different*. This is not something that the cis-male owners of music tech companies I spoke to had ever thought of before – they simply regarded it as neutral, until I gently pointed out that might be their gender bias colouring their judgement.[54]

Asking 'What would women-made music technology be like?' is an interesting thought experiment, and one that I generated some views on from the producers I interviewed. While most couldn't conceive what such a thing would look like, many nonetheless recounted preferences for technologies that allowed them to be, first and foremost, expressive in their music making. 'I'm more interested in the creative process,' Lauren, an artist who was also a music tech educator told me: 'I just fall in love with sounds and things that make sounds [the tech] are just the route to that.' Others cited things like 'the groove', adding 'swing', and other words to describe the emotional tone of the tracks they wanted to make, which supports Isobel Anderson's call to return to artistry in music teaching as we saw previously. During an introduction to music production workshop I attended, Olga instructed us to randomly 'click things in' to the MIDI pattern,[55] such as high-hat sounds and other percussive elements, to over-ride the way the software encourages you to be regular or regimental in your placing of sounds. This is a technique I now use regularly in my own music production, clicking in a string of random triggers for the sound and then removing the ones I don't like later. These freer, less constrained and organic preferences were very much about returning to the body in music making – something which, as we saw earlier, has traditionally excluded women from being seen as natural electronic music producers.[56]

During our conversation Lauren went on to explain how she was 'very drawn to a more tactile approach to music sound making'. She told me: 'I need to get my head out of the screen and go back to just something tactile and tangible to feel inspired.' Likewise, when talking about her creative process, Dana told me she definitely preferred to use hardware, such as drum machines and keyboards, rather than click triggers and notes into software with her mouse because it allowed her to impart 'natural swing' to her music more easily. 'If I use the machines,' she told me, 'it feels different … more straightforward, more organic, in a way?' This was despite her style of music (techno) being very firmly based on a quantized, highly regular, four–four beat which doesn't necessarily *need* any 'swing' to it. Music researchers Sharon Jagger and Helen Turner heard this from their interviews with studio producers too – that women artists gravitated towards what they called 'the softer technologies' and avoid the harder ones.[57] These accounts very much chime with Victoria Armstrong's observations in the music classroom that girls preferred music-making methods that allowed them to express their musicality rather than spending their time learning (what they regarded as) complicated software to compose their pieces. It was like the computer got in the way of their emotional expression and musical ideas in ways that didn't happen for the boys who fully embraced the computer as a tool of composition. Tara Rodgers, who wrote one of the first book-length collections of women's experiences with electronic music, *Pink Noises*, has a monthly newsletter where she declares 'an interest in describing music technology in ways that are tender and speculative'.[58] These are not words we are used to hearing in this field.

'Tender and speculative': expressive interfaces

Interface design is an important strand of the development of music tech. This branch of the industry is concerned with how the musician engages with the technologies of synthesis and related attributes that ultimately produce electronic music. In particular, 'expressive interfaces' enable intuitive connections between the musician's aesthetic emotions and the generation of sound through control mechanisms that use bodily movements and even gestural commands. Kim Bjørn's gorgeous coffee-table book *Push Turn Move: Interface Design in Electronic Music* explores expressive interfaces in-depth, reminding us that they are not actually new, and that they have long been associated with women's electronic music-making. The Theremin is a classic example from the 1920s: music is produced through subtle movements of hands and fingers around two antennae and almost half the virtuoso Theremin players are women.[59]

Another way to quite literally get a grip on your music making is by wearing MiMU gloves: gestures from arms, hands and fingers wirelessly map to MIDI through 17 integrated sensors that free artists to freely perform on stage, rather than run between machines.[60] But, as a MiMU ambassador told me, they allowed her to make music with all her senses in the studio too, 'from my hands to your ears,' she said. Once again, MiMU was the brainchild of a woman – Imogen Heap – who assembled a tech team around her to bring her ideas to life.

It was through an expressive technology conference panel that I met Grace, who I later interviewed about her experiences using (at the time) a revolutionary piece of kit that uses 'MIDI polyphonic expression' (MPE) to translate subtle changes in your touch into aural effects that affect the character of the note that is being played – for example delay, volume, pitch, sustain, reverb, and so on:

> I thought how synaesthesically pleasing it felt, and just felt really overwhelmed by how many dimensions of touch and sounds you'd get just from one finger, and a little wobble just triggers like a completely different movement of a sound.

I had the pleasure of playing around with this instrument in the 'Gear Lab' at Amsterdam Dance Event (ADE) in 2019. Without needing to know any technical details about what I was doing, the movements of my fingertips turned into musical expression intuitively, depending on how I wanted it to sound as I felt my way around the surface of the device.

These are just some examples of emerging 'tactile' and 'gesturally responsive' music technologies that do not look or behave so much like traditional, masculine coded music tech.[61] As a learner I was certainly drawn to play with them because they just didn't look so threatening and complex. Indeed, Hayley – a user of MPE technologies – saw them as an extension of her gender, explaining how she found them 'very intuitive … how you touch it is going to be how it responds, and that to me has like some sort of, like, feminine intuition about it'. This is all a far cry from the rest of the horribly complicated-looking black boxes on the display stands around me in the ADE Gear Lab that produced the same repelling effect in me as my DJ decks had done in my step-daughter.

Expressive interfaces have the potential to bypass traditional 'click and code' ways of writing electronic music into a DAW that can feel inaccessible to women and gender-expansive producers for all or any of the reasons I've discussed in this chapter. Indeed, traditional mainstream music technology has been shown to be racially biased too, because the code and features have the unconscious aesthetic preferences of their creators baked into their architecture.[62] For example, tuning mechanisms are based on 'equal temperament' – a system that underpins European music based on the keys of a piano, but cannot account for the microtonality of music from other cultures, such as those of Arabic countries, Turkey and India. Likewise, the regular 'grid system' of DAWs and, indeed, digital music players used for DJing have a hard time dealing with the irregular percussive beats of African rhythms. It turns out that technology has been able to account for these things since the early 1990s, but because the designers were from Europe and North America they never saw a need for these features, and argued there was no demand.[63] Expressive interfaces are also democratizing in other ways too, for example MiMU gloves have also opened up production to disabled artists because the gloves detect and learn the user's unique gestural patterns. Artists are no longer limited to actions and gestures that their bodies find it difficult or impossible to perform.[64]

Mainstream music tech companies are only just beginning to realize that they may have a potential market of users who appreciate more accessible features. Emma told me a great story about how this plays out in the simplest way for women DJs:

> We did some user tests on DJ mixers and we had [female DJ] from London on the test, and she said, 'Oh, I like where the buttons are because I can use it without having to lean forward so my top doesn't fall down.' And then it was, like, 'This one works really well with my fake nails, I can touch it really easily.' Wow, my mind was blown, this is what happens when you speak to different types of users.

Kallie Marie and one of her interviewees, Andrea Yankovsky, speak of similar design bias in relation to studio mixing desks that are simply too big for them to reach without bending over.[65] The two studio producers describe how having to lean right over the desk makes them vulnerable to unwanted innuendo or groping from behind, and potentially exposes their breasts when viewed from the front – unless they wear 'turtleneck' sweaters. As we saw in Chapter 3, sexism is literally built into the system.

It is disappointing, then, that these devices (and software) don't appear to be particularly successful. Equipment that takes account of differently gendered bodies, is intuitive to operate, and seems to favour feminine ways of making music rarely gets beyond 'niche geek' status and into the mainstream. The device I played with at ADE was discontinued a year after my encounter with it, although the company continued with the variant that resembles a more traditional keyboard. This is probably because it was more familiar to established producers, who we know from Chapter 2 are predominantly cis-gendered men. But while it is disappointing, it is perhaps unsurprising that expressive technologies have not proved popular because it is still men who buy the vast majority of music tech gadgets and these more expressive gadgets don't support masculine music-production identities. This is precisely *because* they are seen as 'feminine technologies'.

Conclusion: Decoding music tech as boys' toys

Associations of technology with masculinity are deeply entrenched which means that for now, it's likely to be true that 'girls just aren't into tech.' Yet. But changing the status quo is only likely to happen when a critical mass of more diverse people enter the industry and push on several fronts. Firstly, the technology itself needs to be – or perceived as – less blokey. This is most likely to happen when it is not only cis men designing things, as we have seen with Imogen Heap's MiMU gloves, and which Hayley summarizes here:

> It'll take a while for a woman to really know her stuff to work her way up into the system before changes will be made to the design of these things. But in order to do that we first have to start educating the women young, who then will get into this space and will then grow up to be the people that make it.

Educating those women and gender-expansive people 'young' is, of course, a challenge when the equipment, language and culture around electronic music production is so masculine, but as we shall see in the next chapter, great strides are being made by initiatives in training, developing and supporting women, trans and non-binary artists in ways that demystify the skills and technology needed to be a good producer. It's also important that women, trans and non-binary people are encouraged to show up as themselves in the industry – like, for example, Sarah Sommers, Carmen and Mona, who unashamedly link technical prowess with femininity. From my interview data, and other industry research too, this seems most likely to happen when parents actively socialize their children in feminist ways and schools pay more attention to the gendered dynamics of their music classrooms and curricula. We all have a part to play in helping dismantle the myth that 'girls just aren't into tech'. Perhaps they're not, but that's almost certainly because nobody told them they could be.

Chapter track: 'Therapist Drift'

'Therapist Drift' was my first techno release, as part of DeepDownDirty Records' 2021 compilation of 'acid-inspired' tracks that they put out to celebrate '303 Day' on 3 March each year. The Roland TB-303 was a synthesizer released in 1981 and designed to emulate the sounds of bass guitars. It did this so badly that the company discontinued it just

Figure 7: Artwork for *Acid Vol 3* compilation featuring 'Therapist Drift' by Dovetail, reproduced with kind permission by DeepDownDirty Records

Source: https://www.beatport.com/track/therapist-drift/14855464

three years later. However, it was very good at making other-worldly squelchy sounds that caught the attention of early dance music producers who could easily buy cheap TB-303s secondhand. The sound of the TB-303 is iconic of early acid house music and people have been using those sounds in their music ever since. I don't own a TB-303 but I do have some software plug-ins for my DAW that make similar noises – so I decided to use one to write and produce 'Therapist Drift' for *DeepDownDirty Acid Vol 3* that label boss and incredible champion for underground dance music (and women) Maya Stone had invited me to be part of.

The reason that I have chosen this track for this chapter is that I didn't have a clue how to operate the plug-ins (which were given to me by a friend) and so I had to muddle my way through, overcoming my gendered reticence to tinkering with settings without knowing what would happen. While I was pondering how to manipulate a sound in the breakdown of the track (the quieter section that slows the energy before building back up to when the bass and kick drum comes back in – 'the drop'), unbeknown to me I had leaned on my laptop and, using a keyboard shortcut I didn't know existed, had stretched the parameters of the sound I was working with to extreme proportions. I panicked as I tried to undo what I'd done, but then listened to it, with delight. It sounds absolutely amazing when played in a club, and it's a great example of how important it is to just experiment, not know what you're doing and make 'creative mistakes'!

8

Women Just Need to Be More Confident

Change the Beat

> Nobody wants to look at all-male line-ups any more. And the only way that that is going to change is by diversifying the record labels, because the record labels are how you get known as an artist. So, if all the record labels are just signing men, then the line-ups are going to be all men because when the labels throw the parties, they can legitimately say 'Well, you know, we only put our producers on the line-up, and women don't send us their music so …' Not having diverse artists on record labels is the root of the problem. Everybody needs to put in the work and everybody needs to make music, that's the way you succeed as an *artist*.
>
> Sydney Blu, Founder of Change the Beat

Change the Beat is the brainchild of veteran DJ and producer Sydney Blu. 'I wanted to start a campaign to increase representation on record labels of women and gender-expansive artists, which is currently something ridiculous like 5 per cent,' she told me during our radio show interview in 2023. 'But I wanted to do something that would be an *actual activation* and not just talk. So, we're doing this through remix competitions which are amazing … we're giving all these women an opportunity to remix the songs by big labels. A lot of these labels, they want to diversify, but they keep saying they never get any demos sent to them by women, trans and non-binary producers, so they're collaborating with us and we're assisting them with A&R and signing music from more diverse artists.'

This is a hard-hitting campaign including global record labels like Hospitality, Anjuna, Desert Hearts, Mau5trap and Drumcode, and the opportunity for *anyone* who does not identify as a cis male to remix music by A-list artists like Nicole Moudaber and Eli & Fur. The initiative has been so successful that it was awarded prestigious support from global online music store Beatport's 'Diversity and Parity Fund' in 2024. As of February 2025, Change the Beat have run 28 competitions attracting thousands of entrants, and 84 winners taking first, second or third place. Most of those tracks have been signed to the record label sponsoring the contest, and most of those have been the producers' first major signing.

To enter, you first join a Discord group which now stands at over a thousand members. 'They have conversations about how they got into the business, what they're doing to further their careers and then one of them might help the other out and vice versa,' Sydney told me. It's this community that's at the heart of Change the Beat, and what it shows is that women and gender-expansive artists *will* send their music to record labels and they *do* have the desire to put themselves forward for opportunities. That community has now sparked Change the Beat's evolution into showcase events, mentorship and education initiatives.

Introduction

If I had to sum up the advice for gender-expansive and women producers I've heard over the years it would be this: 'Just be more confident.' The courage and ability to take a deep breath, put on your big girl panties and go out there and do your thang is a message that rings loud and clear through all the initiatives I've encountered, podcasts I've listened to and interviews I've carried out. Abi, the founder of a collective for women and gender-expansive DJs sums this up as her organization's main mission:

> we teach people to have the confidence to do gigs, get exposure, do radio shows, and feature in our [online] mix series as well, which then connects people with people in other countries. And I guess just once the confidence is within someone, they then can like go out there and be like, 'Actually I *can* do this, and I *want* to do this!', and they can envision themselves on line-ups, and whatever ...

In a similar vein to Change the Beat, Abi's collective aims to address what is widely considered to be a lack of confidence among women and minoritized genders in music – and is the reason why these artists are notoriously bad at putting themselves and their music forward for opportunities, as we shall see later. In this chapter we'll turn the tables on this myth and ask a question to spark a more reparative reading instead: 'What is it about the environment that is so confidence *draining*?' A great example of this is the 'She Said So' networking breakfast that runs every year at Brighton Music Conference (BMC) in the UK. Nikki McNeil, lead for the She Said So Brighton chapter, organizes an early-morning 90-minute meet-up with coffee and pastries each day so that women, trans and non-binary delegates at the conference can have a natter and connect with others like them before they go out into their day and feel like fish out of water. To be fair, BMC is a conference where there are lots of women and gender-expansive folks (until you go to one of the tech panels) and the organizers put a lot of effort into ensuring sessions are delivered by diverse speakers. Nonetheless, we all agreed that starting the day in a friendly, safe environment to talk about music business stuff with other women, trans and non-binary folks was a game-changer for how we felt heading off into the sea of cis men afterwards. Buoyed up, supported, encouraged, and like we truly deserved to be in this industry and take up space, this shows how powerful and important the homosocial networks are that I discussed in Chapter 3. It was just, well, *nice*.

Change the Beat, Abi's collective, the BMC SheSaidSo breakfast, and the many other initiatives I am going to talk about in this chapter seem to suggest that the answer to gender imbalance in electronic music is helping women to be more confident. We know from Chapter 7 that girls and women are not generally socialized to be confident with 'techie' things, and less 'go-getting' than men. From Chapter 3 we also know that women and gender-expansive artists lack the social capital that fosters networks for career advantage. So, they are basically cold-calling gatekeepers to 'sell' offerings they doubt the quality of. This does not sound like a recipe for success, and the response has been a concerted effort to help women learn and grow the confidence they need.

On the face of it, there is absolutely nothing wrong with this – it is a perfectly reasonable, laudable and kind thing to do, and this chapter includes lots of examples of brilliant individuals and collectives in the industry that are doing just that. On the face of it, upskilling minoritized gender artists to be more confident, and own their space, is reparation in the face of the more paranoid readings that being in a minority is all just *awful*. But is 'lacking confidence' the minoritized artist's 'fault', as the deficit implied by the title of this chapter suggests? If we reparatively read 'lack of confidence' itself, perhaps we might arrive at a different interpretation? After all, it is easy to be confident in an environment where you feel you belong and are welcomed, but it's very hard when the reverse is true, as I suggested in Chapter 4, and we shall see in more depth here. Feminist researchers Shani Orgad and Rosalind Gill nail this idea in the introduction to their book *Confidence Culture*: 'living in a society that is gendered by design and systematically undervalues and attacks women and minorities, it would almost be surprising if there were *not* an impact on women's sense of confidence, entitlement, and wellbeing'.[1] It is these ideas that we are going to interrogate within the electronic music industry in this chapter as we dismantle the myth that 'women just need to be more confident'.

'We never get demos from women': producing confidence

Change the Beat inspire women, trans and non-binary artists to take the plunge and share their music when they are normally reticent to do so. When Sydney Blu first launched Change the Beat, it was called '23 by 23', with the catchy aim of increasing representation of women, trans and non-binary artists on record labels to 23 per cent by 2023. During our conversations about it, Sydney recounted the 'push-back' it had received from the industry, who claimed what she was doing was unfair – how could the record labels be expected to magically better their diversity ratios when there just weren't enough good-quality producers out there, and they certainly weren't sending them their music even if they were! Adeline and Imogen, who both worked for global record labels, cited a lack of diversity in the demo tracks received by their labels as the reasons why they launched their positive action campaigns. As Adeline told me, 'People say, why have you got no girls on your label? And the issue we have is that, well, no girls send us their music!' We saw this lament from the big-name male DJ we met in Chapter 2 who asked me to send women producers his way, and I also heard this from Sean and Niall – two of the few men at record labels who agreed to speak with me about diversity issues. Both ran successful, global brands and admitted that, to date, all the artists signed to their labels were cis men. In Sean's case this spanned a 23-year history – something which he was not proud of. He was talking to me because he knew it was time to do something about it.

Adeline's initiative was one of the first to actively solicit submissions from women and gender-expansive producers: 'We put out a call that said, "Look girls, we want you, we're listening, send us your music,"' she told me. 'We didn't think we were going to get many demos – because we don't get a lot of music from female producers normally – but after about 24 hours we had 90 demos, and it was amazing!' Likewise, when Imogen set up her Facebook group for women, trans and non-binary artists making music in a genre where men dominate more than most, she 'expected, like, 50 people to join it'. But, as she went on to tell me, 'it got 1,000 members within two days! It was mad! I was not expecting it at all … that there's women from all over the world in [this genre] and they're talking and you can see them connecting and it's been really nice.'

Every record label and promoter who I have heard speak on a diversity panel at music conferences says the same thing, 'Women don't send us their music – what can we do?'. Even *women*-run record labels report the same thing. Producers Alyson, Tess and Angelica confirmed to me that they rarely receive demos to their labels' inboxes from artists who are not cis-men, and Zara told me the following about her label: 'I wanted it to be girl/boy, boy/girl, alternate every month, but getting submissions from females has been like pulling teeth.' She went on to explain to me that she's tried to tackle this: 'I put a tweet out and people were retweeting it but still nothing, no, actually I got one thing come through, I've got one so far. I purposely want to sign females, but it's hard!'

Alyson was particularly frustrated during our conversation about the lack of commitment and what she described as 'flakiness' exhibited by women who *did* put themselves forward for releases, remixes, gigs and so on, and Ines explained how the response to her competition to win a release on her label was disappointing. 'We weren't inundated, let's say. But we had a lot of enquiries from female artists that didn't follow through. So, I think it was potentially a confidence thing, perhaps, and that's what I find with female producers, it's a confidence thing.'

Belonging and confidence

We know the desire to produce and DJ is there because the classes run by Hayley and Olga's collectives find themselves regularly oversubscribed. Both offer high-quality music production education exclusively to women and gender-expansive people. 'We had different rooms set up with synthesizers and we had all these women coming through the space,' Hayley explained. 'I just thought this is the coolest thing *ever*, teaching all these women synthesis. We had to turn people away, it was packed!' Olga's organization has had 15,000 registrations for their free introduction to music production courses since it began five years ago, and has seen over 100 students take the intensive year-long programme of training that was founded in 2022. In DJing too, Abi's collective receives way more applications to join their yearly roster for early-career artists than they can accommodate. There appears to be no shortage of interest from women, trans and non-binary people wanting to get into electronic music. The artists who have shared their music when gender-specific calls are made, or who join classes where cis men are not involved are clearly not short of confidence – or at least, they don't let their anxieties get in the way of following their dreams.

Contrast this with the figures that we saw in Chapter 6 showing how few women and girls enter formal music technology or audio engineering courses and the picture is clear. Joining a course designed for, taught, and attended exclusively by women and gender-expansive students is considerably more attractive than enrolling on a mixed programme. 'Out of 33 of us on the course, three were girls, including me. I would wait till all the guys left the room to feel comfortable to ask questions. I would be the last person left with my professor,' Liz told me of her experience at university. Others felt out of place because they were older learners and women, returning to college in their 30s. We heard this from Heather in Chapter 3 when she explained how all the young lads just seemed to naturally know more than her, and the fact Nancy was a mum in her late 30s was almost enough to put her off from continuing her studies. Race was an additional factor for Emma in class: 'I'm the only person of colour in this group. Even if people don't treat you differently you just kind of know they're thinking, 'What is she doing here?' I'm not going to ask any questions because I can't be bothered to deal with feeling and looking stupid.

Feeling like you don't belong and/or don't deserve your place in the room is debilitating, as we can see. It limits ability to engage in learning activities, inhibits willingness to put oneself forward for opportunities, and hampers self-esteem. It is an anathema to confidence. It's also so common that an entire discourse has arisen around it: 'imposter syndrome' has become an everyday phrase,[2] and there are no shortage of self-help and coaching interventions that will help you overcome this affliction.[3] Of course, it can be super scary for *anyone* to share their art, since creative offerings generally feel intensely personal labours of love, often referred to as one's 'babies' for that reason. But if you're already in an environment that is making you feel out of place, your anxieties are likely to be way higher, because you are blatantly aware that you *don't* fit in. During our interview, Nancy recounted her experience at a track feedback session at a conference: 'I just wanted the ground to swallow me up,' she said. 'I was absolutely petrified, I couldn't even keep track of what they were saying! I've recorded it and I've never listened back to it, I went into this hole of, like, oh my *God, what the hell am I doing*??'

I remember the first time I shared my music publicly, too, during a producer meet-up in my home town. I was the only woman in the room, in a group of about seven, and probably twice everyone else's age. It took all my bravado to submit my track for review, which was blasted through speakers during a feedback session. Truth be known, if it hadn't been for the fact that the organizer was a personal friend and my first music production tutor, there's no way I would have done it. He'd already reassured me that the track was OK – and in fact, that was the feedback I got from the group too, along with some constructive suggestions on how I might improve it.[4] My experience was a positive and supportive one and it certainly helped me feel less nervous about sharing my music, and engaging more actively in future events. Had the reverse been true, would I have felt I lacked the character to deal with it? Probably. And I wouldn't have been alone. Orgad and Gill devote a chapter of their book to the reach of 'confidence culture' into the workplace.[5] They show how women's apparent lack of confidence has become unquestionably accepted as the reason why there is a gender pay gap (women lack confidence in demanding pay rises or promotions), why their performance is rated below that of men's (they don't shout about their achievements) and why they drop out of their careers when they face adversity (they are not resilient enough to take the knocks). They provide examples from high-flying (white, cis, American, middle-class) women business leaders who suggest their sisters hold back and don't 'get stuck in enough' to learning, decisions, or new projects like the men, contributing to their lack of visibility. Yet during the 2008 global financial crisis it was precisely these qualities of women leaders that were praised within smaller banking institutions and which prevented them from suffering the catastrophic losses experienced by those dominated by male boards.[6]

Shani Orgad and Rosalind Gill also critique how ensuring one always has a ready supply of confidence is a never-ending and ongoing project of self-work. To ensure one continues to be a woman 'who defies adversity by springing back from any crisis or challenge that she is forced to confront'[7] is ameliorative work that should be celebrated and recognized for the effort it takes. But, as acclaimed writers on racism and inclusion Ruchika Tulshyan and Jodi-Ann Buey say, perhaps it would be nice if we all just 'stop telling women they have imposter syndrome'. This is, in fact, the title of their landmark *Harvard Business Review* article which is among the most popular and impactful of all time.[8] They say this because their argument is that confidence and feeling like an imposter are manufactured by a white, American ideal of performance and workplace behaviour. Furthermore, feeling this way is not a *syndrome*, like a disease or illness, but a *response* to the way you are treated, overtly or implicitly.

If we look more closely at the kinds of people who report feeling like an imposter, then, we start to see that it's usually anyone who lacks the social and cultural capital to seamlessly blend in, and often those differences are visible on our bodies, or through our behaviours.[9] Self-proclaimed imposters might be differently gendered from the majority, differently abled or perhaps neurodiverse, they may be racially minoritized folks, and/or queer folks, or those who didn't go to the right school, or live in the right postcode. Psychologist Nellie Tran reminds us that the desire to assimilate (which is basically what imposter syndrome is) is an internalized tool of oppression, because oppression works best when individuals buy into it.[10] When you believe that there is something inherently wrong with you, that *you* need to change in order to be accepted, you'll be motivated to mould yourself to fit. We saw this in Chapter 4 in relation to how women in particular downplay their prettiness and femininity to be more readily accepted in the boys' club, or in Chapter 5 how minoritized genders who feel they are tokenized might work harder just to be seen as good enough.[11] This is not to downplay the brave and impressive work people do when they *feel the fear but do it anyway* (as the famous saying goes), but when you take on this responsibility yourself, you won't even question why the majority players choose not to accept you *as you are*. You won't question the ameliorative work you feel *you* need to undertake to make it happen, because you believe it's just what you have to do.

The need to belong, and be accepted for who you are, also returns us to our discussions of networking in Chapter 3. To recap, there I established the importance of networks in the creative industries, and particularly in electronic music. Having a 'garage band' support network that you can learn from, and share anxieties with, makes you feel less like an interloper, more like you belong and that you are in the right place, for all the right reasons. Not to mention the opportunities that come from feeling more comfortable with the technology, and knowing like-minded people who can open doors to gigs, bookings, collaborations and recording contracts for you. But unlike cis men's networks that form organically through homosocial tendencies, women and gender-expansive people's groups form in *response* to something. They are founded because women, trans, non-binary and gender-queer folks often do not feel safe in mainstream music environments, dominated as they are by cis men, and often white ones at that. In short, men get together to learn and make music for fun with their friends, women do the same in order to 'tool up' and grow armour to enter a world that doesn't welcome them. 'I was surprised how much fun it was to hang out and vibe with other women,' Celene told me. She'd previously worked solo, and when she had taken part in meet-ups with other producers she felt uncomfortable and awkward, despite being a proficient producer already. 'I never looked forward to those things really, it wasn't a chill experience.' Isobel Anderson raises this issue in an episode of her podcast on male-dominated music education spaces.[12] She calls for an end to the pressure on *everyone* to 'perform confidence' around technology, opening up space for the vulnerability that is so essential to learning. This, she argues, benefits *everyone* in music, regardless of their gender.

Confidence? ... Or armour?

But are the people whose experiences we've heard in this chapter (and indeed throughout the book) just snowflakes[13] who need to work on their confidence, heal their imposter syndrome, take a deep breath and just get on with things? After all, what we hear everywhere in electronic music – and saw in Chapter 4 – is that no one is actively *stopping* women, trans or non-binary people from doing anything! They just choose not to put themselves forward – so, what's a dude supposed to do, huh? Women just need to be more confident.

Except that research shows that they already are. Management psychologist Michelle Ryan and her colleagues have found that in male-dominated occupations, women's ambition and drive is no lower than men's at higher education and graduate level.[14] They found that women's decisions to quit their careers were in response to constantly battling their environments – not a lack of ambition. These exit decisions are then explained away as being down to individual women's 'choice', and therefore the system and environment doesn't need to change. Likewise, psychologists from the Netherlands have found strong evidence that working in a male-dominated environment *and* in occupations that are stereotyped as 'men's work' has negative effects on women's career confidence, even when women are equally qualified and experienced as their male counterparts.[15] We have known for a long time that girls (in the Global North, at least) do better when they attend all-girls schools. Not only do they achieve higher academic results than girls from mixed-sex schools, but they exhibit higher propensity to accept risk, innovate more, and show higher levels of leadership. It appears that the environment may have more to do with women's so-called lack of confidence than any innate failing on their part, as Shani Orgad and Rosalind Gill also argue.

Indeed, once we explore women and gender-expansive artists' everyday experiences on the job it becomes clear that they face environments that are not only unfamiliar, and potentially unsupportive, but in many cases they are downright dangerous.[16] During this research, I have heard stories of attempted rape as a result of drink spiking, with the artist only being saved when a passer-by raised an alarm. Another woke after attending an after-party in a state of undress with no memory of the hours before. One of my participants recounted a story of a friend who fled from a recording studio after one of the men she was with slipped some powder into her drink. Many reported feeling unsafe during gigs or when going to 'support' promoters' club nights, as Esther explained in Chapter 3. I heard stories of having to fend off DJ booth invasions and gropes from men – not only from the crowd but also from bar staff and security – all while trying to DJ with their ears covered and their eyes on the decks. Others have told me how they have been booked into dodgy hotels in unsafe areas by promoters and been unable to sleep all night, with others reporting lewd behaviour during meetings with male 'colleagues'. In two cases, I heard of physical threats and accusations from other (male) DJs' wives and girlfriends who were convinced my interviewees were having sex with their partners while at gigs and festivals. This led to promoters declining to book them as they were a 'liability'. But women just need to be more confident, right?

It's not just the big, shocking stories that chip away at artists' confidence either. I have experienced drunk guys invading my space behind the decks in ways that I am certain they would never ever consider if it was a man playing. At one gig a guy leaned over the front of the DJ desk and adjusted a knob while I was playing. I thought he was venue staff, monitoring the sound levels, but when he came behind the decks trying to drunkenly dance with me (while I was mixing), I realized he wasn't. All I could do in the moment was grin and laugh and politely shove him out of my way. Thankfully I was able to signal to security who did remove him from the venue. The other DJs I was with (also women) felt I'd been a bit harsh getting him chucked out. I didn't agree.

Almost every one of the people I interviewed had some kind of story to tell of unsafe or threatening behaviour, either towards themselves, or people they knew. Further examples of how 'just going to work' as a woman, trans or non-binary DJ entails serious hazards are detailed in The Jaguar Foundation/ SONY report.[17] These examples are shocking enough by themselves, but the aftermath is even more so. After raising incidents, artists reported being dropped from line-ups, struggling to get gigs, being disbelieved and/or trivialized, and/or blamed for their experiences. Only one person reported that the club management took any action against a perpetrator.[18] Being called a diva for rejecting men's advances and daring to call out unwanted behaviour was another repeated theme in my interviews. Many employed their own strategies to safeguard themselves – bringing friends or partners to the DJ booth with them as minders, disarming would-be harassers with jokes, smiles or brushing things off as 'just part of the job', as my fellow DJs did in the incident I recounted earlier. Refraining from drinking or taking drugs at after-parties even when they might have liked to do so was another tactic – the choice not to attend the party potentially being career limiting, since this was where a lot of networks were formed and contacts made. Navigating this balance is crucial.

A more subtle but equally damaging outcome of these experiences is the constant vigilance that women and gender-expansive folks have to employ to guard against the *possibility* of being assaulted or harassed. This was also highlighted by Rosalind Duignan-Pearson in her research with South African women DJs[19] who used everyday career strategies that were situationally contingent, ongoing judgement calls, meaning they were constantly on their guard. This 'second guessing' around men's intentions leads to decisions not to accept invitations to collaborate, or jam in the studio, or go for the drinks, coffees or lunches that might result in the kinds of contacts and relationships that provide boosts to their careers. One young, early-stage producer angrily described how she'd been accused of giving off romantic signals to a male colleague when she'd asked him if he'd like to join forces and put on an event with her. A couple of weeks later she'd been enthusiastically invited to write a track with another guy but declined, having felt burned by her previous encounter. She told me that she felt sad that maybe he really *did* just want to work with her and berated herself for not being brave enough to try again. Is this really a lack of bravery? Or just an eminently sensible response?

The microaggressions, mansplaining and doubting of women, and gender-expansive producers' skills that we saw in the previous two chapters are also part of this murky soup. Being accused of lacking talent, not possessing skills or of being a fake is not a psychologically safe environment in which to be your best self and, as artist and music researcher Kallie Marie discusses in her book, this is a major cause of 'career fatigue' causing women to leave the industry.[20] 'You're always feeling you need to do more, and be *better* than the guys,' Zara told me. 'Yes, I do think you always have to be that little bit better than the men,' agreed Lia. '… when you're the only woman on the stage that night, you feel all eyes are on you. You can't fuck up.' This vigilance continues online too, as we saw in Chapter 4, with women's content being subject to considerably more scathing and often sexualized comments than videos and photos shared by men.

Even in the music-related online forums, the environment is not safe, as Jenny explained:

> I've suffered a severe amount of abuse at the hands of some of these quite reputable DJs. Really like, hateful sort of like, online slagging, abuse. So, I have avoided all those groups now. I wouldn't join any of the ones that aren't exclusively women – joining a woman's group, hopefully nobody's going to be having a go at me.

Beyond specific comments, there is an 'air' about many cis-male-dominated online music production forums, as Angelica noted: 'There's a lot of ego, a lot of "Look what I can do!", and lots of technical and very complicated questions – and answers.' I've also noticed this, observing how cis-male artists tend to post unsolicited advice and tips about their own practice – or sharing track deconstruction videos[21] and so on without anyone asking for them – what I call 'producer peacocking'. This is entirely absent from the women and gender-expansive music groups. Instead, self-promotion has a relational or sometimes self-effacing tone, offered with a preface as to why other members might be interested, or even couched in an apology for posting! Tess told me how she had recently joined her first all-women online production workshop run by an artist she really admired and had been truly amazed by the level of friendly, supportive and genuinely warm comments that poured into the chat box during the event. 'It was *completely* different to events I've been to populated by guys,' she remarked. Nadine agreed with this, telling me how online spaces for women and gender-expansive artists 'just have a totally different feel to when you're in a group that's primarily male'.

Confidence through solidarity: safe and brave spaces

The idea of a 'safe space' originates from queer communities, often at the intersection with people of colour, to describe an environment where marginalized folks can come together and truly be themselves together in freedom.[22] These often include spaces to dance, party and celebrate sexual freedom and queer spirit.[23] As Jacinda explained to me, 'It's queer, and especially fetish – parties that are the most respectful. Everything is fundamentally based on consent. You ask if you can touch someone and if they say no, then that's totally accepted.' These are examples of what scholars of organization studies call 'prefigurative organizations', they try to imagine an alternative way of doing things, sometimes as a pure alternative, and sometimes with a view to changing mainstream practice.[24]

However, even prefiguring does not necessarily make these spaces entirely safe, since they can still remain targets for hate attacks, or colonization by the mainstream. As we saw in Chapter 2, disco music began life as a safe space for black gay men and their allies in New York yet was quickly invaded by mainstream commercial interests and the major record labels and clubs, the majority of whom were white, male, heterosexual and cis-gendered. Safe spaces are continually evolving in the face of these pressures – and continuing to exist as a demarcated space for alternative expression comes with risk of being singled out for hate crime. Transgender hate crime, in particular, is on the rise globally, and nightlife is not immune.[25]

India explained why she preferred to DJ in a queer, black-majority club environment: '... being a black woman and wanting to go to a techno rave, I've got to think, 'Is some idiot going to touch my hair?' If I'm going into a majority-white space, especially if people are going to be drunk and that, you have to think about that kind of stuff. And for some people that can be incredibly triggering of something that was way worse.' She described these parties as 'brave space – where people can be brave enough to truly be themselves without fear they are going to be mistreated for how they look, or act'. This idea of bring brave is what first drove the surge in campaigns, initiatives, collectives and organizations that now exist to support and upskill women and gender-expansive creatives in the music industry, such as those introduced at the start of this chapter or mentioned throughout this book, and the many others like them worldwide.[26]

Beyond providing brave and safe spaces to party without fear, initiatives like MPW, Saffron, She Knows Tech, Femme House, Toolroom's 'We are Listening' Academy, The Unheard Academy, and Girls Twiddling Knobs provide education workshops exclusively for gender-expansive and women students, providing online and in-person classroom experiences that avoid the psychological harm described at the start of this chapter. Feeling free to ask those 'stupid questions', feeling among supportive people that share your struggles and who just 'get you' are foundational elements of fostering the confidence that women are accused of lacking. Forging bonds on shared common ground is how homophily works, as we saw in Chapter 3 – I have lost track of how many friends and acquaintances I have made simply through doing this project, for example, sharing my love of electronic music and of learning to DJ and produce. This is how the guys do it – just more organically, much younger, and with far more options to choose from since they are the majority players. Carmen echoed my own experiences of Facebook group '2% RISING' in this regard when we chatted about it during our call, shortly after it was founded: '… it's brilliant because I think we're all helping each other already with this group, I'm seeing such levels of support, and having "listening sessions" to give you helpful feedback on your music, and that's what you need sometimes to build that confidence'. All Carmen is talking about here is the kind of creative confidence that all artists need – belief in the quality and value of their own work, for example, which is a normal part of being an artist, no matter who you are. But artists of minoritized genders have to summon up the guts simply to exist and be safe in the industry even before they *get* to the kind of confidence they need to grow around their work.

Mentoring schemes are also important initiatives in this regard. The most recent programme I've become aware of is Hunna,[27] a network for Middle Eastern and North African DJs, music producers and professionals. Others include Hospital Records' 'Women in Drum and Bass' artist programme,[28] the industry mentoring scheme from global organization She Said So[29] and the 'board development' mentoring available from Women in Ctrl.[30] Others still, such as Change the Beat, are providing tangible opportunities to further individual artists' careers through releases on top record labels, as we saw in the opening vignette to this chapter. Toolroom's We Are Listening campaign does this, too, and also allocates places to these artists on their high-profile party line-ups in clubbing hotspots like Ibiza and Amsterdam. It is *this* kind of concrete action and the resulting exposure that really propels music careers – and although having the confidence to put your metaphorical hat in the ring is undoubtedly part of this, it is clear that having advocates who can put you in front of solid opportunities is probably one of the most valuable dimensions of these organizations. Abi's organization operates as a DJ-booking agency for their roster and her words nicely encapsulate the function and aspiration of many collectives in this space:

> Our overall mission and aim is to diversify the music industry, as broad and as wide as that is, if we can even slightly contribute to getting more girls on the line-up, or getting out there and in the industry, or even just feeling confident within themselves, that's the overall aim, and we do that through everything we do, the platforming, the courses, the connecting people, the mix-series, the little pockets of communities …

This is what gender researcher Karren Knowlton calls the 'trailblazing motivation' for engaging in pro-diversity initiatives.[31] Wanting to make things better for others, rather than oneself, and importantly, for others who have yet to come into the industry, and it's deeply inspiring. Through her research she has found that trailblazing motivations are strongest and most successful when minoritized individuals come together in solidarity.

The ameliorative work of 'fixing women'

The formation of these organizations gathered pace after the hashtag #metoo went viral in 2017. Attached to social media posts calling out sexual violence, harassment and discrimination in all walks of life, but particularly in the screen industries,[32] 19 million people used the hashtag in its first year.[33] This swell in outrage at the sheer scope of the problem and how it is continually hushed up by a male-dominated industry that closes ranks to protect the powerful was matched with a wake-up call from the electronic music industry that something was wildly wrong there too. More than 90 per cent of festival acts were cis-gendered men at that time,[34] and high-profile cases of sexual assault have also continued to come to light. Derrick May,[35] Kamaal Williams,[36] the rapper Diddy[37] and Erik Morillo, who went on to take his own life before he could be brought to court,[38] are just the tip of an iceberg that refuses to melt. The UK's Misogyny in Music report[39] found widespread evidence of a culture of harassment and discrimination that is rife across the music sectors, and recommended that the UK government tackle the dubious and increasingly commonplace use of non-disclosure agreements (NDAs) to silence sexual assault survivors. Zelda Perkins and Julie MacFarlane's 'Can't Buy My Silence' is a campaign to put an end to NDAs being used in this way.

Zelda Perkins was the first person to break her NDA (against Harvey Weinstein) and she has made it her life's work ever since to fight injustice. And that's a problem: the fact that it was cast as *her* problem, and therefore *her* problem to fix, not just for her own sake, but for the hundreds of thousands of women this affects.[40] In fact, all the collectives, initiatives, groups and organizations I've written about in this book are run, managed, funded and resourced by the very people they are designed to help. Addressing their own marginalization is an identity tax on women and gender-expansive people, as I introduced in Chapter 2 when I discussed the time and effort involved in doing A&R work on behalf of cis, white men to hunt out gender-expansive and female artists for them. But, here, it is way more than just a tax. It's ameliorative work at its most all-encompassing. In some cases, it's become artists' full-time careers, leaving little or no time for music production or DJing. 'I set up [the organization] to fund my music as well as help other women – so they didn't have to go through the slog that I did,' Olga told me. 'But now it's taking up all my time and I am finding myself hunting for funding to keep *this* going too.' I'm delighted to say that Olga's organization has well and truly taken off since that day, and she is the recipient of several awards. Running her business as a social enterprise, she has expanded all over the world – but she still has very little time to make or perform her music. In contrast, Zara found that as she got more successful as an artist, time for her activist work had dwindled: 'there's quite a lot to organizing these events, and as me and my partner have progressed in our careers it's got harder.'

Dana explained to me how much hard work it had been building her collective up from nothing, and how she had assembled a team around her to manage a podcast, blog, put on regular parties, run a conference and provide a booking agency for queer and gender-expansive people within her particular genre. A woman with seemingly boundless energy, she justified my suggestions that she had taken on an enormous project by saying she felt *lucky* that she got to be an activist for something she was so passionate about. An unpaid activist, challenging the status quo while the majority white, cis-, heterosexual men do nothing, and she feels *lucky*. It's important to pause here and celebrate the incredible efforts, power and drive these artists have, and their trailblazing motivation. However, with every respect to the amazing work they do, something is very wrong. Zara also referred to running her 'safe space' collective as a 'labour of love'. Vick Bain, Founder of The F List for Music[41] told me how it takes considerable financial investment and at least one day of her time every week to keep the network and directory of female and gender diverse musicians afloat. She has found it exceptionally hard to attract regular sponsors – the search for which is additional ameliorative work. Similarly, others talked of how difficult it has been to raise funding to support their activities, leaving them personally out of pocket or living hand to mouth, as Olga was in her early days. There seems to be a reluctance on the part of the industry to fund diversity initiatives, as Kerri explained of her crowd-funded project: 'It was like getting blood out of a stone – not one of the big guns came forward, I had to go bang on their doors and they just ignored me.' Freya, too, was struggling to raise the money she needed to keep her organization going, and pouring even more time into continually applying for highly competitive grants and funding from arts councils. Yet, as a transgender musician pointedly remarked to me over a coffee after a conference session, '[the big companies] are all biting your hand off to come and sit on their panels, and do their diversity work for them *and they don't even pay you for that.*'

It's partly for these reasons that a major challenge facing these organization was, as Dana explained, 'to take the conversation out of those spaces where you're only talking to people who are sympathetic. You know, how do we actually make change outside those circles, so that big organizations listen to us?' She also told me of the toll that constantly justifying the collective's existence was taking on her: 'What I do find hard, is people patronizing me. A lot of the time I find myself having to justify the existence of [our collective], like, Why? Why do it? Why can we not play the mainstream like everyone else and why should we have this special space?' This constant battling, justifying, and being undermined and belittled is just as much ameliorative work as footing the bill for your organization's conference.

Where are the allies?

So, where are the cis men fighting to change the culture within electronic music alongside marginalized genders? Who from the majority is shouldering the burden of creating an environment in which women and gender-expansive artists can truly and safely be more confident? Even on International Women's Day (IWD), the responsibility for organizing events, social media posts, press releases and other events falls to the women of the business. This made Jacinda extremely angry.

> International Women's Day has become a virtue signalling fest by cis-white dudes and companies who do fuck all for diversity the other 364 days of the year. Last year I was working part time on a short-term contract. It got to 4 pm and my [male] boss fired me an email, asking, 'Why haven't you posted anything for IWD yet??', and I was like 'Okaaay – why is this my job? Where is the content *you've* put together? What's *your* position on women in the industry? What the fuck do *you do* about diversity? *What the fuck do you want me to say about YOUR company??*'

In carrying out the research, I deliberately sought out label owners and male A&R staff to talk to but was usually passed on to a woman – or in one case a non-binary person – to talk to after my initial contact. There were a couple of exceptions, as I mentioned at the start of the chapter, but the only one who really spoke candidly about what *he* had done, was Oscar, from a global and very high-profile record label. 'We put women at the top,' he shrugged, as if it was obvious. 'As soon as [name] was appointed head of A&R we got interest from women. She went out and *found* them. If they weren't ready for the big time, we worked with them until they were.' The idea that making the organization itself more welcoming to people other than white, cis men came as a surprise to Niall, who confessed he hadn't noticed how 'blokey' his label was because half the fans they had were women. He had not connected the fact that all the faces on the website were male, and their range of merchandise did not include women's fit in any of the items, with why they might not be attracting demos from women. This returns us to the importance of representation that we saw in Chapters 3 and 5, only this time it's behind the scenes in relation to positions of power within the record labels themselves, rather than who is performing on the stage. This was summed up simply by Suzie, who preferred to submit her demo tracks to queer and/or women-run labels only: 'If you don't see anyone like you in the management team, if you don't see any faces like yours on their promo, why would you bother sending them your music?' The reasoning for this was not just that the music might not get signed, but that if it *did*, it would mean working with people who were culturally so unlike her that she didn't want to put herself in that position. Suzie did not lack confidence, she was just smart enough to know where she would be safe.

Unfortunately, what happens when queer people only submit music to women- or queer-run labels, and/or DJ at queer or all-women events, is that subcultures form and thrive that might even be described as ghettos. Scholar of alternative organization, Genevieve Shanahan discusses the potential outcome of this as 'insulation degeneration', whereby groups become so separate from the mainstream that they fail to have any impact on the status quo at all.[42] Another variant of this I have noticed is that women tend to remix tracks by other women far more than they do cis men's music.[43] Sure, some of these artists are highly successful ones, and the labels can be high profile, but nonetheless, the impression that's given off is that women can be encouraged into the industry as long as they play nicely among themselves and don't disrupt the 'real' business of men and men's music.

Women talking to women about women?

By turning gender imbalance into a 'women's issue' and delegating responsibility for diversity initiatives to gender-expansive or female members of staff, a reality is reinforced that men need have very little to do with it all (in effect, nothing). They are free to continue making, releasing and performing music unencumbered by the ameliorative work I have described in this chapter, and in every other chapter of this book. I am very aware that I am treading controversial ground in suggesting that, on some level, women's collectives and initiatives might actually be contributing to the very problem they seek to overcome, but this is borne out by evidence. As Dana lamented earlier, the struggle to get anyone other than other women and gender-expansive people to take notice, let alone some responsibility, is tough. I have seen this repeatedly with my own eyes. Very, *very* few of the music industry conference panels on diversity I have spoken at or attended have had more than a dozen attendees, even when they take place at huge, industry-leading events. The numbers of cis men who attend are miniscule. Diversity simply doesn't concern them, and this perception is intensified the more gender diversity is solely seen as women's, or gender-expansive people's work. At one conference my initial delight at being offered the chance to convene an entire panel to share the results of my research soon turned to exasperation when I realized I had been scheduled at the same time as a question-and-answer session with Carl Cox, one of the world's biggest dance music legends. Needless to say, I could count the number of audience members in the room on one hand. Only one was a cis man, and he was my mate.

Even when its well intentioned, ameliorative work is still regarded as *women's* work, best solved by collecting together a bunch of women, perhaps with some gender-expansive people included for good measure. A local promoter who was genuinely keen to diversify their parties and record label asked me recently if I would like to put on an 'all-female' line-up as a special showcase of women's talent. The offer absolutely came from a good place and I was very much heartened to see a young, white, cis man genuinely wanting to use his brand to make a difference. Putting this party on would have required me to find, book and liaise with the artists, source a suitable venue, sell tickets and possibly find the equipment to use too. Ameliorative work that would not only have been unpaid, but would have cost me considerable time, and probably money too. Of course, I am unusual and very privileged in that I work in the music industry in my capacity as a researcher with a well-paid job – but the premise is the same. Diversity – particularly gender diversity – is women's work. Rather than pointing this out directly to the promoter, I suggested that the best way to showcase diverse talent was by putting women and gender-expansive people on the line-ups of the regular parties that *they* organized, and billing them as headliners, as well as including more than one of them per event if possible. 'Do that without mentioning gender in your promo' I told him. 'Just quietly get on with it and give them a platform that's really meaningful ...' I am delighted to say that's what he has done.

Among my participants, feelings on initiatives designed to support women and gender-expansive people that excluded cis men were quite mixed. Olga reflected on this pragmatically: 'It's us who are really being impacted, so it does, in a way have to come from us. It can be helped by society around that, but if we don't speak out then who will?' On the other hand, Yvette summed up quite a common discomfort with gender-exclusive initiatives: 'I think you really have to get away from the gender part of this,' she explained. 'You limit yourself when you're, like, "Oh, I can only connect with other females," because, let's face it, this industry is made up of 92 per cent men!' Alice also considered that the aim of diversity initiatives was '50/50 representation, on line-ups and labels, that's the end goal – not to keep this separation between men and women'. This 'until we get there' sentiment was shared by others too, including Helen, who conceded: 'I guess this all-woman thing is OK because we need it to show, hey, we're out here, maybe. But I don't really like it so much. It's OK for now I guess, but not forever.'

Conclusion: The power of collective action

We've ended on the realization that regardless of whether minoritized genders *actually* lack confidence or not, the responsibility to fix that problem is firmly and squarely on their shoulders. The impact of this is not only that women and gender-expansive folks end up doing all the work (usually for free), but that they also become corralled together. They move in packs – growing secure and successful on their own terms, and within the safe spaces they have created (and hurrah for that!), but segregated from where the real power is: the 'malestream' world of top record labels, and global brands that can propel an artist's career to the next level. These corrals are defined by the very thing that shouldn't be a factor – gender. As well as doing excellent, much-needed work – for which I am incredibly grateful – they also foreground the whole concept of gender, reinforcing that things are different between men and women, and that there is such a thing as a 'female producer'. As I explained in Chapter 5, several of the people I contacted for interviews for this project declined because it would draw attention to them *as* women, and, in several cases, transgender too, when all they wanted to be seen as was *artists*.

But enough of this paranoid gloom and back to the hope of a reparative reading. Despite being labour-intensive and resource-heavy work, these groups of selfless, powerful people *are* making a difference, because it *does* help gender-expansive folks and women to be more confident – at least until the industry becomes a more hospitable place. The success these initiatives have been having is undeniable, whether that is through actively signing music from gender diverse artists to prestigious labels, or providing safe spaces in person and online for education and professional development that enable women, trans and non-binary people to flourish. Without them, confidence doesn't have a chance to take root, let alone bloom, due to the continual isolation, second-guessing, wariness and caution that takes up women and gender-expansive people's bandwidth when the dudes in the room are simply getting on with learning how to make music. As we have seen in this chapter, and throughout the book, these internal processes are absolutely justified, and often necessary to ensure psychological and physical safety. They are not optional responses that can simply be eradicated through affirmations, or mantras, or the power of positive thinking. They are learned survival strategies that it would be foolish to abandon until the environment in which women and gender-expansive people find themselves is really, *truly,* safe. And that's why the women's groups form – in response to these threats. But, unfortunately, this *also* takes us down the road to gendered segregation and a two-tier music industry under the guise of progress. The missions and operation of women and gender-expansive collectives sum up the tension between exploitation and empowerment so clearly – which is why I left this topic to the end of the book, ready to feed into the manifestos for change in the final chapter.

So, to sum up this one, no, women do *not* need to be more confident. Sure, they might *appear* less confident than their male counterparts in male-dominated situations, but is this a failing on their part? The environment they work in needs to be less confidence-*draining* – less dangerous, less isolating and more welcoming. Only then will minoritized genders feel they are not imposters blamed for their own inability to fit in.[44] Only then will they be able to stop the constant and tiring self-work that Shani Orgad and Rosalind Gill explain is the burden of confidence culture. Only then can they quit the ameliorative work and get on with the *real* work of making music and being a creative performer. We *know* this is the case because of the way these same people behave and feel when they are in an all-female and gender-expansive space, as we have seen in this chapter. It's not women's inherent confidence that's the problem – it's the fact that others create spaces that deplete it. And that's what needs to change.

Chapter track: 'Just Dance'

Figure 8: Artwork for 'Just Dance (Dovetail's Funky Breaks Remix)' by Dovetail and Bungalow, author's own artwork

Source: Listen to it at https://soundcloud.com/dovetail_uk/just-dance-dovetails-funky-breaks-remix

'Just Dance' (Dovetail's funky breaks remix) is – as its name suggests – a funky breakbeat remix of Bungalow's original on Wildfire Recordings. The original is slower and has a 4 x 4 house music groove, and I decided to funk it up with a broken beat, and the addition of some jazzy trumpets and a bit more scratching. The vocal stabs are all from the original but I've used them in different ways and given them different emphases – I love the end result and feel confident when I play it as part of my sets. Remixing is fun because you get to do creative things with what's already there (plus add in your own new bits), and in that sense it is very much like collage.[45]

I've chosen this track for this chapter, in particular, because the original was offered up as a remix competition – and I felt confident enough to give it a go. So, where did that confidence to enter come from? Partly from my growing experience and skills in production, but also because of networks. I had played on livestreams with the label owner during the COVID-19 lockdowns, and we shared a connection to the breakbeat genre through Diesel Recordings that I say more about at the end of Chapter 4. I wasn't successful at winning a release slot on the label, but for me that doesn't matter because the fact that I entered at all feels like a win!

9

Conclusion: Manifestos for an Inclusive Industry

GENIE

Grace Goodwin is a researcher, artist mentor, drummer and trustee of the PRS Foundation. She is also the founder of GENIE: Gender Equality Networks In Europe, an online database of organizations, collectives and networks that operate within the music industry.[1] Every time Grace went to a music conference or workshop she met yet more amazing people with platforms and initiatives aimed at bringing about a better gender balance in music. Frustrated by the lack of a central point where she could find all these resources in one place, she set about compiling one herself. GENIE is a great example of ameliorative work in action – Grace has spent huge amounts of unpaid time researching and assembling the database on top of her regular job. Although she's benefitted from this work as a marginalized musician herself, and as a gender-in-music researcher, she was primarily driven by 'trailblazing motivation' – to conjure up GENIE for the benefit of everyone involved in the music industry. Thank you, Grace!

When you check GENIE out, the first thing you might notice is how professional the website is, and how easy it is to search and navigate. This kind of web design doesn't come cheap. All too often platforms and collectives struggle with off-the-shelf and often clunky interfaces (my own included) because they cannot afford bespoke web design. However, when Grace was talking about GENIE at an awards ceremony in the summer of 2024, she was delighted when the woman she was chatting to immediately offered to pay for the costs of the site. 'I'm from SoundCloud,' she said. 'We'd love to sponsor this and cover your costs. How much do you need?'

Somewhat stunned, Grace accepted, and GENIE was born. This is the kind of allyship and industry support that is needed to put real clout behind the promises of diversity we hear all the time. Every industry player says they are inclusive. Every International Women's Day/Trans Day of Visibility/PRIDE/Black History month, every company says they celebrate diversity. *OK, fine. So, tell me again, what it is you actually* **do***?*

The job (and joy) of being an ameliorative worker

The GENIE database shows how *just how much* ameliorative work women and gender-expansive people in this industry do to survive and thrive, purely and simply because of their gender and the wider world's expectations of them. The 423 organizations that appear in the database are almost all run by women, trans or non-binary folk doing the work of ameliorating their own situations. Ameliorative work is rarely cis men's work. They either don't see gender inequality as their problem to fix, don't think that it's appropriate for them to fix, or don't see it as a problem at all. This book has shown that cis men are anxious about advocating in this space, and nervous about speaking up and out on gender inequality for many reasons – as we explored in Chapters 5 and 8. In this final chapter I suggest that these are not good enough reasons for potential allies to say and do nothing, and will propose effective ways for gatekeepers and those in positions of influence to lift their heads from the sand safely, and proudly, to reshape the industry. I'll be putting forward manifestos for stakeholders in the industry to show what everyone can do to help in that reshaping. Whether you are a minoritized gender artist in music yourself, or someone who is in a position to be an ally inside – or outside – the music industry, we are all able to influence change. We can all be 'delicious disruptors',[2] as Christina Malley delightfully expresses it, no matter how small we think that disruption is. We have no way of knowing what effect we will have as our actions ripple out in ways we could never imagine.[3]

Before we begin, it's important to note that women and gender-expansive people doing their own ameliorative work is not always a bad thing providing it comes with a corresponding allocation of power and respect. Although a rare example, Oscar's record label promoting a woman to Head of A&R in Chapter 8 is a great example of how to effect change in a way that actually reshapes the industry from the top. Sure, it is still this person's job to find and develop diverse artists – but she is appropriately rewarded and highly visible in doing so. Ameliorative work is part of her main job, and that's progress, because power and respect are not the reality for the overwhelming majority of people we have met in this book who are suffering emotional exhaustion, fighting to be heard and valued, or just battling to stay psychologically and physically safe. They are labouring for love, spending their own money, time and energy running organizations just to make working life that little bit better for themselves and others, as we saw from the Psy-sisters vignette that opens Chapter 1 and Vick Bain's experience running The F List for Music in Chapter 8. Whatever the form, it's underpaid, undervalued, often invisible, and usually exhausting *work*.

Throughout this book, I have repeatedly suggested that ameliorative work is akin to a 'second shift' or additional job that minoritized individuals have as well as their career as an electronic music artist. They may have this alongside a day job, too, because being a DJ and producer can't earn them enough of a living by itself. Being an electronic music artist in a digital age is tough for *everyone,* but if you're from a marginalized identity it's twice as hard, for all the reasons we have seen. And yet women, trans and non-binary people *still do it*. Black and brown women, queer women, trans women, those who refuse to be defined by gender … all doing what they love regardless of the costs they incur. That's inspirational, and it's a story that deserves to be told, as I have done here. Reclaiming, and 'repairing' the story with hope, when all too often all we see and hear is doom and gloom, has been a central part of the book, even when a lot of what I have presented is also fraught with difficulty, effort, danger and seems hope*less*. And this matters. As feminist writer Rebecca Solnit tells us, hope is not 'the belief that everything was, is or will be fine'. It is also not 'a sunny everything-is-getting-better narrative, though it may be a counter to the everything-is-getting-worse narrative'.[4] Instead, it is a force that demands we take action because without hope, people will give up the fight – celebrating victories, recognizing pockets of progress and seeing good in the world is vital to bring about change.

Hope and power in spite of it all

GENIE, in our opening vignette, is a database full of hope. Four hundred and twenty-three organizations, and counting, all working to bring about change – just scroll through the pages to see image after image of powerful, inspiring women and gender-expansive people.[5] These organizations are doing vital and necessary work. They upskill, provide support, create networks, and offer solidarity and opportunity to artists of marginalized genders. They provide new entrants (and veterans too) with role models, fuelling confidence and self-belief, as we saw in Chapter 8. Sure, the industry needs to be less confidence-*draining* for women and gender-expansive artists, but this doesn't take away from the amazing work these organizations are doing for their members to survive and thrive in ways that cis men take for granted.

As we have seen, cis men take it for granted that they will not be doubted as the authors of their own work just because they have used equipment that transgresses their gender. If they are attractive, no one is going to doubt they know what a compressor is, or how to operate a DJ mixer. It is taken for granted that boys will get stuck in with taking things apart and experimenting without encountering a force-field of socialized convention that makes them physically recoil instead of playfully creating music. The ameliorative work that those outside the socialized bubble have to do is considerable. The bandwidth associated with 'performing confidence', as Isobel Anderson perfectly expresses it in her podcast, is exhausting. Battling feelings that you don't belong, ignoring the little whisper that says, 'What are *you* doing here?', growing louder as you feel stupid for not knowing what the boys already know. Berating yourself when those feelings – and that *work* – is gaslit by someone who tells you that *you* just need to improve your resilience and toughen up. That takes its toll. We know this because of the joy and lightness my participants reported when they were in an environment without those pressures. Ameliorative work saps creativity and is the surest way to stop artists 'putting themselves out there' that I can think of – perhaps apart from being fearful of entering a collaboration, meet-up, studio or DJ booth in case you get assaulted, of course. *Yet these women do it anyway.* They have built strategies to navigate this terrain like bats in the dark – they just *know*. So much so that much of what they do they don't even notice, seeing it as part and parcel of being a minority in this industry.

In a way, then, ameliorative work is a kind of 'hope labour' – a term which creative industry researchers Ewan MacKenzie and Alan MacKinley use to capture the essence of working for free, or at reduced rates that is rife in the creative and cultural industries.[6] This work is driven by the hope that exposure from underpaid labour will lead to more lucrative opportunities in future – and in a way, that's what ameliorative work is all about too. Only this time well-paid gigs and record deals are not all that's hoped for – instead, ameliorative workers are driven by the hope that they'll simply be recognized and respected for who they are and treated on equal terms to everyone else. A fundamental human right, one might say. But hopeful or not, pointing out inappropriate conduct or microaggressions, inequality or bias still takes enormous courage – especially online – where you know you will then have to defend against 'the backlash' that comes from the deeply entrenched myths I have presented in this book. *But still people do it*. Because as well as being exhausting, it's also utterly jubilant. When someone stops short and realizes something they have never noticed before because you gently pointed it out. That's disruption. When *they then change something* as a result? That disruption is delicious.

Delicious disruption

As Christina Malley's ideas remind us, delicious disruption can start with just showing up. Taking up space despite the pressure to look a certain way, or pass as someone you're not. Delicious disruption is also engaging in the verbal jujitsu of deflecting and redirecting microaggressions, and questioning gendered, raced, classed, sexualized and every other kind of comment that makes you feel shit. By being visible – and vocal – women and gender-expansive artists inspire others to join the industry – or not to leave it – and over time this *will* lead to a normalization of diverse genders behind the decks and as producers of music. In time, little boys won't recoil in shock and surprise at their stepmother's DJ equipment because 'girls can't be DJs', and little girls won't be repelled by the technology they need to do that. Change *is* happening and we can see this all around, even if some of it is perhaps performative virtual signalling – for now. I get a sense that my participants who were newer entrants to the industry could tell me less about the challenges they've faced and more about the opportunities they're getting. Although this is not something I formally analysed within my data, maybe this is because they are newbies who have yet to face the door marked 'boys' club' slammed in their face, or maybe we could read that more hopefully – that the door is being left a little more open for them to come in. For now, crossing that threshold undoubtedly comes with the glare of a brighter spotlight and all the challenges that brings, but as we saw in Chapter 5, it also brings opportunities to shine – and the disruptive work that does to gender stereotypes, particularly around technology, is priceless.

I say priceless because, of course, ameliorative work is unpaid, unrecognized *as* work, or if it is recognized – for example, the effort involved in running the collectives and initiatives that GENIE highlights – it's still undervalued and minoritized gender artists are expected to carry it out for free. Grace's experience with Soundcloud sponsoring GENIE's website build is rare – but it's what we need to see more of. The sums of money (or perhaps expertise) these initiatives need to make a drastic difference to their operations and the wellbeing of those who run them is small fry to the bigger industry players in electronic music, yet as we saw in Chapter 8, sponsorship, endorsement and financial patronage is hard to come by.

Conclusion

'Ameliorative work' is a therefore a term that captures the double-edged character of life as a minoritized gender in electronic music – a dance between toil and hope. As I noted in Chapter 1, although I don't believe ameliorative work is confined solely to the music industry, electronic music has proved to be an excellent, in-depth case-study of issues that drive it. These issues may also be apparent in the wider creative and cultural industries and, indeed, in the world of work beyond that, particularly where cis men dominate or hold the balance of power.

According to the *Oxford English Dictionary* to ameliorate means: 'to make (something bad or unsatisfactory) better … reduce the impact or severity of (something negative or unpleasant) … to mitigate, alleviate, soften'.[7] Mitigating, alleviating and softening takes ingenuity, resilience, creativity, bravery and *power*. The act of ameliorating is therefore borne out of an optimism that things can get better. But it is also full of effort and exhaustion, and regularly incurs negative consequences. Emotional, physical, psychological, financial and creative resources are used up in the process, and neither positive nor negative aspects are more important than the other.

I believe we need this concept to balance the disproportionate amount of negative press around being a woman, or gender-expansive artist in electronic music and to celebrate the amazing work and success that is also achieved *despite* the hardships. I hope this book stands as a beacon of hope among the stark and often murky reality of the job. This is important, because a constant focus on the downsides drags us into despair and negativity with very little hope of inspiring future generations of women, trans and gender-expansive people to get involved. It's my contention that ameliorative work is a theory that might explain why gender inequality has proved so stubborn in electronic music, but equally, why women, trans and non-binary people work so hard to *follow their dreams anyway*.

So, with all this in mind, I will end with three manifestos for change in the electronic music industry. Whether you are a woman or gender-expansive artist, and/or someone in a position of influence within the music industry, or a music educator or researcher, there is something you can do.

Manifesto 1: For women, trans and non-binary people working in electronic music

1. Know that you are not alone, no matter how much you feel it.
2. Know that the work you do just to *survive and thrive* as a creative professional is twice as much as a cis man does. You are literally working a double shift, all the time. So at least give yourself credit for that, until someone else does too.
3. Play myth bingo. Pay attention to how many times you hear one of the myths in this book trotted out to you. Bonus points if you can swerve and deflect it back to them!
4. Practise delicious disruption whenever it is safe to do so. Call out, speak up, just *show up as you*. Call on your tribe for back-up if you get caught in a backlash.
5. Seek out connections and find your tribe – don't struggle on your own. There is so much support out there just waiting for you to tap into it. Level up your power through solidarity – and have fun!

6. If you already run an 'ameliorative organization' for minoritized genders in electronic music – *thank you*. I hope this book is a treasure trove of inspiration and evidence to help you write funding applications and secure sponsors.
7. Race, age, class, disability, sexuality are all intersections that keep some women and gender-expansive folks down more than others – see where your privilege is and use it to raise others.
8. Give this book to the gatekeepers in your world. Your manager, agent, record labels, the promoters you deal with, and the lecturers on your course if you're still in school. Bonus points if they are a cis man and double bonus points if you can get them to put their hands in their pockets and buy a copy themselves.
9. Share some of the ideas from this book with your cis-male artist friends. Even better, get them to read it.
10. Know that *you* are amazing for simply showing up every single day and doing what you do, and that this makes a difference *just by itself.* You inspire others and show that change is not only possible, it is happening – *and that's because of you.*

Manifesto 2: For those in a position of influence in the electronic music industry

1. Examine your own thoughts and reactions to the myths I have presented in this book and how they impact minoritized genders. Consider where you hold similar biases and reflect on that.
2. Recognize that the playing field is far from level and do what you can to support marginalized groups – whether that is offering additional A&R development if you are a record label, taking a 'chance' on a woman, trans or non-binary artist by giving them a good slot on your line-up if you are a promoter or festival, or following-up with encouragement to women and gender-expansive artists who don't immediately accept opportunities or respond to calls for contributions.
3. If you are a DJ, find and play music made by people other than cis-gender men in your sets, mixes and on your radio shows. Do this work yourself. You will find plenty of suggestions for how to do this in Chapter 2.
4. If you are a cis man, listen to your female and gender-expansive friends and colleagues. If you are a cis woman, listen to your trans and non-binary friends – ask them what makes them feel safe, and what they find harassing and/or irritating. Their answers may surprise you. Don't trivialize or minimize what they tell you.
5. Make sure your in-person spaces are safe. Check whether your women and trans artists, in particular, are happy with how they're getting to the gig, where they are staying and how they are getting home. Pay

attention to where they will be performing and the risks that might pose – do you have measures in place to protect their safety? Consider this even if you are only putting on a small event – harassment happens everywhere and grassroots venues are far from immune.
6. If you are in a reputational position to do so, consider an inclusion rider *especially if you are a cis man* – or at least try one out. State you will only play parties where there has been a genuine commitment to avoiding all-white cis-male line-ups.
7. Make sure your online spaces are safe. If you are platforming someone from a marginalized group online, police the comments and delete offensive posts. Respond to those who challenge or make remarks about 'positive action' with an informed explanation of why you are doing this. Don't leave this exhausting work to the artist – not least because if you are a cis man, coming from you the words will carry far more weight (unfortunately).
8. Challenge the backlash, don't hide from it, and don't use it as an excuse not to engage in allyship and positive action. Those who challenge positive action and believe in meritocracy are usually fully paid-up members of the myths I have described in this book. Use your platform to educate and inform.
9. Avoid drawing attention to gender unless you need to (and even then, question why you do). I know you mean well, but terms like female or trans DJ/producer, or calling an event line-up/festival stage 'the women's stage' (for example) is not helpful. Never refer to artists as sexy, or hot, or luscious, or anything else that sexualizes them. A good way to check this is to think 'How would this sound if I were describing a cis man?' If it feels weird, then don't do it.
10. Think about your offering. Ask people from marginalized communities if they feel included in your brand. This might be as simple as including photos of marginalized-identity people on your website, adding women's fit sizing to your merch, expanding colours beyond just black and so on.
11. Above all, do this quietly and not for your own glory. If you want to draw attention to your campaigns, ask yourself why that is? Think backstaging, not grandstanding.
12. Offer your services as a mentor to someone who is not like you – let them into your privileged world so they can see how things can be different, and you can see how different things are for them.

Manifesto 3: For educators, researchers and consultants

1. If you teach music technology or production, treat software as a tool for music making rather than an end in its own right – as Isobel Anderson says, 'it's time to bring artistry' back into learning about music in a digital age.

2. Know that girls and boys have been socialized to learn very differently – find out how to make your classroom inclusive.
3. Recognize that girls have had significantly less chances to jam with mates growing up and don't develop the skills that the boys take for granted. Understand that they don't know this and don't get why they feel so far behind.
4. Make it OK to be vulnerable in your classes, *for everyone*, so no one has to perform confidence they don't feel.
5. Engage in outreach work with schools to encourage more girls to consider learning music technology – start young, and entice them in different ways.
6. De-male your curriculum – discuss the work of pioneering women engineers and producers (of which there are many) and refer to their work. Screen documentaries about women in music. Normalize female expertise around technology, especially if you have a majority cis-male cohort and you are a cis male yourself.
7. If you teach courses on work, business or organization – use this book as case material to show how rife inequality is in creative work, and what can be done about it. I promise you it will go down well with your students. It does with mine.
8. If you are a researcher, take the concept of ameliorative work and run with it. Does it travel to other intersections of inequality and identity characteristics? Continue the process of unmasking all the hidden or undervalued work that minorities do as part of their jobs.
9. Take a reparative, appreciative inquiry approach in your own projects. Recognize the creative resilience these folks show, to change the narrative about marginalized groups and help them resist being cast only as victims.
10. If you are a consultant to the industry or commissioned to write a policy report, use the resources and ideas in this book to help support your work (and I'd love to hear from you if you do).

Appendix: Knowing the Industry Inside Out

Because of my involvement with the world of electronic music this was an ethnographic research project. Specifically, it is an organizational ethnography[1] – surfacing and critiquing the processes by which electronic music artists build their careers and make a living, while also being marginalized because of their gender. It is also feminist standpoint research[2] because I was (and am) engaged with the communities involved in order to bring about positive change. I have summarized my data generation activities in Table A1, although the 'always on' character of ethnography does not neatly fit into discrete activity classifications – for example, my time spent in clubs, informal conversations with people on social media via posts and direct messages, and the countless hours I have spent on DJ practice, recording mixes, watching tuition videos on YouTube, and engaging in music production all informed the project in various ways but would be impossible to delineate and quantify.

Insider research

This book is therefore generated from 'insider' research because I have been living the occupational culture of DJing, production and being a woman in the electronic music industry in a variety of roles. I did this through a strategy of 'interrupted involvement'[3] over a six-year period from 2018 to 2024, the time when I was writing this book. However, it is important to note that I didn't quit my job as a professor at the university in order to become an electronic music artist, therefore I can't claim to *truly* understand how it feels for my occupational identity and livelihood to be dependent on this industry and profession – unlike my participants. That said, as we saw in Chapter 2, many DJ/producers also have 'day jobs' alongside their musical careers and as such I was able to empathize

Table A1: Data generation activities

Activity	Date	Details	Data generated
DJ courses	2019	One-week intensive course (all women)	Autoethnographic reflection on learning
	2019	Two x one-to-one sessions with male DJs	
Production courses	2018	Six-week Introduction to Ableton (online) Mixed group	Autoethnographic reflection on learning Music tracks as artefacts
	2020	Music Production course (online, self-paced, all women/gender-expansive)	
	2021	Six-week intermediate production course (online, self-paced, all women/gender-expansive)	
Meet-ups	2019	3 x in-person local production sessions, including one with track feedback (mixed, but male-dominated)	Autoethnographic reflection on participation
	2020	3 x online sessions with all-women/gender-expansive group, including 'listening sessions' and track feedback	
In-person DJ sets	2018–24	9 x festival appearances from grassroots to major commercial events 14 x official events in club/bar environments and several others at informal parties	Ethnographic observation of DJ culture and event management Autoethnographic reflection on experiences
Livestreamed DJ sets	2020–23	12* x DJ sets for festivals, record labels, DJ collectives (*approximate number)	Ethnographic observation of DJ culture and event management in online space Autoethnographic reflection on experiences, particularly around tech
Industry conferences	2019–24	2 x events solely as delegate (2019, one all-women/gender-expansive event) 10 x events as expert panel member, speaker or panel convener. These usually included attending several parties and club nights with music industry contacts	(Auto)ethnographic observations of formal/informal industry activity

APPENDIX

Table A1: Data generation activities (continued)

Activity	Date	Details	Data generated
Industry roles	2019–24	Co-Chair AFEM Diversity and Inclusion group: holding and attending meetings, preparing reports/newsletter content, communicating with membership	(Auto)ethnographic observations of formal/informal industry activity
	2021	Women's night-time safety taskforce member (all women/gender-expansive group)	
	2019–22	Member of all women/gender-expansive DJ collective	(Auto)ethnographic observations of operation of and participation in grassroots volunteer collective
Workshops facilitated	2021, 2024	2 x development events for women/gender-expansive people in music industry	Ethnographic observations of discussions during session
Event organization	2020–24	Member of music performer team for non-profit, community festival	(Auto)ethnographic observations of politics and commercial dimension of event organization
	2021	Organized networking party at industry conference	
Podcast and radio production	2019–23	34 x 2-hour interview and music podcasts as In the Key (formerly In the Key of She) in collaboration with Sisu DJ collective	Analysis of conversations, and observations about politics of representation, censorship and editing (both mine and artists')
	2021 to date	Resident DJ with local radio station, have produced 35 two-hour shows at time of writing showcasing self-producing underground artists (not exclusively women or gender-expansive)	Autoethnographic reflections on learning how to be a radio producer
Development of 'Dovetail' and 'In the Key' brands	2019 to date	Setting up and maintaining social media accounts
Developing and sharing content and promotional materials
Professional photoshoot, writing bio, and curating 'electronic press kit'
Releasing music on independent record labels	Autoethnographic reflections on self-promotion/branding as an artist, and an industry advocate, navigating creative process and gendered politics of industry as an insider.
Formal interviews	2018–23	63 x semi-structured interviews, usually around 90 minutes in length. 44 were with women/gender-expansive producers, 13 were with non-producers running gender inequality initiatives, and six were conversations with cis men gatekeepers (for example, record labels, promoters). See Table A2 for further details.	Approx. 90 hours of audio-recorded discussion about gender in electronic music which was then transcribed for analysis

with their experiences of conflicting identities, squeezed time and energy and so on. I was also fortunate enough to be awarded a fellowship from The Leverhulme Trust to carry out the research between 2019 and 2021 which also allowed me to immerse myself in this world far more fully than I would have been able to while undertaking all my regular university duties. On reflection, during these two years, I 'went native', seeing my various music industry roles as more integral to my professional identity than academia.[4] This was partly because the majority of my fellowship coincided with the COVID-19 pandemic, meaning that contact with the university and my colleagues there was minimal. At the same time my activities as industry professional and consultant, radio presenter and DJ/Producer were growing.

Data quality: analytical distance

The realization I've just mentioned led me to seek 'critical friendship' from an academic colleague from 2020 onwards – Dr Marjana Johansson.[5] Marjana's unfamiliarity with the research context was a valuable counterbalance to my growing naturalization. We met regularly online for long conversations, and she brought an academic and theoretical perspective on the richness of my empirical stories – challenging me on my assumptions and interpretations, facilitating psychological and emotional distance from the data. Indeed, the central idea of the book – ameliorative work – emerged from our conversations over 18 months as we prepared an academic journal article developing and sharpening it as a useful theoretical concept.[6] Distance is important in ethnographic work in order to generate findings.[7] For example, it is not until you 'leave the field' as a researcher that you can conduct analysis that generates patterns arising from quieter stories within the data. Indeed, the whole concept of hope, and the strategy of taking a reparative reading came about once I had resettled into academic life. When I was living and breathing electronic music I was overwhelmed with the negative experiences I was hearing and reading about. Yet with critical distance I could see that to write only about that would be to reproduce a very particular, and potentially damaging, discourse that positioned these brave, sassy, powerful, and inspirational people as powerless victims. This revelation happened in Vienna in 2023 while Marjana and I were there to participate in a conference. Standing in the hallway of the beautiful 'Grande Dame' of a Viennese Airbnb apartment we were sharing, I wailed: 'I can't write something that says "*it's all just shit*", I just *can't*!', and that's when I remembered the work of Eve Sedgwick that my dear friend Ann Rippin had introduced me to only a few weeks before.[8] I skipped the conference dinner and spent the evening reading about reparation instead.

Com-passionate interviews

The formal conversations that generated the data for this project were carried out between 2018 and 2021, with the majority conducted over video call, using Zoom. This was partly due to the restrictions on travel necessitated by the COVID-19 lockdowns, but also proved a useful way to fit in with busy freelance musicians' schedules. Since the pandemic, video interviewing is no longer seen as inferior to face-to-face encounters,[9] and this was certainly my experience. Interviews were immersive and engaging with a high degree of rapport between my participants and myself. This came about in two main ways:

1. Being a new DJ/producer myself allowed me to understand the struggles and joys that were being recounted from what I refer to as a 'com-passionate' position.[10] During these conversations, the participant and I were communicating *with* (com-) passion about the topic which helped them see me as someone who understood and cared about their world.
2. The explicitly engaged agenda for the research, and my commitment to platforming women and gender-expansive artists through 'In the Key' helped them see I was serious about making a difference to their working lives.

The interviews were conversational, and the starting point for the interviews was open. They were broadly biographical, covering childhood and career histories with music, before discussing creative processes, career strategies, and occupational issues such as getting booked for DJ gigs, or signing music to record labels. I didn't assume that the participants felt discriminated against or viewed the industry in gendered terms. After I had completed the first one or two interviews I realized what a goldmine of inspiration and information they were for new DJs and producers, and so around half the conversations were used as the basis for the 'In the Key' radio show.[11] In practice, this meant recording the first half of the interview with the intention of it being for public consumption (45–60 minutes) and then continuing the conversation privately. This led to interesting data around what participants felt comfortable sharing in a public space versus what they told me privately – often about the same incidents. Everything that came after the end of the 'public' recording was guaranteed to be anonymous. A further layer of unexpected analysis arose through the editing process for the shows. The decisions I took about what made 'engaging' content to foreground in the episode, how I edited our natural speech and so on all told me what felt 'appropriate' to be sharing as inspirational 'infotainment'. Finally, the participants themselves exerted editorial control over content and style – I gave everyone the choice to listen to the final edit before it was aired, and sometimes I was asked to remove content, or edit speech, which led to productive discussion about how the participant wanted to be seen professionally.

Table A2: Sample characteristics

Characteristic	Details
Gender identity	63 formal interview participants in total All cis-gendered as far as I am aware, 90% women (n=57), 9% men (n=6), 3% non-binary (n=2)
Age of the women participants	50% in their 30s (20% early 30s, n=11, 30% mid- to late 30s, n=19) 26% in their 20s (n=17) 11% in their 40s (n=7), 6% Over 50s (n=3)
Heritage	36% black/brown/ mixed race (n=23) 63% white ethnicities (n=40)
Location[14]	73% UK (n=46), 8% Berlin (n=5), 6% USA (n=4), 6% Other Europe (n=4), 6% Other global (n=4)
Career experience as a producer	*44 producers in total* 13% Early stage with no music released (n=6) 25% Early stage with some releases (n=11) 52% Established producer with large catalogue of releases (n=23) 9% Veterans with long (20 year+) history in industry (n=4)
Industry roles	DJ (n=41), Producer (n=44), Radio presenter (n=9), Label owner (n=22), Promoter (n=11), Collective/initiative founder (n=19), Teacher/trainer (n=13), Industry support roles (n=5)
Sexuality	15% lesbian/non-binary/queer people (n=9)
Genres (of those who DJed/produced)	35% house/tech-house (n=17), 19% techno (n=9) 16% deep house (n=8), 15% drum & bass/ breakbeat (n=7) 10% downtempo/experimental (n=5)

Table A2 is a summary of my sample. I have chosen not to break demographic and career indicators down further to reduce the likelihood of readers being able to identify specific individuals. Protecting anonymity and minimizing risk of harm to participants is essential when conducting any research, but especially so given the sensitive nature of some of the topics we discussed.[12] The table should be seen a rough guide to the 'shape of the sample', as classifications are often fluid and difficult to determine, for example some early-stage producers had a much longer history as DJs, some with no releases nonetheless had strong production skills, and the extent of commercial success among the producers varied – several established artists still had 'day jobs' to enable them to make a living, for example. In addition, most participants held several industry roles at the same time with differing emphases that shifted over time.

Positionality

The value of ethnographic interviewing comes from the richness of the resulting data that results from a high degree of trust and empathy created during the conversation – they are far from objective encounters. The data that I generated in this project may well be quite different from the data you would generate, as your positionality might lead you to develop different avenues of conversation from the ones I followed. As such, it's important that you know a little more about me, so you can understand how my subject position will have impacted on the data. Some of this you will already have gathered from my stories earlier in the book.

I am a British-born, white, middle-aged, cis-gendered and heterosexual woman from a small southern UK city. I was born into a lower socio-economic household and left formal education with basic qualifications, (much) later diagnosed as neurodiverse with ADHD. I returned to higher education in my mid-20s while parenting two small children, and so began a successful career as an academic, obtaining a PhD in organization studies in my mid-30s and a professorship at 40. Prior to my first full-time lectureship aged 33, I always had multiple jobs at once, juggling work, family and study, and until my mid-30s struggled to make ends meet. With this in mind, I consider myself a 'self-made' person, although I am very much a product of the support I received from friends, partners and institutions along the way. As such I can see how I resonated with the fragmented, challenging lives recounted to me by my participants, but also wholeheartedly bought into their desire to create and succeed as artists. At times this has felt like a wistful longing to 'be like them' and at others, I have enjoyed my position as knowledgeable outsider and, as the research progressed, I realized my umbrella view of the industry was very helpful to the people I was interviewing in terms of making connections, and at times entering into a coaching-style relationship.

I have always been creative and have had a love of art and music, and started to learn DJing and production in my mid- to late 40s, but have had a particular love of electronic music since teenage years and been a 'raver' since I was 30. As intimated throughout the book, my family is characterized by traditional gender roles and I have often rebelled against anything to do with gender studies or women's empowerment for fear of 'upsetting the menfolk', as my grandmother once called it. In many ways this has been a difficult project to have instigated, not least because this was a complete change of research direction for me mid-career, and the first time I have ever worked in collaboration with industry as part of my academic role. Being invited to be a co-chair for a professional body in electronic music was wonderfully affirming of my need to feel useful in the world, but also replete with anxieties and self-doubt too.

What's still to be done?

Aside from the practical manifestos I have outlined in Chapter 9, there are a number of important directions for future investigations that I encourage you to follow if you are a researcher. In this project I chose to focus on women who were already producing music in order to facilitate the appreciate inquiry and 'positive' approach I describe in Chapter 1. I didn't include the voices of women who do not produce music, and so our understanding of their reasons has yet to be explored. I also was unable to formally interview trans women, and the numbers of non-binary people in my interview sample was low. There is a lot more work needed to amplify the voices of gender-expansive artists, not least around the issue of whether they feel comfortable being included with 'the women's campaign'.[13]

Now we know how much ameliorative work minoritized artists have to do on account of their gender, and the forms it takes, it would be interesting and important to know its prevalence across a wider range of people. Examining intersections of age, gender, race, education, genre and so on in more depth, for example, is better excavated through quantitative data, rather than the ethnographic strategy I have used in this project. Throughout the book I have cited results from several larger-scale gender-in-music surveys, but very few focus on the concrete strategies women, trans and non-binary people use in response to the challenges and opportunities they face, and even fewer zoom in on the electronic music industry with its unique challenges of being a DJ and (self-)producer, as I explained in Chapter 1. Numbers are powerful, and having a statistical dataset that covers a wider pool of artists, and perhaps geographies too, would be valuable. It would also allow tracking of trends in ameliorative work over time. As I note in Chapter 9, my hunch is that things are definitely improving for newer entrants to the industry, and in general – but that's a claim that requires further evidence to establish.

Finally, the concept of ameliorative work has untapped potential. How relevant is the idea to other marginalized identity characteristics, for example? Does it characterize life in other creative industries (and, yes, I suspect it does) and/or in occupations beyond the creative sphere? How do the contours of ameliorative work change in different circumstances? What kinds of ameliorative work are undertaken by black folks, or queer folks, or those with disabilities, for example, and do these identity facets throw up unique variations? I invite scholars of diversity to take the concept and run with it.

Notes

Chapter 1

1. Two key sources are Smith et al (2024) and Female:Pressure (2024), but Chapter 2 will present many more.
2. See the methodological summary in the Appendix for more details.
3. The name 'Dovetail' is also personally and musically meaningful to me for reasons I'll let you investigate yourself (Parsley, nd).
4. See the Appendix.
5. I have taken care not to present opinion, or unsubstantiated assertion as facts. Where possible, I have talked to the organizations involved and generally only write about companies and initiatives that are doing good things in this space.
6. Biehl (2019).
7. Butler (2014).
8. For example, see Wolfe (2020), Chapter 3, 'A studio of one's own'.
9. I refer to lots of writers' work throughout the book, but some key texts to highlight from the outset are Tara Rodgers' (2010) collection of interviews with women sound artists and performers in electronic music – one of the first to be published; Rosa Reitsamer's (2011) study of techno and drum and bass DJs; Rebekah Farrugia's (2012) exploration of being a female DJ in electronic dance music; Victoria Armstrong's (2016) account of how music education is gendered, excluding girls at every stage; Contributors to Rebekah Farrugia and Magdalena Olszanowski's (2017) special issue on 'Women and Electronic Dance Music Culture' in the online journal *Dancecult*; Paula Wolfe's (2020) examination of women's creative control in popular music production; Helen Reddington's (2021) book on women sound engineers and studio producers; and Kallie Marie's (2022) annotated conversations with women music producers working in recording studios.
10. The concept of 'ameliorative work' was developed in collaboration with my friend and co-author Dr Marjana Johansson who acted as a sounding board for the ideas I was developing during the research. Please see Parsley and Johansson (2025) for more details.
11. Branch and Rocchi (2015) have a nice philosophical paper about concepts in management research, which unpacks these ideas further, and more broadly these ideas rest on the understanding that language and discourse are what actually create reality. This is known as the 'linguistic turn' in the social sciences – and writers such as Luce Irigaray (1977) and bell hooks (1989) argue how language is deeply gendered, raced and classed. Spivak (1988) questions whether it is even possible for marginalized voices to speak within these dominant discourses. For a more lighthearted look at how new language comes into being – and particularly women writers' roles in that – see Grovier (2020).

12. The saying 'there's nothing so practical as a good theory' supports this. For an account of the origins of this phrase, widely attributed to Kurt Lewin in the 1940s, see Bedeian (2016).
13. This was also highlighted by Rosalind Duignan-Pearson (2019) in her research with South African women DJs who used everyday career strategies that were situationally contingent, ongoing judgement calls, meaning they were constantly on their guard.
14. See, for example, the Catalyst report examining the 'emotional tax' for people of colour in the workplace (Travis and Thorpe-Moscon, 2018).
15. At the time of writing, there are 437 ameliorative work projects listed on the Gender Equality Networks in Europe (GENIE) database and you can read more about this in Chapters 8 and 9.
16. Cooperrider and Witney (2005), Cooperrider (2021)
17. I first encountered these ideas from Debra Meyerson's (2001) article in *Harvard Business Review*. More recently Christina Malley has referred to this as 'delicious disruption' (Malley 2024) and I discuss this further in Chapter 9.
18. Sedgwick (2003), Chapter 4, 'Paranoid Reading and Reparative Reading, or, You're so paranoid, you probably think this essay is about you', reprinted from her 1995 original essay transcript.
19. See Tadajewski et al (2011).
20. Goodman (2022), see also Warren (2010) for a forerunner of these ideas.
21. Fineman (2006)
22. Many were nearer the two-hour mark, and a few were shorter than an hour.
23. An excellent discussion on gender non-conformity and the role of pronouns can be heard in ALOK's conversation with Man Enough (2021).
24. See n 10.
25. This 'hyper-text' approach to reading is something I have always done. Starting at the beginning and working through to the end of a book has often felt too overwhelming and off-putting which I later discovered was due to ADHD. If that's you too, just pick a chapter and read in whatever order you choose – as my coach Susanne Schotanus reminds me, there are no reading police!
26. Many cultural philosophers have talked about the importance of myths in human societies, but my approach in this book is influenced by Roland Barthes' argument in the early 1970s that everyday objects, symbols and language can be 'read' for social and ideological clues that position them as natural, universal, or 'common sense' that supports the status quo (Barthes, 2000).
27. See for example Bathurst and Monin (2010) and the foundational work in this area is Meyer and Rowan (1977).
28. See Mary Phillips and Ann Rippin's fascinating paper tracing the origins of the leadership of Starbucks and in particular the mythology around its 'mermaid' logo (Phillips and Rippin 2010).

Chapter 2

1. Draw the Line Radio Show, https://adarkerwave.com/draw-the-line-radio-show
2. You can listen to our discussion on the recording of the radio show here https://soundcloud.com/dovetail_uk/itkos-episode-20-jacki-e-oct-2020?in=dovetail_uk/sets/in-the-key
3. beatport.com: Beatport is the market-leading record store for electronic music DJs, describing itself as having been 'at the centre of DJ culture' for 20 years ('About Us'). DJs can browse hundreds of thousands of tracks, purchase and download them to their collection, discover new artists and follow their favourites.
4. 'DJ charts' on Beatport are lists of 10 or so tracks that the DJ is currently playing or otherwise enjoying. The idea is that if you enjoy that DJ's style then you will probably enjoy the music they're currently into – and go and buy it.

NOTES

5. blackartistdatabase.co/#/ This links directly to the artists' Bandcamp pages but do check them out on record stores (such as Beatport, Traxsource and so on) too, as often music released on record labels doesn't appear on their Bandcamp pages. BAD was instigated by Niks Delanancy in response to the US riots and BLM protests of 2020. You can hear her talking about it in my conversation with her for my radio show https://soundcloud.com/dovetail_uk/itkos-episode-21-niks-oct-2020?in=dovetail_uk/sets/in-the-key

6. Once you find an artist who looks like a woman or a non-cis man, check them out online and see what pronouns they use, or if you think they are not cis-gendered, check whether they have spoken out on trans issues, for example. You should never out a trans person who does not publicly identify as trans. For excellent commentary on this see https://saffronmusic.co.uk/stories/making-space-exploring-questions-of-trans-and-nonbinary-inclusion/

7. www.inthekey.org/directory The directory was compiled with assistance from Alex Wright (who DJs as Hide the Soul) and Thilini Jayawickrama (who DJs as Thilini).

8. Other directories to peruse include the Dynamics database dynamics-music.com/ that specializes in gender-expansive and female drum and bass, and jungle DJs (not necessarily producers); and The F List for Music https://thef-listmusic.uk/ which is a directory of women, trans and non-binary people across all music genres and all music industry roles. More specialized directories include Soundgirls.org predominantly for audio engineers and studio producers.

9. Jaguar Foundation/SONY Report (2022: 49).

10. I first came across this term in Professor Karen Johnson and Dr Emily Yarrow's work on diversity accreditation committees in Higher Education (Johnson and Yarrow, 2024), but the concept was first introduced in 1994 by black American scholar Amado Padilla (Padilla 1994).

11. See Bindu De Knock's book *The All-Round Musician* for an excellent guide (De Knock, 2021) for more details about contracts. It's also worth noting that large promoters booking for high profile shows often insist that the artist doesn't DJ at another event in the same city for several weeks, or longer.

12. Kitching and Smallbone (2008). The statistics are dated, but the issues raised in this report summarize the complexities of identifying and counting freelance workers (in the UK at least).

13. In the UK, for example, the UK Music Diversity Taskforce, which had a response rate to its 2024 survey of 2,574 people who consider themselves musicians or working in the music industry: https://www.ukmusic.org/wp-content/uploads/2024/06/UK-Music-Diversity-Report-2024.pdf

14. https://www.digitaldjtips.com/census-results-2024/

15. With a bias towards English-speaking countries, given that's where the platform originated.

16. Slide 15, IMS Business Report 2024 (Mulligan and MIDIA Research, 2024).

17. Digital DJ Tips 2024 DJ survey/census (Morse, 2024).

18. Moving others with their music is the number one marker of success for musicians in 2024, according to industry research, with 94 per cent of respondents agreeing to that statement: www.amuse.io/en/successredefined/

19. See Nick Prior's chapter 'The Rise of the New Amateurs' (Prior, 2010) and also Ramburran (2017) on amateur 'laptop musicians'.

20. For an overview of the legal situation in the UK, see the Musicians' Union guidance: https://musiciansunion.org.uk/working-performing/recording-and-broadcasting/music-copyright-performers-rights-in-sound-recordings

21. There are several different types of rights, including performing rights, sound rights, composition rights and neighbouring rights – it's beyond the scope of this book to go into these in detail here, but check out Bindu De Knock's great book (see note 10) and

22. https://blog.songtrust.com/music-publishing-fact-collective-management-organization
23. Sentric Music https://www.sentric.com/ and Ditto Music https://dittomusic.com/en are just two of many music publishers, each with their own differentiated set of services, making it hard to compare them.
24. https://prsformusic.com/press/2021/tipping-the-scales-new-figures-show-more-women-entering-songwriting-profession and https://blog.songtrust.com/songtrusts-client-survey-who-are-our-clients
25. From Vick Bain's 2019 report *Counting the Music Industry* (Bain, 2019)
26. https://breakwindproductions1.bandcamp.com/album/dovetail-ep
27. The economics of digital music streaming was the subject of a UK government independent enquiry in 2021, which is well summarized in White (2022). Spotify's response to the recommendations was to introduce a redistribution of streaming royalty towards more 'professional' artists (1,000 streams or more per track). You can read responses to this from a variety of academic experts on the website of the Centre for Regulation of the Creative Economy (CREATe, 2023).
28. Music distributor Ditto have a useful blog post on this topic (Ditto, 2024).
29. As reported in the 2024 report *Inclusion in the Recording Studio* published annually by the Annenberg Inclusion Initiative (Smith et al, 2024).
30. 2% Rising is a Facebook group founded in 2018 by Katie Tavini, Jen Rookes and Suzie Cooper as a 'safe community on the internet for women & gender-expansive people who produce & engineer music': https://www.facebook.com/groups/2percentrising/
31. Lazar et al (2023) *Fix the Mix* report.
32. Wolfe (2020), Chapter 3, 'A studio of one's own'.
33. See also Kallie Marie's great 2022 book on the lives of women producers working in recording studios (Marie, 2022).
34. Charles Audley, Interview for 'Sisu Presents: In the Key', April 2019, https://soundcloud.com/dovetail_uk/sisu-presents-in-the-key-of-she-with-charles-audley-noisily-exclusive
35. Morse (2016).
36. Find out more about Deevstock here: www.deevstock.com
37. See Haynes and Marshall (2018) on musicians and entrepreneurship.
38. One of the earliest discussions of this is Banks and Hesmondhalgh (2009). It seems to have receded from more recent writing on creative industries, however – possibly because it has now become so normalized.
39. Whitman et al (2025).
40. https://a2d2.net/blogs/blog/the-hardest-working-djs-of-2023
41. In the UK, nightclub numbers and attendance are shown to be in decline, but festivals still number 300 nationally, with 19,500 artists performing there https://ntia.co.uk/the-second-uk-electronic-music-industry-report/
42. https://ntia.co.uk/nte-economy-report-2024/
43. Female:Pressure (2024) FACTS Survey.
44. ROSTR (nd).
45. www.bookmorewomen.com
46. In 2018 I replicated the Book More Women method for some UK festivals for one of my early blog posts about the In the Key project: https://inthekey.org/electronicher-part-two/
47. www.keychange.eu/themovement
48. You can hear more about this from HAAi on this podcast: https://ra.co/podcast/829
49. 'Safety and Inclusion Rider' template: https://inthekey.org/resources/

NOTES

50. Original research undertaken by Sky News in 2023 (Dunford et al, 2023)
51. For example, at the time of writing, these included Charlotte de Witte, Amelie Lens, Nina Kraviz, Deborah de Luca, Peggy Gou, Honey Dijon and Nicole Moudaber.
52. 'Radiomonitor monitors the music played on radio and TV in over 120 countries. This airplay data is used by all major record labels, music broadcasters, media, PR and for royalty management': https://app.radiomonitor.com/home/?username=#aboutus
53. https://womeninctrl.com/gender-disparity-in-radio/
54. https://everynoise.com/gender_tldr.html#:~:text=Overall%2C%20Spotify%20has%2043.6%25%20female,female%20or%20mixed%2Dgender%20artists
55. Bradley (1999)

Chapter 3

1. Listen to the three-part series 'Techno a Social History', by Ash Lauryn, to learn more about both the US and German roots of techno (Lauryn, 2022).
2. A good text that charts the rise of rave culture, and one of the only ones written by a woman, is Sheryl Garrett's *Adventures in Wonderland* (Garrett, 2020).
3. Other texts on the birth of the electronic dance music scene include Reynolds (2013); and Collin (2009). If you prefer documentaries, Patrick Hinton has assembled some cult classics in his *Mixmag* article (Hinton, 2017).
4. The Peace, Love, Unity and Respect Movement was given shape by DJ Frankie Bones' rules for his Storm Rave parties held in New York aircraft hangers at the beginning of the 1990s (see Sterling, 2016).
5. See Jaguar Foundation/SONY (2022: 12–13).
6. There were *some* messages of support on the main festival page – particularly heartening were the ones from men. I reached out to thank as many of them as I could, and made a couple of friends in the process.
7. Lash and Urry (1994), Chapter 5, 'Accumulating signs: the culture industries'.
8. Hooper (2019).
9. Janosov et al (2020a).
10. Clarke et al (2024).
11. Huber (2016).
12. Hooper (2019).
13. AFEM (2021).
14. Knowlton (2024: 4).
15. I thoroughly recommend Peggy Macintosh's excellent privilege-busting checklist from 1988 to help unpack your own privileges (Macintosh, 1998).
16. Project Implicit is global crowdsourced research project that examines the extent of implicit bias across various measures https://implicit.harvard.edu/implicit/takeatest.html. For a discussion of the concept from an ethical standpoint, see Brownstein (2016), and for a good account of the concept's criticisms see Brownstein et al (2020).
17. For an excellent study on the effect of homophily on investment in women's businesses, see Greenberg and Mollick (2017).
18. Benn Jordan's MPW video podcast is here https://www.youtube.com/watch?v=Mzcn78H1ecE and the full video on his YouTube can be viewed here https://www.youtube.com/watch?v=2Ipb81z46kI
19. I took active steps to rectify this, with the help of several wonderful people who put me in contact with their networks. You can see a summary of my interview sample characteristics in the Appendix.
20. Janosov et al (2020b). They also note that mentoring is not a predictor of getting into the very top elites, however.

21 Hooper (2019: 137). Emma Hooper's (2019) chapter is one of the only music industry studies I have found that examines the influence of the boys' club as it operates through homosociality.
22 Criado-Perez (2019).
23 https://www.healthline.com/health/average-hand-size#adults
24 Potocnik, M. (2024).
25 Wreyford (2015: 93).
26 EdExcel, cited in Criado-Perez (2019: 18).
27 Friedmann and Efrat-Treister (2023), see also Fine (2010) Chapter 5.
28 Hangartner et al (2021).
29 Jackson and Oliver (2003).
30 MU (2024: 27).
31 Morris et al (2024).
32 See Grugulis and Stoyanova (2012) and Wreyford (2015) for accounts of this in the screen industries.
33 Abtan (2016: 56).
34 Kill (2020: 90).
35 Smith (2024).
36 Tanner (2022).
37 Abtan (2016: 55).
38 See Laura Bates, *Fix the System not the Women* (2022), and for scholarly research identifying the normalizing of gendered incidents, see Kim and Meister (2022).
39 MacKenzie and MacKinlay (2021).
40 Galop (an LGBTQ+ anti-abuse charity in the UK) has seen a 65 per cent rise in requests for support from trans people who have experienced abuse, and argues that the England and Wales statistics woefully underestimate the problem, despite also recording a rise (GALOP, 2023). See also Home Office (2023).

Chapter 4

1 In the US the direct/indirect distinction is known as 'disparate treatment and disparate impact', but the premise is the same.
2 Campbell and Smith (2023) note that this is in itself a crude distinction that doesn't sufficiently take account of the morality of discriminatory acts.
3 Jaguar Foundation/SONY (2022: 27), quote by Riva.
4 Taking the financial loss herself, the irony of being a woman, working for free to support women in the industry as a woman was not lost on either of us.
5 For companies employing less than 250 people, there is no requirement to report what they pay men and women under the UK Gender Pay Gap Reporting rules (Gov.UK, 2024)
6 The 'majors' are SONY, Warner and Universal, as defined by the Association of Independent Music as having 5 per cent market share globally. All other labels are technically 'independent', but some are also huge concerns, such as Atlantic, Columbia, Epic, RCA and so on. Generally, electronic dance music is not released on the majors – but their share is growing as 'commercial EDM' becomes big business.
7 This information was requested from artist managers, agents, booking agencies, promoters and so on ,who were contacted using professional networks and close contacts.
8 For example, see Jaguar Foundation/SONY report (2022: 36).
9 European Data Journalism Network (2020).
10 Digital culture feminists Nicolas Carah and Amy Dobson refer to this as 'algorithmic hotness' (Carah and Dobson, 2016).

NOTES

11. This is a tension at the heart of modern feminism. Third wave feminism asserts that women have the right to behave however they choose, including DJing topless, seeing these as 'sex-positive' actions. More traditional views of feminism would see this as exploitation conditioned by neoliberal patriarchal structures and the male gaze. In other words, the so-called 'freedom' of sex-positivity is actually a form of oppression and exploitation which perpetuates inequality – as Olive considers it here. 'Getting your boobs out' might be your choice, but it's also playing to (cis, straight) male desire. Angela McRobbie's book *The Aftermath of Feminism* is a good place to read more about this difficult debate (McRobbie, 2009).
12. This has led to a whole economy of skill based on homage to the past and legacy equipment that affects how modern DJs see themselves (Foroughi et al, 2024).
13. www.imdb.com/title/tt11906012/
14. Beard (2018).
15. Beard (2018: 8).
16. For a harrowing read about contemporary abuse endured by women who speak out about anything remotely gender-related on social media, see Chapter 14 of Mary Ann Sieghart's book, *The Authority Gap* (Sieghart 2021). I should warn that the comments you will read there may be triggering– that was certainly the case for me.
17. Baudrillard (1983). It is also the set of ideas behind the film *The Matrix*. For a light-hearted explanation see Magdalen Rose's YouTube video which I very much enjoyed: youtube.com/watch?v=h7urGFiy_3g
18. Gawronski et al (2003) present a thorough, albeit it jargon-heavy review and study of how this happens.
19. For a review of the complicated intersectional dynamics at play in relation to light skin and privilege, see Phoenix and Craddock (2023).
20. See especially O'Shea (2016: 213) and also discussed eloquently by Biehl (2024: 51) in relation to norms around leadership and what the bodies of leaders 'should' look like.
21. A derogatory term for 'the hanging fat that swings from an obese woman's upper arms when they are raised and shaken while shouting "Bingo!" during a tournament', but which has entered common parlance (in the UK at least). https://www.urbandictionary.com/define.php?term=bingo%20wing
22. For those unfamiliar with dance music patter, 'Throw your hands in the air like you just don't care' is a disco/hip-hop-inspired instruction meted out by DJs and popularized by Cameo in the 1980s' in their hit single 'Word Up'. The internet is inconclusive as to its origins, but as one comment on the 'Ask MetaFilter' thread I read points out – it probably has origins in gospel music or the music of enslaved, black people, like so many of the motifs used in modern dance music: https://ask.metafilter.com/112061/Where-does-this-phrase-come-from
23. I'm pleased to say that I am now much more accepting of my ageing body and, several years on, look back at this photo with the wish that I still looked this young and slim!
24. Parsley and Sambrook, working paper, 'Embodying the patriarchy'. The idea of self-governance comes from the work of French philosopher Michel Foucault, and in particular the way that disciplining regimes work through the body in what he calls 'biopolitics'. Power-laden social norms and expectation agendas (for example looking a certain way) work through our bodies as we literally alter our flesh, chemistry and so on to confirm to them. See Repo (2016) for a fuller discussion of biopolitics and gender.
25. O'Grady and Madill (2019)
26. This is far less likely the further into the underground community you go, where clubbers are way more diverse than at commercial events.

27. His name is Nick Hayes, and his Instagram account can be accessed here: https://www.instagram.com/the_last_dj_
28. 2024 Women Musicians Insight Report (Musicians Census, 2024: 11).
29. Etzkowitz and Ranga (2011).
30. My favourite rendition of this song is by Annie Lennox, which you can listen to (and watch) here: https://www.youtube.com/watch?v=pfk8kLJMab0
31. These were also issues raised by Kallie Marie's professional studio engineers (Marie, 2022: 69–83).
32. See https://pregnantthenscrewed.com/ for a UK-focused glimpse into the level of workplace pregnancy discrimination that is still happening today across all industries and sectors.
33. At the time of writing, the video and post from Amelie Lens is available to see here https://www.instagram.com/amelie_lens/reel/C-GWbs5OEK1/ but I realize that social media content is dynamic so this may not be a permanent reference.
34. 2024 Women Musicians Insight Report (Musicians Census, 2024: 27–29).
35. In 2018 audio engineer Olga Fitzroy instigated a campaign to raise awareness of the 'motherhood penalty' in music, specifically to the UK, calling for an extension of shared parental leave entitlement to parents where both are self-employed (Fitzroy, 2018). This is also discussed in Reddington (2021: 116). As far as I am able to ascertain there has been no change in the law around this.
36. Musicians Census (2024:38).
37. For further reading I recommend on this Anne Karpf's little book *How to Age* (Karpf, 2014), and Sharon Blackie's *Hagitude* (Blackie, 2023), which you can also find out more about here https://hagitude.org/

Chapter 5

1. Faragher (2023) is an accessible overview of the difference between positive action and positive discrimination in a UK context from a practitioner perspective. For a good academic overview see Broderick (2022), and for a global comparison of these measures from an academic law perspective see Oppenheimer (2019).
2. Jagger and Turner (2020: 257).
3. Knowlton et al (2022).
4. You can listen to that episode here https://soundcloud.com/dovetail_uk/sisu-presents-in-the-key-of-she-with-charles-audley-noisily-exclusive
5. Knowlton et al (2022: 7).
6. The heading for this section is a play on the 'Normal Not Novelty' name that the (now disbanded) Red Bull campaign for gender equality in dance music used when I first began this research, and it sums up the issues so well.
7. See Kirsch (2022) and Miliopoulou and Kapareliotis (2021).
8. For more on the idea of the 'Queen Bee', and particularly the role of context in encouraging such behaviours, see Derks et al (2011).
9. Mavin and Yusupova (2020).
10. Ironically, using the beat sync button actually opens up higher-level skills of editing on the fly, looping and cutting parts of several tracks simultaneously, for example – fully harnessing the creative potential of digital DJing. This story is told in much more depth in my article on the gendering of the sensory skills of learning to be a DJ (Parsley, 2022).
11. https://ra.co/dj/girlsdontsync
12. I first encountered this idea from scholar Marilyn Davidson's work on women in management (Davidson and Burke, 1994) framed as the 'salience of gender'. See also Rosalind Duignan-Pearson (2019) on this in her study of women DJs in South Africa.

NOTES

13 See, for example, Jones et al (2014), Kuchynka et al (2017) and Hideg and Shen (2019).
14 See also the discussion in Chapter 3 about implicit bias as an excuse for explicit action.
15 Knowlton (2024).

Chapter 6

1   Merrich (2021).
2   Mixing and mastering are processes that really shape and polish the final track: 'mixing' refers to the balance of sounds within the music and how they sit in 'space' when you listen to them; and 'mastering' is a bit of a dark art, where frequencies are boosted, cut, compressed, limited and so on to make the music as crisp and as full as possible.
3   See also Biehl (2024: 48–51) on the damaging dynamics of 'passing'.
4   In fact, ghost producing can be a very lucrative income stream for producers. One of my earlier interviewees told me he earns in the region of £25,000 a year from producing for other people. As an introvert with little interest in fame and fortune himself, he is, by and large, happy to let someone else take the credit because he's proud that his music is out there in a way it could never be under his own name. In 2018, *Mixmag* published a fascinating and insightful article into this practice (Raven, 2018), but it still remains a dark side to the underground electronic music scene.
5   See Kallie Marie's great book on the lives of women producers working in recording studios (Marie, 2022).
6   Good sources to learn about what is involved in self-producing electronic music are Wolfe (2020), Chapter 3, 'A studio of one's own', and Prior (2018). For instruction on how to actually produce electronic music – see the further resources list that accompanies this book on the In the Key website at www.inthekey.org/minor-keys-book
7   See, for example, Richards (2017) on the influence of maker communities, and their relationship with gender imbalance (Richards, 2016); Chapter 17, 'Artist', in Brewster and Broughton (2022) on the shift from DJ to producer through sampling, edit and remix culture; and Reitsamer (2011) on the DIY origins of DJ/production as a career.
8   For a quick introduction see Hagen (2024), and for more scholarly, critical accounts consult Harkins and Prior (2022), Prior (2018), and Ramburran (2017).
9   A mash-up is where you mix two or more (often very different) tracks together to create fun, or surprising, versions. An edit is the same kind of process, but usually done in a DAW rather than live while performing. What sets an 'edit' apart from a remix or a full production is that an edit is just chopping up and moving pieces of the original full track whereas in remixing or producing from scratch you work with each element of the music individually (see also Brewster and Broughton, 2022, Chapter 17).
10 Reitsamer (2011: 37).
11 These and many other resources are listed at www.inthekey.org/minor-keys-book
12 Jagger and Turner (2020).
13 Jagger and Turner (2020: 260).
14 Thompson (2020).
15 Fine (2010, 2017). *Delusions of Gender* focuses generally on the nature/nature debate and brain-sex, and *Testosterone Rex* is a more in-depth consideration of the rise in hormonal explanations for differences between men and women. Both books are a delight, not least because they are laugh-out-loud funny, which is somewhat unusual for scientific literature!
16 Fine (2010: 16–21).
17 Fine (2010: 171).
18 Fine (2010), Chapter 15, 'The "seductive allure" of neuroscience'.
19 A succinct summary of this process is given in Fine (2010: 236).
20 Fine (2010), Chapter 16, 'Unravelling hardwiring'.

[21] Farrugia (2012: 127).
[22] Statistics from the Work and Opportunities for Women Report on Unpaid and Unrecognised Labour (WOW, 2021).
[23] ILO (2018).
[24] Office for National Statistics (ONS, 2016).
[25] For an overview of recent research, see Hogenboom (2021).
[26] A recent review of studies on these topics was undertaken by Natalia Reich-Stiebert and her colleagues (Reich-Steibert et al, 2023).
[27] Farrugia (2012: 129).

Chapter 7

[1] Producer and researcher Kallie Marie found the same pattern in her research with studio producers (Marie, 2022: Chapter 4), and Helen Reddington also mentions hearing this from her interviews with women sound engineers (Reddington, 2021: 23).
[2] See Fine (2010), Chapter 18, for some stark evidence of implicit gender stereotypes in parenting that support this.
[3] The first of two bonus episodes of Isobel Anderson's 'Girls Twiddling Knobs' podcast includes thought-provoking observations on gender balance in the music technology classroom (Anderson, 2023a).
[4] For a fuller discussion of these ideas see Parsley (2022).
[5] To learn more about the gendered history of our senses, I recommend David Howes (2004) book, Constance Classen's (1997) paper and her (1998) book from which I will draw more later. Historian Sasha Rasmussen's blog post on the *History Journal*'s website is also a nice read (Rasmussen, 2021).
[6] Women's inferiority and unsuitability for anything to do with thinking, argument or cerebral life (politics, education, public life, you name it) has been variously 'proven' over the years in what now seem to be highly amusing ways – from having smaller, lighter brains, more delicate brain fibres, excesses of bodily fluids, and lighter spinal columns, to deterministic hormone levels and differentially activated brains and the existence of particular genes. For a systematic and amusing demolition of all these theses, see Fine (2010, 2017).
[7] Grosz (1994).
[8] Classen (1998: 66).
[9] Classen (1997: 4).
[10] Howes (2004).
[11] Farrugia (2012: 21).
[12] Wolfe (2020: 111).
[13] Reddington (2021: 100–101).
[14] On our home amplifier these showed the level of treble and bass frequencies being sent to the speakers, and the needles twitched in time with the music – the aim being to get them to swing and bounce within a certain range marked on the panel behind them. Twiddling with these was probably my earliest introduction to audio mixing.
[15] Interestingly I never regarded the equipment associated with my gran and mum's hobbies – such as a weaving loom, a sewing machine, a pottery kiln and lace-making equipment – as 'technology' at all.
[16] I am pleased to say that I finally got my wish, aged 50, when my friends and family clubbed together to buy me a Korg Minilogue XD.
[17] Many of the artists in this study have no musical training whatsoever – and those who were classically trained saw that as a double-edged sword with the potential to constrain their creativity, as they had internalized accepted ways of doing things.

18 Doubleday (2008: 19).
19 Armstrong (2016: 31–32).
20 Wolfe (2020: 13).
21 Reddington (2021: 152). Interestingly this seems to be changing with a recent renaissance of vocals in beat-heavy genres such as a techno and tech-house.
22 We see this throughout all sorts of occupations – caring, nursing, teaching, home management, customer service, cleaning – anything that is associated with so-called 'women's skills' of nurturing, bodily expertise, using one's emotions to persuade or calm others and so on is generally low-status, low-paid and presumed to be low skilled. These kinds of roles are only performed by men when they have no choice, such as migrant workers or those living in poverty. For more on this in a UK context, see Florrison and Gable (2022).
23 Reddington (2021), Chapter 6, 'Ventriloquism'.
24 Armstrong (2016: 64).
25 https://unesdoc.unesco.org/ark:/48223/pf0000389406
26 https://professionalprograms.mit.edu/blog/leadership/the-gender-gap-in-stem/
27 For a thorough discussion of the roots of gender inequality, you can't get better than Simone de Beauvoir's *The Second Sex*, published in 1949 (De Beauvoir, 1997), and more recently, Mary Beard's (2018) short book *Women and Power: A Manifesto* gives a comprehensive account of how women came to be excluded from the public sphere and why it's so hard for this to change.
28 Huber (2016), Chapters 3 and 4.
29 American psychologist and industrial engineer Lillian Gilbreth was foundational in arguing that the work of the 'housewife' was a complex job as difficult as any man's in the workplace (Gilbreth, 1927). Often eclipsed by her husband's work, Lillian is credited with inventing the modern, efficient kitchen as we know it today, using the principles of scientific management, which you can read more about on her Wikipedia page.
30 The introduction to Cordelia's Fine's (2010) book *Delusions of Gender* brilliantly charts the history of this.
31 Women's access to finance is still a large determinant of gender gaps globally; for example, according to the International Monetary Fund (Morsy, 2020), only 37 per cent of women in sub-Saharan Africa have their own bank account, which is largely due to internalized gender roles by the women themselves and family dynamics.
32 This is a necessarily brief potted history of female intellectual subjugation, and alternative accounts of women's achievement in history abound, such as Sadie Plant's alternative feminine history of technology (Plant, 1997), and in music see the Women in Sound, Women on Sound project (WISWOS, nd), Tara Rodgers' (2010) *Pink Noises*, the film 'Sisters with Transistors (https://sisterswithtransistors.com/), and Johann Merrich's (2021) book on the history of women in electronic music around the world.
33 Prior (2018: 88). See also the discussion on p 111 of Paula Wolfe's (2020) book *Women in the Studio*.
34 Anderson (2023a).
35 Brereton et al (2020).
36 Bayton (1997: 42).
37 Music researcher Simon Waters (2016: 66–67) suggests that one way we might start to overcome this is to recruit students into music technology courses 'from subject areas more explicitly concerned to embrace inter-sensorial exploration … after all Art schools have never struggled to recruit women'.
38 Anderson (2023a).
39 Bayton (1997: 42).
40 Armstrong (2016: 50)

41. Isobel has an interesting approach to teaching music production in her courses that I return to in Chapter 9 as part of the manifesto (Anderson, 2023b).
42. See https://www.edmprod.com/electronic-music-production-glossary/ for a comprehensive glossary.
43. Sharon Jagger and Helen Turner refer to this as the 'cool capital of music production' (Jagger and Turner, 2020: 255) – and indeed I realize I have used the word 'cool' a lot in this chapter.
44. For more about 'somatic norms' (Puwar, 2021) and how certain bodies and identities seem to be a 'natural fit' for certain occupations, see Ashcraft (2013); and for a fuller discussion of these dynamics, see Parsley (2022) and Parsley and Johansson (2025).
45. See, for example, Yodovich (2021) and Wray (2020).
46. I took a few classes with my friend Gary Wood, and then with MPW (Music Production for Women) to learn in an all-female/ gender-expansive space. For details on MPW, see the further resources list that accompanies this book on the In the Key website at: www.inthekey.org/minor-keys-book
47. Helen Reddington quotes journalist Art Tavana on the idea that GarageBand is a 'gateway DAW' before moving on to more sophisticated software, and because it came preloaded on Apple's laptops for many years it has been heralded as a great democratizer in music production. For a critique of this idea, see Harkins and Prior (2022), who call for a closer look at how *socialization* around cheaper and more accessible equipment still follows traditional socio-economic, racialized and gendered patterns.
48. You can watch how she does this on her Instagram channel https://www.instagram.com/sarahsommers.bimboprincess/reel/C6MinZEoVD5/
49. In 2021 Mattel launched 'Music Producer' as their 'career-of-the-year' doll to highlight the gender gap in music production (see Chapter 2 for stats on this). I am pleased to say that there is a black version of Producer Barbie and a white version https://corporate.mattel.com/news/barbie-launches-new-music-producer-doll-to-highlight-the-gender-gap-in-the-industry
50. This contrasts with the experiences of women in male-dominated industries who report a paradox of simultaneously being *invisible* as professional experts while they are *highly* visible as women on account of there being very few of them (Lewis and Simpson, 2010).
51. Armstrong (2016), see particularly pp 31 and 104. I'm not saying here that tech affirms ALL masculine identities – but the archetype of the nerd/geek is male.
52. Anderson (2023a).
53. Virginia Caputo's work, cited in Armstrong (2016); see also Anderson (2023a).
54. I am delighted to say that at least one of the companies I spoke to has since involved a more diverse pool of beta testers for their products as a result of speaking with me about this.
55. MIDI stands for Musical Instrument Digital Interface and is the instruction you give to software to start/stop or otherwise manipulate a sound that you have instructed it to play. It means that you can swap and change the sounds, effects or groove patterns without losing the cadence and arrangement of your track.
56. For a fuller discussion see Parsley (2022).
57. Jagger and Turner (2020: 254–256).
58. https://www.analogtara.net/
59. https://en.wikipedia.org/wiki/Category:Theremin_players
60. Visit the MiMU website https://mimugloves.com/gloves/ or watch a demonstration of them performed by founder Imogen Heap here https://www.youtube.com/watch?v=CvyVQqCO8pY&t=8s
61. For more examples see *Push, Turn, Move* by Kim Björn, now in its second edition (Björn, 2021), or visit the 'New Interfaces for Musical Expression' website, https://nime.pubpub.org/

NOTES

62. https://nime.pubpub.org/pub/wkeb4nv4/release/1
63. This idea and the following detail comes from Tom Faber's fascinating research (Faber, 2021).
64. Personal communication with MiMU development team and also a demonstration of how the gloves help musicians with disabilities from musician Kris Halpin here: https://www.drakemusic.org/video/mimu-gloves-demo-by-kris-halpin/
65. Kallie Marie (2022: 45).

Chapter 8

1. Orgad and Gill (2022: 9).
2. The term 'imposter phenomenon' was first used in research on high-achieving women in the 1970s by psychotherapists Pauline Clance and Suzanne Imes (Clance and Imes, 1978).
3. I won't single out any resources here but just do a YouTube or Amazon search for 'overcoming imposter syndrome' and you'll get the idea. Shani Orgad and Rosalind Gill also undertake careful and sensitive critique of several of these texts throughout their book (Orgad and Gill, 2022).
4. The track is called 'Almost Like' and was released on DaCosta Records in 2021. You can find out more about this track at the end of Chapter 3.
5. Orgad and Gill (2022), Chapter 2, 'Confidence at Work'.
6. Palvia et al (2015).
7. Orgad and Gill (2022: 56).
8. Tulshyan and Burey (2021a, 2021b); Brown (2021).
9. Hewertson and Tissa (2022).
10. Tran (2023).
11. See also Jagger and Turner (2020: 257).
12. Anderson (2023b).
13. Urban language moves so fast that 'snowflake' may not be a common term by the time you are reading this. Just in case, at the time of writing, relevant definitions of 'snowflake' from the Urban Dictionary include 'a very sensitive person. Someone who is easily hurt or offended by the statements or actions of others', and 'an insult, used to mean that a person is too easily insulted or is too sensitive to the opinions, often used by people from the alt-right' https://www.urbandictionary.com/define.php?term=Snowflake
14. See discussion on p 559 in Ryan and Morgenroth (2024).
15. Van Veleen et al (2019).
16. Because what follows is so sensitive, and was generously confided to me despite being traumatic for those involved, I have not attributed these real stories to any individual person to ensure their identities are completely protected.
17. Jaguar Foundation/SONY report (2022).
18. Eva Petersen refers to the unique characteristics of the music workplace as 'lawless spaces'. Her research particularly focuses on the experience of being on tour where having to sleep on tour buses, and the gendered politics of dressing rooms and green rooms all feel beyond the law, falling under the hackneyed phrase 'what goes on on tour stay on tour' (Petersen, 2024).
19. Duignan-Pearson (2019).
20. Marie (2022: 83).
21. These are where the artist shares a video of a screen-recording of them showing how they put their music together in their DAW – layering effects, setting controls, manipulating samples and mixing and so on – to give an insight into their creative process.
22. For a well-researched and informative account detailing the history of the term 'safe space' in relation to homosexuality, see Fusion Staff (2015).

23   At the time this book goes to print, cultural anthropologist and DJ Anjali Prashar-Savoie is writing a fascinating insider's account of work and activism in queer nightlife that will be published by Velocity Press in 2026. I highly recommend it.
24   See, for example, Schiller-Merkens (2024).
25   For example, see O'Shea (2020), Herrera (2023) and Abdellatif (2024).
26   See the GENIE database for a comprehensive list – featured as the opening vignette in Chapter 9: https://geniedatabase.com/
27   https://mdlbeast.com/events/xp-music-futures-24/hunna
28   www.hospitalrecords.com/equality-and-inclusion
29   https://shesaid.so/mentoring
30   https://womeninctrl.com/
31   Knowlton (2024).
32   https://metoomvmt.org/get-to-know-us/history-inception/ And for an account of how the hashtag went viral after actor Alyssa Milano urged women to come forward following the breaking news about Harvey Weinstein, see: /www.pewresearch.org/short-reads/2018/10/11/how-social-media-users-have-discussed-sexual-harassment-since-metoo-went-viral/
33   Drewitt et al (2021).
34   In the first FACTS survey in 2013 – 9.2 per cent of festival acts were women (Female: Pressure, 2024)
35   Beaumont-Thomas (2020).
36   Shukla and Ross (2024).
37   Bushard (2024).
38   Lowe (2020).
39   https://publications.parliament.uk/pa/cm5804/cmselect/cmwomeq/129/report.html
40   In the UK, estimates for NDAs applied to the harassment and discrimination claims raised by pregnant women stand at nearly 500,000 according to research by Pregnant Then Screwed, and reported in the *The Independent* newspaper (Oppenheimer 2024).
41   As well as other genres, The F-List of Music has over 1,000 electronic artists, DJs, producers and engineers listed in its directory and it regularly runs music production workshops: https://thef-listmusic.uk
42   Shanahan (2024).
43   Diesel Recordings are a notable exception here (see https://dieselrecordings.com/).
44   Ryan and Morgenroth (2024).
45   Collage was also the method I used to make sense of my experiences during the research and I have written about this in more depth elsewhere (Parsley and Acevedo 2024).

Chapter 9

1   You can find the GENIE database at https://geniedatabase.com/
2   Delicious disruption is mentioned in Christina Malley's Substack article, which you can access at the following link. https://christinamalley.substack.com/p/thoughts-from-2024 At the time of writing, she promises to post more about this idea in future, so do subscribe to her Substack and see how that develops.
3   These ideas come from Ralph Stacey's complexity theory of change whereby he sees most organizational change programmes falling into a zone where the best you can do as a change agent is to make tiny adjustment and see what effects they have – an approach inspired by chaos theory. His founding book on this was published in 1992 (Stacey, 1992) but he wrote many more texts before his death in 2021, and the internet is full of useful applications of the ideas to different contexts.
4   Solnit (2016: vi).

5. For a specifically UK focused resource, visit the 'Sister organisations' page at The F List for Music https://thef-listmusic.uk/who-we-are/sister-organisations/
6. MacKenzie and McKinlay (2021).
7. *Oxford English Dictionary*, 'Ameliorate' /www.oed.com/dictionary/ameliorate_v?tl=true

Appendix

1. See contributions to Kostera and Harding (2021) and Pandeli et al (2022) for a flavour of the fascinating research on organizational life that is undertaken using ethnographic methods.
2. For example, Wood (2009).
3. Sambrook et al (2023)
4. See Weller (2022) on this, albeit in a very different context.
5. Dr Marjana Johansson's university profile is here: https://www.gla.ac.uk/schools/business/staff/marjanajohansson/
6. Parsley and Johansson (2025).
7. This is particularly so in relation to autoethnography, for example, see Ellis et al (2010).
8. Ann died suddenly, only a few weeks after our time in Vienna, and I never got the chance to tell her how transformative I had found her suggestion. I dedicate this dimension of the book to her.
9. De Villiers et al (2022).
10. Parsley (2022).
11. Aired in collaboration with DJ collective Sisu on Threads radio under the original project name 'In the Key of She'. Episodes are accessible through the front page of the In the Key website www.inthekey.org
12. The research received a favourable ethical opinion from the University of Portsmouth prior to the interviews commencing under reference number BAL/2018/E532/Warren.
13. See Newham (nd) for a great discussion of this from the perspective of queer, trans and non-binary perspectives.
14. I have chosen to use this instead of 'nationality' because several participants had multiple nationalities, and had moved to work in a different country/city from that in which they were born and raised.

References

Abdellatif, Amal (2024) 'Beyond the genitalia: What is a hu-WO-man?', *Organization*, 31(5): 846–848.

Abtan, Freida (2016) 'Where is she? Finding the women in electronic music culture', *Contemporary Music Review*, Vol 35(1): 53–60.

AFEM (Association for Electronic Music) (2021) *AFEM Gender Diversity in the Electronic Music Industry Report*, AFEM, https://associationforelectronicmusic.org/2021/12/20/afem-diversity-inclusion-working-group-present-the-gender-diversity-in-the-electronic-music-industry-report/

Anderson, Isobel (2023a) '[Bonus Episode] Teaching women music technology part one: Why we have failed so far', *Girls Twiddling Knobs Podcast*, www.girlstwiddlingknobs.com/podcast/episode/79aed4b5/bonus-episode-teaching-women-music-technology-part-1-why-have-we-failed-so-far

Anderson, Isobel (2023b) '[Bonus Episode] Teaching Women music technology part two: My unique approach', *Girls Twiddling Knobs Podcast*, www.girlstwiddlingknobs.com/podcast/episode/7d7b5170/bonus-episode-teaching-women-music-technology-part-2-my-unique-approach

Armstrong, Victoria (2016) *Technology and the Gendering of Music Education*, Routledge.

Ashcraft, Karen (2013) 'The glass slipper: "incorporating" occupational identities in management studies', *Academy of Management Review*, 38(1): 6–31.

Bain, Vick (2019) *Counting the Music Industry: The Gender Gap*, https://vbain.co.uk/research/

Banks, Mark and Hesmondhalgh, David (2009) 'Looking for work in creative industries policy', *International Journal of Cultural Policy*, 15(4): 415–430.

Barthes, Roland (2000) *Mythologies*, tr. Anne Lavers, Vintage Books.

Bates, Laura (2022) *Fix the System not the Women*, Simon and Schuster.

Bathurst, Ralph and Monin, Nanette (2010) 'Finding myth and motive in language: A narrative of organizational change', *Journal of Management Inquiry*, 19(3): 262–272.

Baudrillard, Jean (1983) *Simulations*, Semiotext(e).

REFERENCES

Bayton, M. (1997) 'Women and the electric guitar', in S. Whiteley (ed) *Sexing the Groove: Popular Music and Gender*, Routledge, pp 37–49.

Beard, Mary (2018) *Women and Power: A Manifesto*, Profile Books.

Beaumont-Thomas, Ben (2020) 'Techno DJ Derrick May accused of sexual assault by four women', *The Guardian,* 12 November, www.theguardian.com/music/2020/nov/12/techno-dj-derrick-may-accused-of-sexual-assault-by-four-women

Bedeian, Arthur (2016) 'A note on the aphorism "there is nothing as practical as a good theory"', *Journal of Management History*, 2(2): 236–242.

bell hooks (1989) *Talking Back: Thinking Feminist, Thinking Black*, Between the Lines.

Biehl, Brigitte (2019) '"In the mix": Relational leadership explored through an analysis of techno DJs and dancers', *Leadership*, 15(3): 339–359.

Biehl, Brigitte (2024) *Bodies, Emotions, Success: Leadership Lessons from The Kardashians*, Emerald.

Björn, Kim (2021) *Push, Turn, Move: Interface Design in Electronic Music* (2nd edition), BJ Books.

Blackie, Sharon (2023) *Hagitude: Reimagining the Second Half of Life*, September Publishing.

Bradley, Harriet (1999) *Gender and Power in the Workplace*, MacMillan.

Branch, John and Rocchi, Francesco (2015) 'Concept development: A primer', *Philosophy of Management*, 14: 111–133.

Brereton, Jude, Daffern, Helen, Young, Kat and Lovedee-Turner, Michael (2020) 'Addressing gender equality in music production: Current challenges, opportunities for change, and recommendations' in R. Hepworth-Sawyer, J. Hodgson, L. King, and M. Marrington (eds) *Gender in Music Production*, Routledge, pp 219–250.

Brewster, Bill and Broughton, Frank (2022) *Last Night a DJ Saved my Life: The History of the Disc Jockey*, White Rabbit.

Broderick, Andrea (2022) 'Positive discrimination and affirmative action' in C. Binder, M. Nowak, J. Hofbauer and P. Janig (eds) *Elgar Encyclopaedia of Human Rights*, Edward Elgar.

Brown, Brene (2021) 'Jodi-Ann Burey and Ruchika T. Malhotra on imposter syndrome', *Dare to Lead Podcast*, 11 October, https://brenebrown.com/podcast/imposter-syndrome/

Brownstein, Michael (2016) 'Context and the ethics of implicit bias', in M. Brownstein and J. Saul (eds), *Implicit Bias and Philosophy, Volume 2*, Oxford University Press, pp 215–234.

Brownstein, Michael, Madva, Alex and Gawronski, Bertram (2020) 'Understanding implicit bias: Putting the criticism into perspective', *Pacific Philosophical Quarterly*, 101(2): 276–307.

Bushard, Brian (2024) 'April Lampros accuses Sean 'Diddy' Combs of sexual assault in new lawsuit—following these six other suits', *Forbes*, 24 May, www.forbes.com/sites/brianbushard/2024/05/24/seventh-woman-accuses-sean-diddy-combs-of-sexual-assault-in-new-lawsuit-following-these-other-suits/?sh=787e820858dc

Butler, Mark (2014) *Playing with Something That Runs: Technology, Improvisation, and Composition in DJ and Laptop Performance*, Oxford University Press.

Campbell, C. and Smith, D. (2023) 'Distinguishing between direct and indirect discrimination', *Modern Law Review*, 86(2): 307–330.

Carah, Nicholas and Dobson, Amy (2016) 'Algorithmic hotness: Young women's "promotion" and "reconnaissance" work via social media body images', *Social Media + Society*, 2(4): 1–10.

Clance, Pauline and Imes, Suzanne (1978) 'The imposter phenomenon in high achieving women: dynamics and therapeutic intervention', *Psychotherapy Theory, Research and Practice*, 15(3): 1–8.

Clarke, Jean, Hurst, Cheryl and Tomlinson, Jennifer (2024) 'Maintaining the Meritocracy Myth: A critical discourse analytic study of leaders' talk about merit and gender in academia', *Organization Studies*, 45(5), 635–660.

Classen, Constance (1997) 'Foundations for an anthropology of the senses', *International Social Science Journal*, 49(153): 401–412.

Classen, Constance (1998) *The Colour of Angels: Cosmology, Gender and the Aesthetic Imagination*, Routledge.

Collin, M. (2009) *Altered State: The Story of Ecstasy Culture and Acid House* (2nd edition), Serpent's Tail.

Cooperrider, David (2021) *Prospective Theory: Appreciative Inquiry: Toward a Methodology for Understanding and Enhancing Organizational Innovation*, NRD Publishing.

Cooperrider, David and Witney, Diana (2005) *Appreciate Inquiry: A Positive Revolution in Change*, Berrett-Koehler.

CREATe (2023) 'Rethinking royalties: Spotify's new streaming threshold', Centre for the Regulation of Creative Economy, www.create.ac.uk/blog/2023/11/24/rethinking-royalties-spotifys-new-streaming-threshold/

Criado-Perez, Caroline (2019) *Invisible Women: Exposing Data Bias in a World Designed for Men*, Penguin Random House.

Davidson, Marilyn and Burke, Ronald (1994) *Women in Management: Current Research Issues* (1st edition), Sage.

De Beauvoir, Simone (1997) *The Second Sex*, Vintage.

De Knock, Bindu (2021) *The All-Round Musician: How to Create a Sustainable Career in the Music Business*, Crosslink Legal, https://allroundmusician.com/

Derks, Belle, Ellemers, Naomi, van laar, Colette and de Groot, Kim (2011) 'Do sexist organizational cultures create the Queen Bee?' *British Journal of Social Psychology*, 50: 519–535.

De Villiers, Charl, Farooq, Mohammed B. and Molinari, Matteo (2022) 'Qualitative research interviews using online video technology – challenges and opportunities', *Meditari Accountancy Research* 30(6): 1764–1782.

Ditto (2024) 'How to Make Money as a Music Producer in 2024', https://dittomusic.com/en/blog/how-to-make-money-as-a-music-producer

Doubleday, Veronica (2008) 'Sounds of power: An overview of musical instruments and gender', *Ethnomusicology Forum*, 17(1), 3–39.

Drewitt, Chloe, Oxlad, Melissa, and Aougoustinos, Martha (2021) 'Breaking the silence on sexual harassment and assault: An analysis of #MeToo tweets', *Computers in Human Behaviour*, 123, 106896.

Duignan-Pearson, Rosalind (2019) '"Before you're a DJ, you're a woman": Navigating gendered space, society and music as a female DJ in Johannesburg', *Journal of African Cultural Studies*, 31(1): 7–23.

Dunford, Daniel, Keay, Lara and Peplow, Gemma (2023) 'Why female headliners are still too big a "risk" for top festivals like Glastonbury', *Sky News*, https://news.sky.com/story/why-are-only-17-of-uk-festival-headliners-female-in-2023-12854240#

Ellis, Carolyn, Adams, Tony E. and Bochner, Arthur (2010) 'Autoethnography: An overview', *Forum: Qualitative Social Research*, 12(1), https://doi.org/10.17169/fqs-12.1.1589

Etzkowitz, Henry and Ranga, Marina (2011) 'Gender dynamics in science and technology: from the "Leaky Pipeline" to the "Vanish Box"', *Cahiers économiques de Bruxelles*, 54: 131–147.

European Data Journalism Network (2020) 'Undress or fail: Instagram's algorithm strong-arms users into showing skin', www.europeandatajournalism.eu/cp_data_news/undress-or-fail-instagram-s-algorithm-strong-arms-users-into-showing-skin/

Faber, Tom (2021) 'Decolonizing electronic music starts with its software', *Pitchfork,* 25 February, https://pitchfork.com/thepitch/decolonizing-electronic-music-starts-with-its-software/

Faragher, Jo (2023) 'What's the difference between positive action and positive discrimination?', *Personnel Today*, personneltoday.com/hr/difference-between-positive-action-examples-and-positive-discrimination/

Farrugia, Rebekah (2012) *Beyond the Dance Floor: Female DJs, Technology and Electronic Dance Music Culture*, Intellect.

Farrugia, Rebekah and Olszanowski, Magdalena (2017) *Dancecult: The Journal of Electronic Dance Music Culture*, 9(1), Special issue on Women in Electronic Dance Music, https://dj.dancecult.net/index.php/dancecult/issue/view/97

Female:Pressure (2024) FACTS Survey, https://femalepressure.wordpress.com/

Fine, Cordelia (2010) *Delusions of Gender: The Real Difference Behind Sex Differences*, Icon Books.

Fine, Cordelia (2017) *Testosterone Rex: Unmasking the Myths of Our Gendered Minds*, Icon Books.

Fineman, Stephen (2006) 'On being positive: Points and counterpoints', *Academy of Management Review*, 31(2): 270–291.

Fitzroy, Olga (2018) 'Award-winning engineer Olga Fitzroy on why the biz should embrace shared parental leave to help close the gender pay gap', *MusicWeek*, www.musicweek.com/opinion/read/award-winning-engineer-olga-fitzroy-on-why-the-biz-should-embrace-shared-parental-leave-to-help-close-the-gender-pay-gap/071144

Florrison and Gable (2022) 'The gender gap: Insecure work in the UK', *Work Foundation*, https://www.lancaster.ac.uk/work-foundation/publications/the-gender-gap-insecure-work-in-the-uk

Foroughi, Hamid, Eisenman, Micki and Parsley, Samantha (2024) 'Old Skool spinning and syncing: Memory, technologies, and occupational membership in a DJ community', *Journal of Management Studies*, https://doi:10.1111/joms.13086

Friedmann, Enav and Efrat-Treister, Dorit (2023) 'Gender bias in stem hiring: implicit in-group gender favoritism among men managers', *Gender & Society*, 37(1): 32–64.

Fusion Staff (2015) 'What's a 'safe space'? A look at the phrase's 50-year history', *Splinter*, 11 November, www.splinter.com/what-s-a-safe-space-a-look-at-the-phrases-50-year-hi-1793852786

GALOP (2023) 'Galop's statement on the 2022–2023 Official Statistics for Hate Crime', https://galop.org.uk/galops-statement-on-the-2022-2023-official-statistics-for-hate-crime/

Garrett, Sheryl (2020) *Adventures in Wonderland: Acid House, Rave and the UK Club Explosion* (2nd edition), TCL Publishing.

Gawronski, Betram, Geschke, Daniel and Banse, Rainer (2003) 'Implicit bias in impression formation: associations influence the construal of individuating information', *European Journal of Social Psychology*, 33(5): 573–589.

Gilbreth, Lilian (1927) *The Home-Maker and her Job*, D. Appleton.

Goldin, C. and Rouse, C. (2000) 'Orchestrating impartiality: the impact of "blind" auditions on female musicians', *The American Economic Review*, 90(4): 715–741.

Goodman, Whitney (2022) *Toxic Positivity: How to Embrace Every Emotion in a Happy-Obsessed World*, Orion Spring.

Gov.UK (2024) 'Gender Pay Gap Reporting: Guidance for Employers', UK Government Statutory Guidance, gov.uk/government/publications/gender-pay-gap-reporting-guidance-for-employers

Greenberg, Jason and Mollick, Ethan (2017) 'Activist choice homophily and the crowdfunding of female founders', *Administrative Science Quarterly*, 62(2): 341–374.

Grosz, E. (1994) *Volatile Bodies*, Taylor & Francis.

Grovier, Kelly (2020) 'The Women who Created a new Language' *BBC Culture* www.bbc.com/culture/article/20200507-the-women-who-created-a-new-language

Grugulis, Irena and Stoyanova, Dimitrinka (2012) 'Social capital and networks in film and TV: Jobs for the boys?', *Organization Studies*, 33(10): 1311–1331.

Hagen, Dave (2024) 'How electronic music production changed the music industry', *Dark Horse Institute Blog*, https://darkhorseinstitute.com/how-electronic-music-pro duction-changed-the-music-industry

Hangartner, Dominik, Kopp, Daniel and Siegenthaler, Michael (2021) 'Monitoring hiring discrimination through online recruitment platforms', *Nature*, 589, 572–576.

Harkins, Paul and Prior, Nick (2022) '(Dis)locating democratization: music technologies in practice', *Popular Music and Society*, 45(1): 84–103, https://doi.org/10.1080/03007766.2021.1984023

Haynes, Jo and Marshall, Lee (2018) 'Reluctant entrepreneurs: Musicians and entrepreneurship in the 'new' music industry', *The British Journal of Sociology*, 69(2): 459–482.

Herrera, Isabella (2023) 'The fight for queer nightlife in an era of political violence', *Pitchfork*, 13 June, https://pitchfork.com/features/article/thefight-for-queer-nightlife-in-an-era-of-political-violence/

Hewertson, Helen and Tissa, Faith (2022) 'Intersectional imposter syndrome: how imposterism affects marginalised groups', in M. Addison, M. Breeze and Y. Taylor (eds), *The Palgrave Handbook of Imposter Syndrome in Higher Education*, Palgrave.

Hideg, Ivona and Shen, Winny (2019) 'Why still so few? A theoretical model of the role of benevolent sexism and career support in the continued underrepresentation of women in leadership positions', *Journal of Leadership & Organizational Studies*, 26(3): 287–303.

Hinton, Patrick (2017) 'A history of rave in dance music documentaries', *Mixmag*, https://mixmag.net/feature/a-history-of-rave-in-dance-musicdocumentaries

Hogenboom, M. (2021) 'The hidden load: How "thinking of everything" holds mums back', *BBC Worklife*, www.bbc.com/worklife/article/20210518-the-hidden-load-how-thinking-of-everything-holds-mums-back

Home Office (2023) 'Hate crime, England and Wales, 2022 to 2023 second edition' *Official Statistics*, https://www.gov.uk/government/statistics/hate-crime-england-and-wales-2022-to-2023

Hooper, E. (2019) 'The Gatekeeper Gap: Searching for solutions to the UK's ongoing gender imbalance in music creation', in S. Raine and C. Strong (eds), *Towards Gender Equality in the Music Industry. Education, Practice and Strategies for Change*, Bloomsbury Academic, pp 131–144.

Howes, David (2004) *Sensual Relations: Engaging the Senses in Culture and Social Theory*. University of Michigan Press.

Huber, J. (2016) *On the Origins of Gender Inequality*, Routledge.

Herrera, Isabella (2023) 'The fight for queer nightlife in an era of political violence', *Pitchfork*, 13 June, https://pitchfork.com/features/article/the-fight-for-queer-nightlife-in-an-era-of-political-violence/

Hinton, Patrick (2017) 'A history of rave in dance music documentaries', *Mixmag*, https://mixmag.net/feature/a-history-of-rave-in-dance-music-documentaries

Home Office (2023) 'Hate crime, England and Wales, 2022 to 2023 second edition', Official Statistics, https://www.gov.uk/government/statistics/hate-crime-england-and-wales-2022-to-2023

Huber, J. (2016) *On the Origins of Gender Inequality*, Routledge.

ILO (International Labour Organization) (2018) *Care Work and Care Jobs for the Future of Decent Work*, https://www.ilo.org/sites/default/files/wcmsp5/groups/public/@dgreports/@dcomm/@publ/documents/publication/wcms_633135.pdf

Irigaray, Luce (1977) *This Sex Which Is Not One*, Cornell University Press.

Jackson, John and Oliver, Tony (2003) 'Personal networks theory and the arts: A literature review with special reference to entrepreneurial popular musicians', *The Journal of Arts Management, Law, and Society*, 33(3): 240–256.

Jagger, Sharon and Turner, Helen (2020) 'The female music producer and the leveraging of difference', in R. Hepworth-Sawyer, J. Hodgson, L. King and M. Marrington (eds), *Gender in Music Production*, Routledge, pp 251–268.

Jaguar Foundation/SONY (2022) 'Progressing Gender Representation in UK Dance Music', https://inthekey.org/resources/

Janosov, Milán, Battiston, Federico and Sinatra, Roberta (2020a) 'Success and luck in creative careers', *EPJ Data Science*, 9(9), https://doi.org/10.1140/epjds/s13688-020-00227-w

Janosov, Milán, Musciotto, Federico, Battiston, Federico and Iniguez, Gerardo (2020b) 'Elites, communities and the limited benefits of mentorship in electronic music', *Scientific Reports*, 10: 3136.

Johnston, Karen and Yarrow, Emily (2024) 'Active representation and identity taxation: unintended outcome of representative labour?', *Public Management Review*, 26(4): 970–987.

Jones, Kristen, Stewart, Kathy, King, Eden, Botsford Morgan, Whitney; Gilrane, Veronica and Hylton, Kimberley (2014) 'Negative consequence of benevolent sexism on efficacy and performance', *Gender in Management: An International Journal*, 29(3): 171–189.

Karpf, Anne (2014) *How to Age*, Pan Macmillan.

Kill, Rebecca (2020) 'Hey boy, hey girl, superstar DJ, here we go … Exploring the experience of female and non-binary DJs in the UK music scene', in R. Hepworth-Sawyer, J. Hodgson, L. King and M. Marrington (eds), *Gender in Music Production*, Routledge, pp 82–96.

Kim, Jennifer and Meister, Alyson (2022) 'Microaggressions, interrupted: The experience and effects of gender microaggressions for women in STEM', *Journal of Business Ethics*, 185(3): 513–531.

Kirsch (2022) 'Revolution from above? Female directors' equality-related actions in organizations', *Business and Society*, 61(3): 572–605.

Kitching, John and Smallbone, David (2008) *Defining and Estimating the Size of the UK Freelance Workforce: A Report for the Professional Contractors Group*, https://eprints.kingston.ac.uk/id/eprint/3880/1/Kitching-J-3880.pdf

Knowlton, Karren (2024) 'Trailblazing motivation and marginalized group members: changing expectations to pave the way for others', *Organization Science*, https://doi.org/10.1287/orsc.2021.15624

Knowlton, Karren, Carlton, Andrew and Grant, Adam (2022) 'Help (un)wanted: Why the most powerful allies are the most likely to stumble – and when they fulfill their potential', *Research in Organizational Behavior*, 42 (supplement): Article 100180.

Kostera, Monica and Harding, Nancy (2021) *Organizational Ethnography*, Edward Elgar.

Kuchynka, Sophie, Salomon, Kristen, Bosson, Jennifer, El-Hout, Mona, Kiebel, Elizabeth, Cooperman, Claudia and Toomey, Ran (2017) 'Hostile and benevolent sexism and college women's STEM outcomes', *Psychology of Women Quarterly*, 42(1): 72–87.

Lash, Scott and Urry, John (1994) *Economies of Signs and Space*, Sage Publications.

Lauryn, Ash (2022) 'Techno: A Social History', *BBC Radio 4*, https://www.bbc.co.uk/programmes/m00199y6

Lazar, Emily, Appleton, Beth, Smyth, Meghan, Keel, Beverley, Malachi, Carolyn, Hamlin, Jordan, Rodriguez-Bonilla, Gabriela and Kok, Jasmine (2023) *Fix the Mix: Annual Report*, https://www.mtsu.edu/media/fix.pdf

Lewis, Patricia and Simpson, Ruth (2010) 'Introduction: Theoretical insights into the practices of revealing and concealing gender within organizations', in P. Lewis and R. Simpson (eds), *Revealing and Concealing Gender: Issues of Visibility in Organizations*, Palgrave, pp 1–22.

Lowe, Abby (2020) 'Opinion: Erick Morillo's death exposed ugly truths about DJs, power and fame', *Beatportal*, 8 September, www.beatportal.com/articles/2984-opinion-erick-morillos-death-exposed-ugly-truths-about-djs-power-and-fame

Macintosh, Peggy (1988) 'White privilege and male privilege: A personal account of coming to see correspondences through work in Women's Studies' *SEED*, https://www.nationalseedproject.org/Key-SEED-Texts/white-privilege-and-male-privilege

Mackenzie, Ewan and McKinlay, Alan (2021) 'Hope labour and the psychic life of cultural work', *Human Relations*, 74(11): 1841–1863.

Malley, Christina (2024) 'Thoughts from 2024', *Exposure,* https://christinamalley.substack.com/p/thoughts-from-2024

Man Enough (2021) 'ALOK: The urgent need for compassion', *The Man Enough Podcast,* www.youtube.com/watch?app=desktop&v=Tq3C9R8HNUQ

Marie, Kallie (2022) *Conversations with Women in Music Production: The Interviews*, Backbeat Books.

Mavin, Sharon and Yusupova, Marina (2020) 'Competition and gender: Time's up on essentialist knowledge production', *Management Learning*, 52(1) 86–108.

McRobbie, Angela (2009) *The Aftermath of Feminism: Gender, Culture and Social Change*, Sage.

Merrich, Johann (2021) *A Short History of Electronic Music and its Women Protagonists*, Arcana.

Meyer, John and Rowan, Brian (1977) 'Institutionalized Organizations: Formal Structure as Myth and Ceremony' *American Journal of Sociology*, 83(2): 340–363.

Meyerson, Debra (2001) 'Radical change, the quiet way', *Harvard Business Review*, https://hbr.org/2001/10/radical-change-the-quiet-way

Miliopoulou, G. and Kapareliotis, I. (2021) 'The toll of success: Female leaders in the "women-friendly" Greek advertising agencies', *Gender, Work and Organization*, 28: 1741–1765.

Morris, Jonathan, Islam, Gazi and Davies, J. (2024) 'The search for meaningful work under neo-bureaucracy: Work precarity in freelance TV', *Organization*, https://doi.org/10.1177/13505084241236454

Morse, Phil (2016) *Rock The Dancefloor: The Proven Five-step Formula for Total DJing Success*, Rethink Press.

Morse, Phil (2024) 'Here are the results from our 2024 census, the biggest dj survey in the world' *Digital DJ Tips*, www.digitaldjtips.com/census-results-2024/

Morsy, Hanan (2020) 'Access to finance: Why aren't women leaning in?', *International Monetary Fund Finance and Development Magazine*, www.imf.org/en/Publications/fandd/issues/2020/03/africa-gender-gap-access-to-finance-morsy

Mulligan, Mark and MIDIA Research (2024) *The IMS Business Report 2024: An Annual Study of the Electronic Music Industry*, www.internationalmusicsummit.com/business-report

Musicians Census (2024) *Women Musicians Insight Report*, www.musicianscensus.co.uk/insight-reports

Newham, Joni (nd) 'Making space: Exploring questions of trans and non-binary inclusion in the music industry' *Saffron*, https://saffronmusic.co.uk/stories/making-space-exploring-questions-of-trans-and-nonbinary-inclusion/

O'Grady, Alice and Madill, Anna (2019) 'Being And performing "older" woman in electronic dance movement culture', *Dancecult: The Journal of Electronic Dance Music Culture*, 11(1): 7–29. https://dj.dancecult.net/index.php/dancecult/article/view/1130/973

ONS (Office for National Statistics) (2016) 'Women shoulder the responsibility of 'unpaid work', ons.gov.uk/employmentandlabourmarket/peopleinwork/earningsandworkinghours/articles/womenshouldertheresponsibilityofunpaidwork/2016-11-10

Oppenheimer, David B. (2019) 'The ubiquity of positive measures for addressing systemic discrimination and inequality: a comparative global perspective'. *Brill Research Perspectives in Comparative Discrimination Law*, 3 (3–4): 1–114.

Oppenheimer, Maya (2024) 'Almost half a million women gagged after workplace discrimination, bullying or harassment', *The Independent*, 14 May, www.independent.co.uk/news/uk/home-news/nda-work-discrimination-bullying-harassment-b2544220.html

Orgad, Shani and Gill, Rosalind (2022) *Confidence Culture*, Duke University Press.

O'Shea, Saoirse Caitlin (2016) 'I am not that Caitlin: A critique of both the transphobic media reaction to Caitlyn Jenner's *Vanity Fair* cover shoot and of passing', *Culture and Organization*, 25(3): 202–216.

O'Shea, Saoirse Caitlin (2020) 'Working at gender', *Gender, Work and Organization*, 27(6): 1438–1449.

Padilla, Amado (1994) 'Research News and Comment: Ethnic Minority Scholars; Research, and Mentoring: Current and Future Issues', *Educational Researcher*, 23(4): 24–27.

Palvia, Ajay, Vähämaa, Emilia and Vähämaa, Sami (2015) 'Are female CEOs and chairwomen more conservative and risk averse? Evidence from the banking industry during the financial crisis', *Journal of Business Ethics*, 131: 577–594.

Pandeli, Jenna, Sutherland, Neil and Gaggiotti, Hugo (2022) *Organizational Ethnography: An Experiential and Practice Guide*. Routledge.

Parsley, Samantha (nd) 'Dovetail: Come out and fly', *In the Key*, https://inthekey.org/dovetail-come-out-and-fly/

Parsley, Samantha (2022) 'Feeling your way as an occupational minority: The gendered sensilisation of women electronic music artists', *Management Learning*, 53(4): 697–717.

Parsley, Samantha and Acevedo, Beatriz (2024) 'Pieces of me, letters from us: Collage-making as embodied reflection in autoethnography', *Culture and Organization*, online first at https://doi.org/10.1080/14759551.2024.2394450

Parsley, Samantha and Johansson, Marjana (2025) 'A slog, a push and a labour of love: How women electronic music artists navigate gendered in/visibility in a creative industry through "ameliorative work"', *Organization*, online first at https://journals.sagepub.com/doi/10.1177/13505084251348689

Perry, Grayson (2017) *The Descent of Man*, Penguin Books.

Petersen, Eva (2024) 'Get your writs out: Experiences of women working as musicians in lawless performance spaces', paper presented to the F-List Gender in Music Research Hub Research Hour, 25 October.

Phillips, Mary and Rippin, Ann (2010) 'Howard and the mermaid: abjection and the Starbucks' Foundation memoir', *Organization*, 17(4): 481–499.

Phoenix, A. and Craddock, N. (2023) 'Complicating the idea of light-skin privilege in the UK', in R. Hall and N. Mishra (eds), *The Routledge International Handbook of Colorism*, Routledge.

Plant, Sadie (1997) *Zeros + Ones: Digital Women and the New Technoculture*, Fourth Estate.

Potocnik, Metka (2024) 'Exposing gender bias in intellectual property law: The UK music industries', in S.D. Jamar and L. Mtima (eds), *Handbook of Intellectual Property and Social Justice: Access, Inclusion, Empowerment*, Cambridge University Press, pp 473–496.

Prior, Nick (2010) 'The rise of the new amateurs' in L. Grindstaff, L. Ming-Cheng and J. Hall (eds), *Handbook of Cultural Sociology*, Routledge, pp 340–348.

Prior, Nick (2018) Popular Music, Digital Technology and Society, Sage.

Puwar, Nirmal (2021) 'The force of the somatic norm: women as space invaders in the UK Parliament', in M. Shirin, M. Gluhovic, S. Jestrovic, and M. Seward (eds), *Oxford Handbook of Politics and Performance*, Oxford University Press, pp 251–264.

Ramburran, Shara (2017) '"DJ hit that button": Amateur laptop musicians in contemporary music and society', in R. Mantie and G. Smith (eds), *The Oxford Handbook of Music Making and Leisure*, Oxford University Press, pp 585–600.

Rasmussen, Sasha (2021) 'What it feels like for a girl: Gendering the history of the senses', *History Journal*, https://historyjournal.org.uk/2021/02/10/what-it-feels-like-for-a-girl-gendering-the-history-of-the-senses/

Raven, Ben (2018) 'Ghostwriters in the former USSR are turning Western DJs into stars', *Mixmag*, https://mixmag.net/feature/ghostwriting-in-the-former-ussr

Reddington, Helen (2021) *She's at the Controls: Sound Engineering, Production and Gender Ventriloquism in the 21st Century*, Equinox.

Reich-Stiebert, Natalia, Froehlich, Laura and Voltmer, Jan-Bennett (2023) 'Gendered mental labor: a systematic literature review on the cognitive dimension of unpaid work within the household and childcare', *Sex Roles*, 88(11–12): 475–494, https://doi.org/10.1007/s11199-023-01362-0

Reitsamer, Rosa (2011) 'The DIY careers of techno and drum 'n' bass DJs in Vienna', *Dancecult: Journal of Electronic Dance Music Culture*, 3(1): 28–43.

Repo, Jemima (2016) *The Biopolitics of Gender*, Oxford University Press.

Reynolds, Simon (2013) *Energy Flash: A Journey Through Rave Music and Dance Culture* (2nd edition), Faber & Faber.

Richards, John (2016) 'Shifting gender in electronic music: DIY and maker communities', *Contemporary Music Review*, 35(1): 40–52.

Richards, John (2017) 'DIY and Maker Communities in Electronic Music'. In N. Collins and J. d'Escrivan (eds), *The Cambridge Companion to Electronic Music*, Cambridge University Press, pp 238–257.

Rodgers, Tara (2010) *Pink Noises: Women on Electronic Music and Sound*, Duke University Press.

ROSTR (nd) 'Who's Behind Coachella 2024? The industry (and data) behind the line-up', https://hq.rostr.cc/reports/who-booked-coachella/2024

Ryan, Michelle and Morgenroth, Thekla (2024) 'Why we should stop trying to fix women: How context shapes and constrains women's career trajectories' *Annual Review of Psychology*, 75: 555–572.

Sambrook, Sally, Hillier, Charlotte and Doloriet, Clair (2023) ' "That's not a proper ethnography": a hybrid "propportune" ethnography to study nurses' perceptions of organizational culture in a British hospital', *Journal of Organizational Ethnography*, 13(1): 63–78.

Schiller-Merkens, Simone (2024) 'Prefiguring an alternative economy: Understanding prefigurative organizing and its struggles', *Organization*, 31(3): 458–476.

Sedgwick, Eve (2003) *Touching Feeling: Affect, Pedagogy, Performativity*, Duke University Press.

Shanahan, Geneveive (2024) 'Two routes to degeneration, two routes to utopia: The impure critical performativity of alternative organizing', *Organization*, https://doi.org/10.1177/13505084231223639

Shukla, Anu and Ross, Annabel Ross (2024) 'Kamaal Williams accused of alleged sexual assault by three women', *Resident Advisor*, https://ra.co/features/4325

Siegart, Mary Ann (2021) *The Authority Gap: Why Women Are Still Taken Less Seriously Than Men and What We Can Do About it*, Penguin Books.

Smith, Brad (2024) 'The protective power of hope and belonging in the workplace', *Strategic HR Review*, https://doi.org/10.1108/SHR-07-2024-0054

Smith, Stacy L., Pieper, Katherine, Hernandez, Karla and Wheeler, Sam (2024) *Inclusion in the Recording Studio? Gender & Race/Ethnicity of Artists, Songwriters & Producers across 1,200 Popular Songs from 2012 to 2023*, USC Annenberg Inclusion Initiative, https://assets.uscannenberg.org/docs/aii-inclusion-recording-studio-20240130.pdf

Solnit, Rebecca (2016) *Hope in the Dark: Untold Stories, Wild Possibilities*, Canongate.

Spivak, Gayatri (1988) 'Can the subaltern speak?' in C. Nelson and L. Grossberg (eds), *Marxism and the Interpretation of Culture*, Macmillan.

Stacey, Ralph (1992) *Managing the Unknowable: Strategic Boundaries Between Order and Chaos in Organizations*, Wiley.

Sterling, Scott (2016) 'Frankie Bones on the origins of PLUR'. *Insomniac*, www.insomniac.com/magazine/frankie-bones-on-the-origins-of-plur/

Tadajewski, Mark, Maclaran, Pauline, Parsons, Elizabeth and Parker, Martin (2011) *Key Concepts in Critical Management Studies*, Sage.

Tanner, Emily, Epler, Rhett and Tanner, John (2022) 'Masking the Role or masking the toll? The effects of career fit on salesperson burnout', *Journal of Business-to-Business Marketing*, 29(3–4): 335–352.

Thompson, Louise (2020) 'Gender in music production: Perspective through a feminine lens', in R. Hepworth-Sawyer, J. Hodgson, L. King and M. Marrington (eds), *Gender in Music Production*, Routledge, pp 199–216.

Tran, Nellie (2023) 'From imposter phenomenon to infiltrator experience: Decolonizing the mind to claim space and reclaim self', *Peace and Conflict: Journal of Peace Psychology*, 29(2): 184–193.

Travis, Dnika J. and Thorpe-Moscon, Jennifer (2018) 'Day-to-day experiences of emotional tax among women and men of color in the workplace', *Catalyst*. www.catalyst.org/research/day-to-day-experiences-of-emotional-tax-among-women-and-men-of-color-in-the-workplace/

Tulshyan, Ruchika and Burey, Jodi-Ann (2021a) 'Stop telling women they have imposter syndrome', *Harvard Business Review*, 11 February, https://hbr.org/2021/02/stop-telling-women-they-have-imposter-syndrome

Tulshyan, Ruchika and Burey, Jodi-Ann (2021b) 'End imposter syndrome in your workplace', 14 July, https://hbr.org/2021/07/end-imposter-syndrome-in-your-workplace

Van Veelen, Ruth, Derks, Belle and Endedijk, Maaike (2019) 'Double trouble: How being outnumbered and negatively stereotyped threatens career outcomes of women in STEM', *Frontiers in Psychology*, 10, Article 150: 1–18.

Warren, Samantha (2010) 'What's wrong with being positive?' in A. Linley, S. Harrington and N. Page (eds), *The Oxford Handbook of Positive Psychology and Work*, Oxford University Press, pp 313–322.

Waters, Simon (2016) 'Engendering hope: A person-centred reflection on technology and gender', *Contemporary Music Review*, 35(1): 61–70.

Weller, Sarah-Louise (2022) 'Too close for comfort? The challenges and unexpected consequence of immersed ethnography' in J. Pandeli, N. Sutherland and H. Gaggiotti (eds), *Organizational Ethnography: An Experiential and Practice Guide*, Routledge, pp 34–49.

White, Andrew (2022) 'The DCMS Committee's inquiry on the economics of music streaming and its implications for artists', *Cultural Trends*, 32(3): 325–339.

Whitman, Kate, Cox, Joe and Parsley, Samantha (2025) 'Hitting the right note: Using AI experiments to investigate gendered consumer preferences in music'. Paper presented to the 16th International Music Business Research Association Conference, University of Hertfordshire, 11–13 June.

Wolfe, Paula (2020) *Women in the Studio: Creativity, Control and Gender in Popular Music Sound Production*, Ashgate.

Wood, Julia T. (2009) 'Feminist standpoint theory', *Encyclopedia of Communication Theory*, SAGE Reference Online, https://edge.sagepub.com/system/files/77593_2.2ref.pdf

WOW (Work and Opportunities for Women Report) (2021) *Unpaid and Unrecognised: How Business Can Realise the Benefits of Tackling Women's Invisible Labour*, https://assets.publishing.service.gov.uk/media/60ae4501d3bf7f7383db35fc/Unpaid-and-Unrecognised1.pdf

Wray, Rebecca (2020) '#NotMyFandom: The gendered nature of a misogynistic backlash in science fiction fandom', *Psychology of Women & Equalities Review*, 3(1/2): 78–81.

Wreyford, Natalie (2015) 'Birds of a Feather: Informal recruitment practices and gendered outcomes for screenwriting work in the UK film industry' in B. Conor, R. Gill and S. Taylor (eds), *Gender and Creative Labour*, Wiley, Blackwell, pp 84–96.

Yodovich, Neta (2021) 'Defining conditional belonging: the case of female science fiction fans', *Sociology*, 55(5): 871–887.

Index

References to figures appear in *italic* type; those in **bold** type refer to tables. References to endnotes show both the page number and the note number (55n40).

A

A&R function and representatives 21, 41, 86, 91–92, 95, 131, 144, 146, 153
Ableton xi, 120
Ableton Live 84
abuse 55n40, 61n16
  misogynistic 64–65
academic scholarship and work in electronic music industry ix, xi, 3, 21
acceptability 123
acid house music 128, 129
activism *see* paranoid readings
activists 145
administration publishing deal 25
affirmative action *see* positive action
after-parties 140
ageing in the electronic music industry 68, 72–73
airbrushing 67
algorithmic hotness 62n10
allies 79, 146–147
allyship 80–81, 89, 153, 159
  see also GENIE
ameliorative work and workers 2, 6–8, 7n15, 12, 13, 14, 19, 20–21, 29, 32, 34–35, 40, 47, 48, 62–65, 78, 79–80, 81–82, 83, 84, 85, 87, 93, 99, 109, 111, 122, 137, 138, 144–147, 148, 150, 152, 153–154, 155, 156–157, 158, 160, 164, 168
Amnesia 11
Amsterdam Dance Event 38, 43
  Gear Lab 126, 127
analytical distance 164
Anderson, Isobel 117, 118, 124, 138, 155
Annenberg Inclusion Initiative 26
Apple 97, 120, 120n47
appreciative inquiry 8–9, 14, 160, 168
archetypal geek/nerd 123n51
Aria, Xylo 36, 49
Armstrong, Victoria 114, 118, 123

artistry of music production 118
artists, recognized affiliation with labels 22
artists and repertoire function and representatives *see* A&R function and representatives
audio engineering 52, 98
  see also sound design and engineering
audio recording 112
Audley, Charles 28
authenticity and quality 24, 94, 98–99

B

backlash 82, 88, 159
backstaging 159
BAD *see* Black Artists Database
Bandcamp 19n5, 26
Barbie 121
barriers to entry 120
Barthes, Roland 11n26
Bassica 75
BBC radio stations, national 33
beatmatching 84
Beatport 19, 19n3
  Diversity and Parity Fund 132
  DJ charts 19, 19n4
  Top 100 Breaks Releases chart 82, 90
  Top 100 releases chart 26
bedroom producers 22, 24
belonging and confidence 135–138
benevolent sexism 86
bias, implicit and explicit 8, 10, 45, 46n16, 46–48, 51, 66, 85, 86n14, 95
Billboard songs in US, counting of women's and non-binary folks' numbers in top 26–27
Billboard Top 100 27
Bimbo Princess, The *see* Sommers, Sarah
biopolitics 68n24
Black Artists Database (BAD) 19, 19n5
Blu, Sydney 131, 134

ND

BMC *see* Brighton Music Conference
body, symbolism of the 65–67
body image 67–68
Bones, Frankie 39n4
booking agents 32
Book More Women 31, 31n46
Boom 31
brains, differences in female and male 102–103, 115, 124
brave spaces 142–144
breakbeat artists and scene 74–75
breastfeeding and childrearing 115
Brighton Music Conference (BMC) 133
British Broadcasting Corporation radio stations, national *see* BBC radio stations, national
bro culture 48–52, 53, 54–55, 56, 93, 95
  challenging 7
  and masculine character 10, 109–110
  perpetuation of 12
Bungalow
  Just Dance
    Funky Breaks Remix *150*, 150, 151

C

cancel culture 81
Can't Buy My Silence campaign 144
career continuity, maintaining 71
career experiences of women electronic music DJs/ producers 3
career fatigue 143
catalogue of own releases 28
CDJ 63
  'beat sync' button 84, 84n10
change agent 153n3
Change the Beat 131–132, 133, 134, 143
childcare, absence of in the workplace 71
children and work 71
choice, conscious 111
cis-gendered interviewees and interviewer 9–10
cis men 158
  acceptance of technically knowledgeable individuals 123
  anxieties about involvement in ameliorative work 44, 153
  as definers of the world of electronic music 6, 20, 30, 33, 34, 43, 138, 146, 156
  as producers and performers of electronic music 18, 19, 27, 40, 154
  preferential judgement and treatment of 12, 47, 55, 56, 62, 65, 72, 73, 85, 95, 100, 134
  reverse discrimination against 13
CMO *see* collective rights management organization
Coachella 31

collaboration 98
collective action, power of 148–150
collective rights management organization (CMO) 25, 34
collectives and initiatives 14
  women and gender-expansive 88, 132–133, 135, 143, 145, 147, 148, 149
  see also GENIE; Psibindi; Psy-sisters collective
competition between women 83
complexity theory of change 153n3
conditioning, inbuilt 111
confidence culture in the workplace 136–137, 150
confidence of women 13–14, 47, 79, 120, 131–150, 155, 160
contact books 20
contracts, negotiation of 31, 59–60, 61
contractual arrangements, liberal 5
copyright law 50
corrective measures 78, 88
Cox, Carl 147
critical management studies tradition 8–9
cult of toxic positivity 9
cultural industries, new 40–41

D

DaCosta Records 57, 136n4
dance 28
dance music culture, belief in inclusiveness of 39
dance music playlists 34
dance music stations 33
  see also Kiss; Kiss Fresh
data quality 164
DAWs *see* digital audio workstations
de Witte, Charlotte 43
decision making 45
DeepDownDirty Acid Vol 3 129, *129*
DeepDownDirty Records 128, *129*
Deevstock 28
delicious disruption and disruptors 8n17, 153, 155–156, 157
design bias, overcoming 127
Diesel Recordings 74, 75, 151
deskilling 52
Detroit techno, origins of 39
difference 30, 39, 43, 79, 87, 101, 103, 104, 105, 115, 123, 137, 148, 149, 156, 158, 165
digital audio workstations (DAWs) 4, 24, 27, 58, 84, 92, 95–96, 98, 99, 111, 120, 120n47, 126–127, 129, 141n21
  see also Ableton; Logic
Digital DJ Tips 28, 96
  Census 23, 24
digital DJing 63, 84n10
  accessibility of viii

199

digital equipment 63
digital music players *see* CDJ
digital music streaming, economics of 26n27
Dijon, Honey 30
disc jockeys *see* DJs
disciplining regimes 68n24
disco music 39, 142
"Discover Weekly" playlists 34
discrimination 88
  direct 61
  indirect 61
  unconscious 12
distance, analytical 164
diversification 77, 79–80, 131–132, 148
diversity and inclusion 33, 49, 87–88, 146, 147, 148, 153
diversity bookings 78, 83, 84, 85–86, 88, 93
diversity conditions 31–32
diversity initiatives 145, 148
diversity panels 134–135
diversity ratios 134
diversity work 145
DJ booking agencies 143
DJ changeovers 53–54
DJ charts 19
  landing pages 19
DJ controllers 96
DJ equipment 82, 96
DJ gigs, bookings for 91
DJ lifestyle 28
DJ Mag Top 100 DJs list 29–30, 49
DJane Mag survey 29
DJing 22n11, 158
  as work and source of financial return ix, 26, 142
  gendered visual culture of 68
  and motherhood 70–72
  and music production 4–5, 23–24, 28, 29–30, 96
  and pregnancy 72
  topless 63, 63n11
DJs (disc jockeys)
  dressing down of 63–64
  lack of female 1
  use of promos to find music to play 20
do-it-yourself music-making and counter-culture 4–5
dominant discourses 6n11
Dovetail viii, 3
  Almost Like 57, 57–58, 136n4
  Fall Away 106, 106–107
  Just Dance
    Funky Breaks Remix 150, 150–151
  Keep Your Disdance 35, 36, 89
  Lift 51 15
  1984 74, 74–75
  Sea Organ 89, 89–90

Therapist Drift 128–130, *129*
  see also Parsley, Samantha
Draw the Line 16–17, 18–19
drum machines 113
drums
  male affinity for 117
  programming of 36
Dynamics database 19n8

E

economy
  of skill 63n12
  of smiles 101
edit 96n9
Eilish, Billie 73
electronic dance music 15, 39, 62, 68, 114
  see also Jaguar Foundation/ SONY report, The
electronic music
  artists ix, 16, 19, 154, 161
  as a meritocracy 39–40
  equipment 119–121, 120n47, 154–155
  industry ix, 4–5
  made by women viii
  production viii, 24–25, 34, 52, 91–92, 111
    association of with men 102–104, 109
    and career success 95–97
    gender imbalance in 133
  tracks, who credited on 26–28
engineering training, lack of female interest and participation in 116–117
engineers, working with 97–100
EQing 113
equality legislation 78
equalization *see* EQing
erasure 73
Everynoise website and analysis 33, 34
exclusion and belonging 53–55
expectations 122
expert opinion 112
exploitation 63n11
expressive technology 13

F

F List for Music, The 19n8
Facebook groups and postings 2, 27, 37, 40, 49, 64, 66, 67, 94, 134, 143
FACTS survey run by Female:Pressure 30–31
featuring on tracks 28
female body and reproductive capacities 115
female DJ course 76–77, 84
female electronic music producers 121–123
feminine identities 100–102
feminine technologies 127–128
femininity 62, 63, 137
feminist determination 110–111
feminist standpoint research 161
feminist upbringing 111

INDEX

festivals, performance at 30n41, 30–33, 34, 77, 96, 144
financial returns from DJing and electronic music production 25–26
Fix the Mix 27
Foucault, Michel 68n24
freelance production of electronic music 12, 22, 22n12, 23
friendship, critical 164
funding and finance 144–145

G

Galop 55n40
garage band 138
GarageBand xi, 120, 120n47
gatekeepers and gatekeeping 13, 43, 44, 47, 51, 56, 60, 65, 79, 81, 88, 93, 96, 133, 158
gender
  as binary construct 10
  as reason for blame 85
  foregrounding of 149, 159
  salience of 85n12
gender bias 111
gender differences in unpaid work 104
gender discrimination in the electronic music industry 59–73
gender-diverse artists, finding music made by 20
gender diversity 81, 147
  across festivals 30–31
Gender Diversity survey 45
Gender Equality Networks In Europe
  see GENIE
gender fluidity 10
gender identity and expression 103
gender inequality in the electronic music industry 2, 10, 11, 36, 153, 157
gender issues and occupational inequality 8
gender minimization strategy 66
gender minorities' music, finding 20–21
gender-neutral terms 10
gender norms 84–85
  during childhood, transgression of traditional 109–110
gender pay gaps/differentials 61
gender relations 5
gender representation, improving 21
gender research ix–x
gender-sensitive language 10
gender stereotypes 62, 109, 110
  see also stereotypes
gendered economy of the senses 112
gendered marketing 112
gendered play expectations, disruption of 110
gendered preferences 122
gendered segregation 149
gendered socialization 13

gendering of music and (music) technology 111–114
genetic code, transmission of predispositions in 10
GENIE (Gender Equality Networks in Europe) 7n15, 152–153, 154, 156
German rave origins of electronic music culture 39
ghettos 147
ghost producers and producing 93–95, 95n4, 97–100, 105
Gilbreth, Lillian 115n29
Girls Don't Sync 84
Goldin, Claudia 51
good music 12, 37–57, 60
Goodwin, Grace 152, 156
graphic equalizer 113
groove 52
guitar, playing of 114

H

HAAi 31, 32
hardware, use of to create music 125
hardware synthesizer 90
harp, playing of 114
harassment and discrimination claims raised by pregnant women 144n40
hate attacks 142
Hayes, Nick 69n27
Heap, Imogen 126, 128
He.She.They 11
hi-fidelity music equipment as domain of men 112, 113
Hilton, Paris 63
hobbies and interests, gendering of 104
home production and studios 22, 24, 27
homophily 48, 49, 52, 142–143
  see also bro culture; sausage fest
homosociality 49, 52
hope 164
  labour 55, 155
  and power 154–155
Hospital Records
  Women in Drum and Bass artist programme 143
Hunna 143
hyper-femininity 121–123
hyper-reality 65
hyper-sexuality 62
hyper-visibility 82, 83
  see also visibility

I

identity 51, 56
identity tax and taxation 13, 21, 34, 144
images of artists 62
  curation and circulation of 65–68

impact, disparate *see* indirect *under* discrimination
impostor syndrome 136n2, 137, 149
In the Key
  Producer Directory 19
  radio show 28, 57, 165
  project 31n46, 36, 37–38, 99, 109, 165
In the Key (of She): Women, Technology and Cultural Technology xi, 41
inclusion clauses and riders 31–32, 80, 159
inclusiveness 159
income 50
independent ethos and electronic music 5
industry support 153
  see also GENIE
inequality 11, 63n11, 73, 160
Instagram 62, 64, 69n27, 77, 94, 122
intellectual property (IP) law 50
interface design 125–128
interfaces, expressive 125–128
International Encyclopaedia of Women Composers 50
International Women's Day 79, 89, 146
internship, unpaid 46
interrupted involvement 161
intersections 158
interviewing underground DJs viii
IP law *see* intellectual property law

J

Jacki-E 16–17, 18–19, 28
Jaguar 31–32
Jaguar Foundation/ SONY report, The 28, 33–34, 61, 140
Janosov, Milán 49
Johansson, Dr Marjana 164
Jordan, Benn 49
judgements, explicit 47

K

Katie, Meat *see* Pember, Mark
keyboards 113, 117
Keychange initiative 31
Kiss 33
Kiss Fresh 33
Kraviz, Nina 30, 67

L

label rosters 22
language, gendered 6n11, 10
learning and education in music technology and production 111, 116–118, 128, 135–136, 138, 142, 160
Lens, Amelie 67
Lift 51 14–15
linguistic turn 6n11
listening sessions 143
Logic 92, 97–98

logic of authenticity 98–99
  see also authenticity and quality
Lopez, Jennifer 70
Lowering the Tone 41

M

#metoo movement 10, 144
MacFarlane, Julie 144
male desire 63n11
male dominance of science, technology, engineering and mathematics (STEM) fields 114, 116
male gaze 63n11
manifestos
  for educators, researchers and consultants 159–160
  for those in a position of influence in the electronic music industry 158–159
  for women, trans and non-binary people working in electronic music 157–158
marginalization of women as electronic music artists ix, 116, 144
marginalized identity and voices 6n11, 154
market forces 41, 44–45, 61–62
marketability 60–61
markets, routes to 5
masculine identity and objectivity 112
masculinity 116
masculinization of sight and hearing 112
mash-up 96n9
mastering engineer 98
Matrix, The 66n17
Mattel 121n49
McNeil, Nikki 133
media lawyers 59–60, 61
men
  and masculinity, association of with 'higher faculties' of sight and hearing 112
  targeting of in advertising 112
  see also cis men
mentorship and mentoring schemes 49, 49n20, 143, 159
meritocracy, making of and belief in 41–48, 60, 159
metaphors, masculine-sounding 119
MIDI (Musical Instrument Digital Interface) 124n55, 126
MIDI polyphonic expression (MPE) technologies 126
MiMU gloves 126, 127, 128
minoritized genders 12, 29, 40, 73, 76, 111, 132, 133, 137, 143, 148, 149, 156, 158
misogynistic abuse 64–65
Misogyny in Music report 144
mixing and mastering 94n2
Mixmag 38
model DJs 63
motherhood penalty in music 72n35

INDEX

motivation 80, 81
  trailblazing 88, 89, 143–144, 145, 152
Moving the Needle 27
MPE technologies *see* MIDI polyphonic expression technologies
MPW *see* Music Production for Women
MU *see* Musicians' Union
Music Data Analyst *Viberate* 31
music equipment, good quality 113
music groups, women and gender-expansive 141
music instruments, gendering of 113–114
music played on radio, prevalence of women, trans and non-binary artists in 33–34
Music Producer 121n49
music production 96n9
  and gender 103–104
  online course in 36
  software 24
Music Production for Women (MPW) 36, 49, 120n46
music publishers 25, 34
music rights 25
music technologies, 'tactile' and 'gesturally responsive' 126
music technology
  education and gender 116–117, 160
  and masculinity 108–128
  reducing the masculinity of 123–125
music workplace, presence of children in 71
Musical Instrument Digital Interface *see* MIDI
musical training 113n17
Musicians' Union (MU) 53, 68, 72
myth of meritocracy 39–40
myths 11–14, 16, 17, 30, 34, 35, 39–40, 65, 72, 73, 78, 93, 99, 122, 128, 133, 134, 157, 158, 159

N

nature and nurture, difference between 103
NDAs *see* non-disclosure agreements
negativity 71
negotiations, legal 59–60, 61
neoliberal patriarchal structures 63n11
networks and connections 12, 40–41, 49, 52–53, 54–56, 133, 138, 140
  see also GENIE
neural pathways 124
neuroscience 103, 115
New York disco, origins of 39
New York Philharmonic Orchestra 51
Nightwave
  'Boiler Room' set and TV channel 64
Noisily Festival 28, 32–33, 81
non-disclosure agreements (NDAs) 144, 144n40
normalization 88, 156
  of self-exploitation 29n38

O

objectivity 113
Official Charts Company 28
online environments, lack of safety for women in 141
online music production forums and groups 141
online spaces, safe 159
organizational change programmes 153n3
organizational ethnography 161
O2 venues 29
oppression 63n11, 137
Orwell, George
  Nineteen Eighty-Four 74
outreach work with schools 160
outsourcing roles 98

P

paranoid readings 8–9, 29, 133
parental leave entitlement, shared 72n35
parenthood and work 72
parenting, transgressive 116
parenting norms 109
Parsley, Samantha
  audio mixing 113n14
  data generation activities **162–163**
    development of Dovetail and In the Key brands **163**
    DJ courses **162**
    DJ sets, livestreamed and in-person **162**
    event organization **163**
    formal interviews **163**
    industry conferences **162**
    industry roles **163**
    meet-ups **162**
    podcast and radio production **163**
    production courses **162**
    workshops facilitated **163**
  DJing and body image 67–68
  ethnographic work and research project 161, 164
  Fall Away 106–107
  insider research 161, **162–163**, 164
  interviews 165–167, 168
    sample characteristics 166, **166**
  Just Dance
    Funky Breaks Remix 150–151
  Keep Your Disdance 36, 82, 89, 120
  Lift 51 14–15
  1984 74–75
  positionality 166–167
  receipt of Research Fellowship from The Leverhulme Trust xi, 164
  record label experience 80–81
  Sea Organ 82, 89–90
  submitting of tracks for review 135
  see also Dovetail
patent 50

patriarchy, embodied 68
Peace, Love and Unity Movement 39n4
peace, love, unity and respect *see* PLUR
Pember, Mark 41
Perfectionism 23
performance of electronic music, gender balance in 16–35
performers in music venues 29–30
Performing Rights Society (PRS) 25
  Foundation 152
Perkins, Zelda 144
photo-editing and photo-editor software 67, 68
physical appearance of minoritized artists 59–66
piano, playing of 113, 114
pioneers of electronic music 93
platforms 19, 148
  see also GENIE
PLUR (peace, love, unity and respect) 39
podcasts 41, 49, 68, 85, 110, 120, 132, 138, 155, 163
  see also Lowering the Tone
political act of recognition 10
pop/rock music 27
positive action 12–13, 76–89, 159, 161
  activities undertaken to solve inequality 73
  campaigns 134
  initiatives and organizations 88
positive discrimination 78
power
  and power dynamics 11, 74, 81
  and respect 153
predispositions 103
preferential treatment 78
prefigurative organizations 142
Pregnant Then Screwed 144n40
pregnant women, harassment and discrimination claims raised by 144n40
prejudice, explicit 47
prestige 50
privilege 45–46, 48, 158
Producer Barbie 121n49
producer peacocking 141
professional recording studios 27, 95, 96
professionalism and professionals 23, 24, 98
'profile-raising' compilations 19
Project Implicit 46n16
promos and promo distribution services 20
promoters 76, 77, 148
promotional copies 20
promotional material, sexualization and patronizing 118
pronouns 9–11, 19n6, 118
PRS *see* Performing Rights Society
PRS Foundation *see* Foundation *under* Performing Rights Society
Psibindi 1–2, 14

psychoactive drugs, effects of 15
Psy-sisters collective 1–2, 7, 14
psytrance scene 1–2

Q

queer identity 66–67
queer parties 141–142

R

race and racism in the electronic music industry 45, 62, 64, 66, 70, 86–87, 126–127, 136, 142
Radiomonitor 33, 33n52
Radio 1 33
radio shows 16, 18
  see also *Draw the Line*
Rampling, Danny 68
rationality 112
raves 5
record labels 20, 21, 79, 81–83, 91, 92, 131, 132, 134, 135, 146, 148
record producers and engineers, decentralization of 41
recording studios 24
recruitment of female students into music technology courses 117n37
remix competitions 131, 132
remixers and remixing 21, 96n9, 150, 151
reparative reading 9
representation
  of gender-expansive artists and diverse individuals 87–88, 131–132, 146
  marginalization of 32–33
  of women 65–67, 131–132, 146
reproductive capacities of cis women's bodies 115
resistance of marginalization and oppression 9
responsibility for unpaid domestic and caring labour, gender differences in 104
reverse discrimination 12–13
reward 29
rock and metal genres 33
Roland TB-303 128–129
role models 111
Roman and Greek society, criticism of women's voices in Ancient 64
Rouse, Cecilia 51
royalties 25–26, 50, 61

S

safe spaces 141–144, 145, 158–159
sausage fest 48
  see also bro culture
scientific management 115n29
self-belief 79
self-exploitation 29
self-governance 68, 68n24
sex-positive actions 63n11

self-producers and self-production 4, 27, 95, 96, 99
self-promotion 141
self-report surveys 22, 61
self-teaching 111
self-work 137, 149–150
sensory divide between men and women 112
sex-positivity, freedom of 63n11
sexual attractiveness of minoritized artists 59, 62, 63–64
  see also physical appearance of minoritized artists
sexualization 159
Shawnonymous
  1984 74, 74–75
She Said So 49, 133, 143
simulations 65–66
singers, women's affinity for 114, 117
sisterhood 40
Sisu xi, **163**
skill, economy of 63n12
skills 3, 4, 114n22, 160
  development of 58, 79, 128, 151, 160, 166
  honing of 41
  lack of 73, 93, 99, 105, 141
  learning of 63, 76
  necessary 54, 84, 96, 98, 100, 115
  personal contacts across 41
  proving of 93, 103
  questioning and undermining of female 8, 13, 51, 64, 78, 94, 95, 140
  simplification of 63
  valued and protected by bro culture 52, 112, 114
social capital 133
social expectations of genders 103
social media
  coverage and algorithms 62
  posts 65n16, 144
  profiles 19
social norms and expectation agendas, power-laden 68n24
social power, gendering by 111–112
socialization 111, 113, 120n47, 128, 133, 155, 160
socialized differences between genders 105
socio-economic status 45–46
software, use of 125, 159
software design 52, 124
software plug-ins 129
solidarity 14, 141–144, 157
Sommers, Sarah 121, 123
Songtrust 25
SoundCloud 77, 152, 156
sound design and engineering 52, 58
  see also audio engineering
Soundgirls.org 19n8

sounds, quality and originality of 51
Spotify 26n27, 33, 34
Stacey, Ralph 153n3
stereotype-busting behaviours, individual 88
stereotypes 13, 46, 63
  see also gender stereotypes
stock samples 58
Stone, Maya 129
Storm Rave parties 39n4
streamed music, prevalence of women, trans and non-binary artists in 33–34
streaming royalty, redistribution of 26n27
structural inequality 18, 34–35
  in the electronic music industry 12, 34–35, 44–45
studio mixing desks, overcoming design bias in 127
subcultures 147
success, benchmarks of 24, 24n18
support for marginalized groups 158
support networks 7–8
  see also Psy-sisters collective
supporting the night 55–56
survival strategies 149
symbolism of the body 65–67
synthesizers 113, 128–129, 135
  male affinity for 117
  see also Roland TB-303

T
talent 38, 40, 50, 56
  production of as a gendered process 12
  scouting out and finding 20–21
tech-heavy creative industries and tech-related education, under-representation of women in 13
technical language 117–119
technical prowess 51–52
technical skills 13
technologies 13, 113
technology 101
  association of with cis-gendered men 47, 93, 102
  dependence of electronic music production and performance 5
  exposure to while growing up 108, 110
  and gender 103, 105, 113
  historical gendering of 116
  use of 13
Theremin 125
third wave feminism 63n11
303 Day 128
tokenism 76–77, 78, 137
Toolroom
  We Are Listening campaign 143
Top 50 electronic tracks 28
Top 100 radio airplay chart 33
tours as lawless spaces 140n18

track
  breakdown of 129
  deconstruction videos 141n21
  mastering the 98
tracklists 19
tracks
  featuring on 28
  remixing of 147
  signing of individual 22
  submitting of for review 135
trans and non-binary people 10, 19n6, 45, 55n40
  see also minoritized genders
transgender hate crime 142
treatment, disparate *see* direct *under* discrimination
trolling 2, 63, 64, 65
2% Rising 27, 27n30, 143

U

UK acid house raves, origins of 39
UK Electronic Music Report 33
UK Gender Pay Gap Reporting rules 61n5
UK Music Diversity Taskforce 22n13
UN Gender Norms Index 26
underground community 69n26
underground music producers and scene 5, 24, 25, 29, 93, 94–95, 95n4, 129
Underplayed (directed by Stacey Lee) 64
unequal treatment 88
Union Club (Vauxhall, 2013) 1
United Nations Gender Norms Index *see* UN Gender Norms Index
University of Portsmouth 51
US electronic dance music culture, origins of 39

V

vertical disintegration 40
virtue signalling 79, 81, 146, 156
visibility 69, 86, 137
  see also hyper-visibility
vulnerabilities 85, 127, 138, 160

W

We Are Listening campaign 143
Wildfire Recordings 150
women
  as passive consumers of the radio 112
  DJs viii, 12, 17, 19, 63, 104, 119, 127, 140
  in electronic music 10
  and gender-expansive people 10
  music producers and production viii–ix, 11–12, 16–36
  (in)visibility as female professional experts 122n50
  see also minoritized genders
Women in CTRL 33, 143
Women in Drum and Bass artist programme 143
Women Musicians Insight Report 72
women's content, criticism of 64
Women's History Month 79
work 48, 55, 56, 157, 161, 164
  doubting of women's 93
work environments, contending with discouraging and dangerous 138–141, 140n18, 146
work ethic 42
workplace pregnancy discrimination 72n32
works, female and male association with 114

Y

YouTube 49, 86

www.ingramcontent.com/pod-product-compliance
Lightning Source LLC
Chambersburg PA
CBHW071158070526
44584CB00019B/2842